Rachel Reeves is Labour MP for Leeds West. She was elected to the House of Commons in 2010 and was a member of Ed Miliband's Shadow Cabinet from 2011 to 2015. Prior to her parliamentary career, she worked as an economist.

'The fierce guardian of Gaitskell through the turmoil of the 1950s, she then became an utterly loyal minister to Wilson. A tough, even ruthless, member of the NEC, while adored by her constituency; socially conservative yet she helped deliver Roy Jenkins' transformational agenda at the Home Office; though a grammar school girl, she called for and drove through Tony Crosland's comprehensive education plans. This engaging, intriguing, scrupulous and well-researched study of Alice Bacon rightly "recovers" her life as a significant, and until now relatively obscure, player in the 1950s and 1960s Labour party.' – **Baroness (Patricia) Hollis, author of** *Jennie Lee: A Life*

'Rachel Reeves has not only brought to life one of Labour's unsung heroines but, through Alice Bacon's story, she's given us her unique take on the party in the heady days after 1945. A loving biography – part social history, part detective work – this is an intimate story of Labour in the last century, written by one of the women who could drive it ahead in this.' – **Allegra Stratton, National Editor, ITV News**

'Alice was a true party stalwart, devoting her weekends to party meetings and functions across the country, defending the historic and best interests of the party on the NEC, and encouraging young activists like myself who were weened in the women's section of the party and then the League of Youth to devote ourselves to politics too. Rachel Reeves, who has also committed herself to the cause of Labour, has shown foresight in writing this book and brought to life this fascinating, at times divided, but most of all transformative period of Labour history.' – **Baroness (Betty) Boothroyd, former Speaker of the House of Commons**

'Rachel Reeves has offered a fascinating insight into the political life of Leeds' first female MP. This thought-provoking story about Alice Bacon's remarkable career has many echoes of the tensions in today's Labour party.' – **Anushka Asthana, Political Editor, the** *Guardian*

'Alice Bacon was a remarkable political pioneer who, in her own words did "everything that a male MP does. And a little bit more". In doing so, she blazed a trail for every single one of Labour's current 100 female MPs – including her biographer, Rachel Reeves herself.' – **Cathy Newman, Presenter, Channel 4 News**

'This book is a great, and timely, read. At a time when all-ability schooling is under threat as never before, we need to salute formidable women like Alice Bacon, who helped to usher in the comprehensive revolution – still the most important, progressive education reform of the last century.' – **Fiona Millar, author of** *The Secret World of the Working Mother*

'Rachel Reeves' biography of Leeds Labour MP Alice Bacon, one of Labour's women pioneers in the House of Commons, combines immaculate scholarship with endearing humanity. The story of the early women MPs is at last being told. Rachel has added enormously to our knowledge and understanding.' – **Mary Honeyball MEP, author of** *Parliamentary Pioneers: Labour Women MPs 1918–1945*

'This book is both a good read and a long-overdue recognition of one of the stalwarts of the Labour Party. The contribution made by Alice Bacon to the party and country was significant in so many ways we are only now recognising.' – **Bernard Atha CBE, former Lord Mayor of Leeds**

'An inspiring and compelling account of one of the unsung heroines of post-war, Labour Britain. With admiration, political insight and historical honesty, Reeves recounts the gritty, determined, and highly principled life of her predecessor Alice Bacon as a female, Leeds Labour MP. A truly rewarding read for historians, Labour Party supporters, and Yorkshire patriots.' – **Tristram Hunt MP, author of** *Ten Cities that Made an Empire*

'*Alice in Westminster* is the very readable tale of a little-known politician who was part of making huge and lasting changes to Britain. Rachel's account of Alice's life and determination proves that politics isn't just the art of the possible, but the practice of getting things done, and a timely reminder that Labour's current dilemmas are far from new. Politicians who made the headlines happen should be remembered too.' – **Laura Kuenssberg, Political Editor, BBC News**

'A well-researched and affectionate portrait of one of Labour's less-celebrated heroines. Readable and scholarly, Reeves' most welcome biography brings Alice Bacon and her distinctive brand of practical socialism vividly to life. It deserves to be read widely by students of Labour Party history, as well as by those fascinated by women's long march to equality in twentieth-century British politics.' – **Dr Helen McCarthy, author of** *Women of the World: The Rise of the Female Diplomat*

'Alice Bacon's "loyalty was first and foremost to the Labour Party, not to any faction within it", writes Rachel Reeves of the first woman to represent Leeds. The now little-known Bacon was the "terror of the Trotskyites" during another period of Labour internecine conflict, a notorious backroom operator, one of the 'five giants … in charge of fixing elections in favour of the Gaitskelite right wing', she nevertheless served Harold Wilson as a minister at the Home office and Department of Education. A grammar-school girl who taught in a secondary modern before becoming an MP, she was a virulent advocate of comprehensive education – "levelling up" she called it – and which she helped become a reality. In the end "government for Alice was about delivery for working-class families."' – **Lisa Martineau, author of *Politics & Power: Barbara Castle, a Biography***

'The fascinating story of Yorkshire MP Alice Bacon as told by Rachel Reeves is one of behind-the-scenes determination and influence in post-war Labour politics. Devoted to Hugh Gaitskell she made her mark both in her party and in government while never forgetting where she came from.' – **Jo Coburn, BBC *Daily Politics* Presenter**

Alice in Westminster

The Political Life of Alice Bacon

RACHEL REEVES

with

RICHARD CARR

Published in 2017 by
I.B.Tauris & Co. Ltd
London • New York
www.ibtauris.com

ISBN: 978 1 78453 768 5
eISBN: 978 1 78672 151 8
ePDF: 978 1 78673 151 7

A full CIP record for this book is available from the British Library
A full CIP record is available from the Library of Congress

Library of Congress Catalog Card Number: available

Typeset by Fakenham Prepress Solutions, Fakenham, Norfolk NR21 8NN
Printed and bound in Sweden by ScandBook AB

CONTENTS

ILLUSTRATIONS

1. Alice as a young girl, c.1917. Private collection.
2. Alice teaching, c.1932. Alice's experiences in interwar secondary moderns informed her views on education. She came to publicly advocate the comprehensive system far earlier than other leading Labour lights. Private collection.
3. Alice celebrates her victory in Leeds, 1945. © Yorkshire Post Newspapers.
4. To the future Councillor Bernard Atha, the 1945 election result was a 'new dawn akin to the second coming'. Here a still-shocked Alice, with her mother Charlotte (Lottie) Bacon, takes in the margin of her victory. Private collection.
5. Alice's mission was always to get Labour into government. Here she is with Prime Minister Clement Attlee in the late 1940s. Private collection.
6. In 1945 Alice was one of fifteen Labour women MPs elected to Parliament for the first time. © National Portrait Gallery.
7. Alice with Herbert Morrison (centre) c.1949. Morrison, active on the Labour right, was always a firm friend. © Getty Images.
8. Alice with Herbert Morrison and her mother, c.1950. Morrison once remarked that 'the farther you live North from London the better time and the better food you have.' Here he had Alice's mother, Lottie Bacon (centre), very much in mind. Private collection.
9. Alice's family was always proud of her achievements. Here her mother (right) inspects her CBE, awarded in 1953. Private collection.
10. Elections needed organising and publicity. Morgan Phillips and Alice discuss both here in 1959. © Getty Images.

11. The 1960 Labour Party Conference was fraught for Hugh Gaitskell (pictured here wearing dark glasses). At least he had his closest political confidant, Alice, sat to his right. Private collection.
12. Leeds United. Leeds MPs Denis Healey, Alice Bacon, Hugh Gaitskell and Charlie Pannell (pictured left to right) were always close – both in terms of their politics and their constituencies. Private collection.
13. Alice with Hugh Gaitskell, *c*.1960. Alice would dearly have loved to have seen a Gaitskell premiership. But she supported his successor, Harold Wilson, despite their differences. Private collection.
14. Alice with Hugh Gaitskell *c*.1960. © Yorkshire Post Newspapers.
15. Alice was a model constituency MP, as emphasised in her 1964 election leaflet. Private collection.
16. Alice enters Downing Street for the first time after the Labour victory in 1964. Six years of ministerial office, and significant achievements at the Home Office and Education, would follow. Private collection.
17. Membership of the National Executive Committee provided three decades of influence for Alice. Here she is speaking at the 1965 Party Conference in Blackpool. © Getty Images.
18. The 1967 Party Conference in Scarborough saw Alice declare it 'absolutely unthinkable' that children should have their educational paths divided at the age of 11. She is flanked by Barbara Castle and Harold Wilson. © Getty Images.
19. Alice meeting Queen Elizabeth II in November 1966. The miner's daughter had come a long way. Private collection.
20. Alice with Harold Wilson at the 1970 Labour Party Conference. © Yorkshire Post Newspapers.
21. Alice works from one of the ministerial red boxes at her home in Normanton, June 1970. © Yorkshire Post Newspapers.
22. Alice, pictured her towards the end of her Commons career. © Yorkshire Post Newspapers.
23. The House of Lords was never quite Alice's scene after she was elevated in 1970. But she was happy to join Dora, Baroness Gaitskell, and Michael Milner, another Labour minister from Leeds, in the upper chamber. © Getty Images.

ACKNOWLEDGEMENTS

There are many people who have ensured that this book was written.

First, my co-author, Richard Carr, who I have been working with for five years. Richard, who is a senior lecturer in history and politics at Anglia Ruskin University, has painstakingly been through archives, NEC minutes and conference speeches to find out who Alice was and what made her so important to the history of the Labour Party. It has been a pleasure working with him.

In Yorkshire, Bernard Atha, a brilliant Leeds City Councillor for 50 years and huge font of knowledge on Leeds Labour Party history, has been a big help and I have enjoyed many hours talking to Bernard about Alice as well as Labour Party and Leeds history. Constituents of Alice and local party members including Frank Pullan have also helped me to understand Alice the constituency MP.

Elaine Bacon, a cousin of Alice, kindly shared with me photos of Alice, a tape recording of a BBC interview, newspaper clippings and other letters and fragments that Alice passed on. Michael Meadowcroft, whose excellent lecture series at Leeds Library included a lecture on Alice, has also been incredibly generous with source material and pictures.

Former MPs including Betty Boothroyd, Shirley Williams, David Steel, Roy Hattersley, Tam Dalyell, Dick Taverne and Jack Straw all have memories of Alice in Parliament and as a minister, and have shared their huge experience and knowledge of politics and Parliament in the 1960s and 1970s. Leeds-born Gerald Kaufman MP gave a generous amount of time and was able to describe Alice as a constituency MP and national politician.

I also treasure the conversations I had with former MPs Denis Healey, Geoffrey Lofthouse and Walter Harrison (who Ed Balls and Yvette Cooper introduced me to), all of whom were both close colleagues and good friends of Alice.

Members of the House of Lords including Lord Bernard Donoughue, who has written a fantastic foreword to this book, former Labour Party General Secretary Lord Tom Sawyer and Baroness Joyce Gould, author of *The Witchfinder General: A Political Odyssey*, have all helped me better position Alice in the party's divided politics of her time.

This book describes, among other things, the important relationship between Alice Bacon and Hugh Gaitskell. I am incredibly grateful to Hugh Gaitskell's daughter Julia McNeal and her husband Peter for talking to me about Alice and sharing photographs, and to their son Hugh for putting us in touch.

From the excellent Labour History Group, many thanks to Greg Rosen for reading earlier versions of the manuscript and for steering me in the direction of lots of good books. Thanks to John Grayson for writing the fantastic book *Solid Labour* which describes Alice so well, to Keith Laybourn from Huddersfield University who I met with for tea and conversation at Kirkstall Abbey to learn more about Yorkshire politics in the post-war period, and to John Goodchild who helped me better understand Alice's native Normanton.

Thank you also to the treasure chest that is the People's History Museum and the excellent staff at the House of Commons Library for their research help. And thanks especially to the National Union of Teachers and Leeds University for their generous support in making this book possible, as well as to Sir David Garrard, for his ongoing support.

In my office I would like to thank Nick Quin and Nick Garland both of whom have helped type, read, find source material and lots more of the things that ensure books get written. In a similar vein a huge thank you to my editor Jo Godfrey, a Yorkshire-woman who saw something in Alice and in me that deserved to be published, and to the team at I.B. Tauris and Fakenham Prepress for getting the book printed and published.

And finally, to my dad Graham Reeves who helped inspire me by his own history writing, and to my husband Nicholas Joicey who encouraged me to keep writing over the last few years in between Shadow Cabinet jobs, electioneering and having two children.

Rachel Reeves
August 2016

FOREWORD

Alice Bacon MP's priority was to secure a majority Labour government which could build a society that enhanced the welfare of British working people.

Alice was born into the early twentieth-century Yorkshire coal industry. She was rooted in the practical problems which concerned her fellow citizens – homes, schools, industrial injuries, job insecurity, pay inadequacy or inequality – rather than the Marxist theoretical dogma which obsessed the far-left and was often far removed from working-class concerns. Those working people who Alice supported had strong collective values of family, work ethic, community neighbourliness, usually organised into strong trade unions, with all the satisfaction of social security which went with those values. Alice and her West Yorkshire political world were what might now be called 'Blue Labour', neither Fabian metropolitan liberal nor dogmatic hard left. They were pragmatic, dealing with the real problems facing real people in a harsh capitalist world.

Entering the Commons in 1945 with the great post-war Attlee government, she was dedicated to supporting its massive programme of reform, giving those millions who had suffered in the economic slump of the 1930s and from the subsequent wartime deprivations the prospect of a happier, more secure and more prosperous life. For her, the 1945 Labour manifesto was a political gospel: 'they deserve and must be assured a happier future .... Labour regards their welfare as a sacred trust.' Her next 50 years of political life in the Commons and the House of Lords were devoted to carrying out that pledge. Achieving that transformation of the lives of millions of British working people in one generation (with the consent and cooperation of all our post-war parliamentary parties) was primarily a triumph for moderate, pragmatic, parliamentary socialism, which Alice Bacon personified.

She was a model constituency MP and the first woman member representing her ever-loyal Leeds (a city where Rachel now sits as the second woman MP), solving her constituents' problems at regular surgeries (not as common then as now), serving sandwiches at social events and addressing meetings of hundreds of Labour supporters. At each election she fought, through to 1970, she outperformed Labour's national swing. Locals knew her as 'our Alice'.

She was joined from Leeds in the Commons after 1945 by a golden generation of Labour colleagues: Hugh Gaitskell, Denis Healey and Charlie Pannell (followed later by Merlyn Rees). Her relations with future party leader Gaitskell were crucial to him, both in protecting his Leeds constituency base and between 1960 and 1962 in supporting his fight to save the party he loved from the intrusions of the hard left. In the latter battle, Alice was a rock of support on the National Executive Committee (altogether for 30 years) and in her assiduous work to prevent Trotskyite infiltration at constituency level. The lessons from this for the party today are clear.

Gaitskell's own inner social circle was mainly composed of Oxbridge Fabians with a Hampstead tinge. But as party leader he knew he also needed a wider legion of political foot soldiers such as Alice, from Blue Labour pragmatism, and the sensible right-wing trade unions who understood that the best defence for the welfare of working people was a moderate Labour movement which could gain a majority to elect Labour governments that legislate on Labour values.

As a Labour historian Rachel Reeves provides, through her description of Alice's parliamentary career, an excellent analysis of Harold Wilson's 1964–70 policies in the social fields of housing, education and Home Office reform. Her time as a Minister of State under Home Secretary Roy Jenkins oversaw a remarkable wave of changes which transformed British society, removing the death penalty, legalising abortion, liberalising race relations and decriminalising homosexuality. Alice herself was, like many working-class people, socially conservative and instinctively cautious on much social policy. But she proved consistently liberal in executing the legislative practicalities of those reforms and in overcoming the Commons resistance of some Tory reactionaries. Because she instinctively understood the concerns of working-class communities facing the threats from crime and mass immigration, she was more able to carry them with her in a liberal direction by argument rather than by lecturing them sanctimoniously on their alleged bigotry and prejudices. She was never really close to Roy Jenkins, without whose driving leadership these reforms would not then have occurred. Roy was too metropolitanly intellectual, too socially upward moving, too liberal and Liberal for her taste. But her detailed pragmatic support in Whitehall and in Westminster was vital to the successful execution of that great reform programme.

On education she played an even bigger role. Alice had taught at a pre-war secondary modern school (I declare an interest here, having experienced a time as a pupil in a post-war secondary modern school) and she was again the key junior minister at the departmental pit face. She wholeheartedly supported Anthony Crosland in his campaign to introduce the comprehensive school system. Providing the crucial momentum for ending selection at secondary level in the late 1960s was probably Alice Bacon's single greatest political impact and legacy.

Alice now perhaps reads as a figure from a very distant political age. Forty years of economic globalisation and open markets have changed the British working world. Reduced economic and social protection, less national and class consciousness, with mass migration of cheap labour and the virtual disappearance of our heavy-industry production and extractive industries, followed by the consequential freezing of lower wage levels and diminished job security for traditional working- and even middle-class groups, have dissolved that working-class society which Alice personified and represented.

Her Labour Party, and the challenges which face it today, have also changed beyond recognition. Labour now seems much less concerned with the practical issues of working life which so worried Alice. Such issues still exist, though in a changed form. For working people, feeling the acute pressures and insecurities of their daily working lives, many of their hardships seem to them to have been made more acute by society's pursuit of progressive, liberal principles, globalisation and the free movement of labour. Too often they have to pay the price, in terms of frozen wages and job insecurity from immigrant competition, schools and medical services under pressure from population growth, higher energy prices from green taxes, etc. Hence the Labour elite has grown removed from its foot soldiers. The Alice Bacons no longer automatically identify with Labour or devote their lives to it as she did.

It is clear that the new globalised economy creates as many, though different kinds of, problems for the new social structures of British working people as did the harsh capitalism of the nineteenth and twentieth centuries. In some ways it was simpler then (though not easier in political-power terms) for Alice Bacon's Labour generation to construct party agendas and manifestos in response to the problems of that earlier capitalist economy. Today's society is more complex, commoditised and less-easily defined than it was earlier. But the problems facing working people today often seem to them similarly difficult, despite the greater surrounding wealth. The challenge facing Rachel Reeves' generation of Labour politicians is to analyse afresh the issues facing working people today and to bring to them the same political devotion which Alice did in her time. They need to create a new philosophy and policy agenda relevant to the lives of working people. Clem Attlee, Hugh Gaitskell, Harold Wilson and Tony Blair showed in their different ways that it could be done. Each needed their Alice Bacons to carry it out.

This is an excellent biography of a fine Labour politician, whose main life commitments were to the Labour movement, to Leeds and to securing a more equal place for women in British political life. They were noble ambitions. Alice Bacon was sound, solid and sensible in her work and her values. She is a role model for anyone entering the very changed world of British politics today.

Bernard Donoughue
August 2016

ABBREVIATIONS

AEU – Amalgamated Engineers Union
ALRA – Abortion Law Reform Association
BMA – British Medical Association
CDS – Campaign for Democratic Socialism
CLP – Constituency Labour Party
DEA – Department of Economic Affairs
DES – Department of Education and Science
HLRS – Homosexual Law Reform Society
LEA – Local Educational Authority
LOY – Labour League of Youth
MFGB – Miners' Federation of Great Britain
NALT – National Association of Labour Teachers
NEC – National Executive Committee
NUT – National Union of Teachers
PLP – Parliamentary Labour Party
PWLB – Public Works' Loan Board
SDP – Social Democratic Party
SEA – Socialist Education Association
TGWU – Transport and General Workers Union
TUC – Trades Union Congress

TIMELINE

1909   Alice born in Normanton, Yorkshire.
1925   Alice joins the Labour Party.
1926   First political speech.
1927   Alice leaves school, and begins teacher training at Stockwell College.
1933   Alice is defeated as a candidate in elections for the West Riding Urban District Council.
1935   Alice meets Hugh Gaitskell for the first time.
1937   Alice secures a degree in public administration from the University of London.
1938   Adopted as parliamentary candidate for Leeds North East.
1939   First mention of Alice in *The Times*.
1941   Elected to the National Executive Committee (NEC) of the Labour Party. Active in National Association of Labour Teachers (NALT) and National Union of Teachers (NUT) during the war.
1942   Elected to the NEC of the NALT as northern delegate.
1945   Elected Member of Parliament for Leeds North East. Labour wins a landslide majority of 145 seats.
1946   Alice helps broker a new deal between the Labour and Co-operative parties.
1951   Labour loses office – de facto Conservative majority of 22.
1951   Alice serves as chairman of the NEC for the Party Conference in Scarborough.
1953   Awarded the CBE. Alice splits with Gaitskell over private schools at Labour Party Conference.

1954   Alice offers to resign from Organisation Sub-Committee on Labour's
         NEC; she recants after being urged to reconsider by Morgan Phillips.

1955   Boundary reshuffle sees Alice move parliamentary seats to Leeds
         South East. Tories increase majority to 60. Hugh Gaitskell
         elected Labour leader in place of Attlee.

1956   Alice, as chairman of the Publicity and Political Education
         Sub-Committee of the NEC, begins to report on the party's media
         and public perception. Khrushchev speaks at Labour's NEC; Alice
         incurs Gaitskell's displeasure by making a critical speech.

1959   Alice appointed, in effect, Shadow Minister of State at the
         Home Office. Tories win third straight election by a further
         increased majority (100).

1959   Gaitskell attempts to rewrite Clause IV of the Labour Party's
–60   constitution – the commitment to wholesale nationalisation –
         without success.

1960   To Alice's delight, Harold Wilson is unsuccessful in challenging
         Hugh Gaitskell for the Labour leadership.

1963   Gaitskell dies, Harold Wilson elected Labour leader.

1964   Labour wins the 1964 general election, with a majority of just four
         seats. Alice appointed Minister of State at the Home Office. She
         serves under Frank Soskice (1964–5) and Roy Jenkins (1965–7).

1965   Tony Crosland introduces Circular 10/65 on comprehensive
         education. Passage of the Murder (Abolition of the Death
         Penalty) Act. Alice renews her vice presidency of the Socialist
         Education Association (formerly NALT).

1966   Labour increase their majority to 96 seats. Alice becomes a
         member of the Privy Council.

1967   Legislation passed to decriminalise homosexuality and abortion.
         Reforms over divorce (1969) and increasing the provisions of the
         Race Relations Act (1968) follow Alice leaving the department.

1967   Alice moved in reshuffle to the Department of Education and
         Science. There she promises to coerce councils into adopting
         comprehensive education if necessary.

1970   Labour lose office to a Conservative majority of 31. Alice
         retires as an MP and is ennobled as Baroness Bacon in Wilson's
         dissolution honours list.

1972   Awarded honorary degree from the University of Leeds. Poulson
         scandal – which Alice had pursued before the 1970 election –
         breaks, leading to the resignation of Reginald Maudling.

1986   Last speech in the House of Lords.

1993   Dies, aged 83.

INTRODUCTION

In the early hours of 7 May 2010 I stood up to give my acceptance speech having been elected as the new Member of Parliament for Leeds West. The other seven successful candidates in Leeds constituencies that night were all men. In fact, it was the first time in 40 years that a woman had been elected in Leeds. Only one woman had ever been elected as a Leeds MP before. That woman was Alice Bacon, MP for Leeds North East and then Leeds South East, between 1945 and 1970.

Alice was not the first female candidate for Parliament in Leeds. A Miss Grant stood for the Liberals in 1922 and Mrs Penny for Labour in 1924, but Alice Bacon was the first, and only, woman to be elected as an MP in Leeds until 2010. A city comprising now over three-quarters of a million people had only ever seen one female representative in the House of Commons until 2010.

As well as paying tribute to my immediate predecessor, I paid tribute to Alice when I stood on the stage that evening. Alice had come from a coal-mining community, a few miles south-east of Leeds in Normanton. Her dad had been a miner, union official and West Yorkshire County Councillor. Politics was in her blood. She loved the party and devoted her life to it. She wasn't someone for grand theories or tub-thumping speeches, but professionally, and diligently, she worked her way up from infant school teacher, youth activist and parliamentary candidate in what looked like a safe Conservative seat to become an MP, chair of Labour's National Executive Committee, Minister of State at the Department for Education and at the Home Office and then finally serving in the House of Lords as Baroness Bacon of Normanton and the West Riding.

I was intrigued by Alice. By the time I was elected, 20 per cent of MPs were women. When Alice first won her seat in 1945 only 38 women had ever been elected to Parliament in the 26 years they had been repre-sented in the House of Commons. How did a working-class girl in a community where most women would stay at home or, even if they had been to the grammar school, were likely to do clerical work rather than political representation, become a politician? Did her parents encourage her? What did the local Labour Party make of a woman in her twenties (as she was when she was selected) wanting to be an MP? What did her constituents think of the first two women to be elected MPs in Yorkshire (Muriel Nichol was elected on the same day in Bradford)? What was Parliament like for these pioneers? Did she have a family to support her? What issues did she champion?

So, with no biography of her yet written, I set out to learn more. My own local councillor in Kirkstall, West Leeds, Bernard Atha, had been a member of the party since the 1940s. He remembered Alice, but more than that, he had been her election agent for a while. He still had photos of Alice and told me stories of meeting Alice's mum and dad at their bungalow in Normanton. He had been at the selection meeting when Leeds South East chose Alice as their parliamentary candidate back in 1955, when a boundary review abolished the Leeds North East seat which Alice had held for the previous decade. In fact, Bernard went along to the meeting with the intention of stopping Alice, whom he regarded as being on the right of the party.

Bernard Atha put me in touch with Elaine Bacon, a cousin of Alice's, who had the letters, photos and news clippings that Alice left when she died – not having had any children of her own to pass on her memories and papers to. Among this collection were photos of Alice with political greats including Attlee, Morrison and Gaitskell, as well as letters from Churchill, Eden and Violet Attlee. Best of all was a cassette recording of an interview that Alice did for the BBC in the 1980s. It was the first time I had heard Alice's voice – described by many as 'grating', although more by people in London than from her native West Yorkshire.

Alice entered Parliament as an unmarried woman, and that was how she ended her life too. Alice, unlike other pioneering female parliamen-tarians such as Barbara Castle, did not have a husband to provide support and neither did she ever have a family of her own. It was because Alice had been a woman MP that first drew her to my attention, but Alice did not regard herself as a 'woman' MP. Although, as she remarked in a BBC radio interview after standing down from Parliament, 'a woman MP has to do everything that a male MP does. And a little bit more'. Comments about her voice ('grating', according to Richard Crossman amongst many) and her appearance ('homely, simple [and] plump' according to the *Evening Standard*'s Robert Carvel) were much more common for women MPs than the men, and even her mentor, Herbert Morrison, suggested that women stick to women's issues in Parliament rather than, for example, the perceived 'manly' domain of defence. Even if there was some reluctance to pigeonhole herself, Alice certainly took part in all the events and social life of the women's section of the Labour Party. Alice wrote at the time of her election victory for the publication *The Labour Woman* that '… it so happens that it has fallen to the young men and women of my generation to translate into reality the hopes and visions of the pioneers of the Labour Party and to be the custodians of the future'. These young men and women included 21 Labour women in the 1945 Parliament. Alice recalled 'walking' rather than 'talking' legislation through Parliament, as MPs walked night after night through the division lobbies with their large parliamentary majority to take forward commitments to create a National Health Service, the welfare state and a programme of housebuilding.

Part of the role of women MPs was to address party members at women's conferences and rallies. In Yorkshire these gatherings attracted hundreds, and sometimes thousands, of Labour activists to Leeds Town Hall or other venues across the county. Rather different to Labour women's conferences today, Betty Boothroyd remembers as a young woman winning the Labour women's rally beauty contest in Filey. The prize was a book written by Attlee and presented by Yorkshire MP Alice Bacon!

To really understand Alice you had to understand Normanton and West Yorkshire mining communities in the interwar years. Normanton was Alice's hinterland, and it was where Alice learned politics from her father. Her first speech had been in the Normanton Railway Men's Club. Her first advice surgeries were held almost 20 years before she became an MP in a working-men's club helping miners, who often could not read or write, to fill in forms for compensation for industrial injuries. Alice was a rare female figure in the working-men's clubs. It was only because of her father's position in the union, and her mother's job in the club kitchens making sandwiches, that ensured Alice was there at all. But it was in these clubs that Alice undertook her political apprenticeship.

To get a feeling for Alice's story and her home life, one Saturday morning I met with John Goodchild in the bowels of Wakefield Library.

Diligently, conscientiously, John had been telling the story of Wakefield and collecting facts, figures, books and letters to bring it to life. He knew of Alice, and had heard her speak at political rallies, but he also knew the story of Normanton, a mining town that grew exponentially in the years leading up to Alice's birth, with workers coming in from Ireland, Scotland and Wales as more coal was discovered and the demand for young men to work in the pits increased. Alice's family were originally from Staffordshire but travelled to West Yorkshire to find work in the booming mining industry. Alice's father, Benjamin Bacon, worked at the Whitwood Colliery, a modern and innovative mine with homes designed and built for the workers by architect Edward Voysey. But it was a tough job: strikes were common during Alice's early years and although work was plentiful, life was never easy for the Bacons or for their friends and neighbours.

The house where Alice lived was built on coal. A pillar of the black stuff lay beneath their home, and the four male inhabitants of the house – Alice's father Benjamin, her grandfather, uncle and a lodger – all worked down the pit. Benjamin Bacon wanted Alice to know what his work was and what their community was built on. As the rising tide of dissatisfaction about pay and conditions that would eventually produce the General Strike was brewing, her father took the teenage Alice down to see how he spent his working days. It was a memory seared on Alice's mind – she described later that she 'went down the mine into its inner workings and almost terrifying darkness'. Alice never forgot her roots or what and who she was in politics for. In 1925, aged 16, Alice joined the Labour Party. Her political journey had begun.

After activism in her union, the National Union of Teachers, the National Association of Labour Teachers and the League of Youth, and several years working as a school teacher in Normanton, Alice was selected as Labour's candidate in Leeds North East. It was a constituency with a Tory majority of over 10,000, and as Gerald Kaufman, now a Manchester MP, reflects, the local Labour Party probably wouldn't have selected a young woman if they thought there was any prospect of getting a Labour MP. But that was before the war and the Labour landslide that was to follow. Kaufman first met Alice (who became his MP) when he was a teenager at Leeds Grammar School and remembers running to the Town Hall in Leeds after the 1945 general election to see the results. Alice had managed to overturn a five-figure Tory majority with a 23 per cent swing from Conservative to Labour. Aged 35, Alice had become an MP.

Alice's Yorkshire roots and humble beginnings were her political driving force. Her maiden speech in the House of Commons was on compensation for industrial injuries, and in it she referred to her early years in a coal-mining community and the deformities and scars workers risked from just doing their jobs. A Tory MP said that the bill before Parliament was 'not socialism'. Alice replied that she wasn't sure about that, but what it most certainly did was limit the excesses of capitalism. Alice's colleagues in Leeds, Normanton and Westminster all agree that it was Alice's early years that had the biggest influence on her politics – from schools, to work, to housing. Former deputy chief whip and Wakefield MP Walter Harrison remembered Alice from Parliament, but also from growing up in Normanton. I first met Walter at Ed Balls and Yvette Cooper's summer garden party in Pontefract and I later met him at his home in Normanton where he told me about Alice's love for, and loyalty to, the party. Walter knew Alice from Wakefield Labour Party, Alice knew his parents, and Walter knew hers. They were both from solid Labour families. Walter was an electrician before he was an MP and helped Alice around the house, including fitting an electric fire 'according to the regulations'. Upon his election Alice remarked in the House of Commons tea room that she had 'lost her electrician'. But Walter continued to serve as Alice's electrician for the rest of her life. Walter died shortly after I interviewed him, but he will now always be remembered for the portrayal of him in James Graham's *This House* which was a sell-out at the National Theatre, documenting the 1974–9 government as its majority gradually evaporated.

Alice is remembered most of all in Leeds for being a good and conscientious Member of Parliament. Frank Pullan, who I met at Hilary Benn's constituency party office in the centre of Leeds, had been a party member and constituent of Alice's. Frank, among others, remembers Alice's constituency advice surgeries at the Corn Exchange in Leeds. These became slightly legendary affairs in one of the most iconic buildings in the City. All of Alice's election manifestos after 1945 refer to Alice's casework as 'no problem is too big or small', and her advice surgeries were dubbed as 'Any Problems?' But as well as the day-to-day work of an inner-city MP, Labour stalwarts from Leeds, including Pullan and also Baroness Joyce Gould, remember the battles in Leeds Labour Party in the 1950s and 1960s between right and left for the heart and soul – and control – of the party. Firmly on Labour's right, Alice was at the centre of these battles.

After some publicity about my plan to write a book, people wrote and phoned me to tell me about their memories of Alice, her kindness to them or their family, her meticulous approach to case work which earned her the respect of political rivals and enemies as much as her supporters. As well as her famous advice surgeries, Alice is remembered for driving around her constituency in her convertible, red Rover, the only reference to luxury in Alice's modest life that I can find. This red Rover became something of a local talking point. Voters would tease her 'Where's your car?' if she ever arrived at a meeting or to see a constituent on foot. It served as an affectionate trademark – never a sign of ostentatiousness, but rather a means by which she could be recognised by a constituency which always held her in high regard. Although Alice died almost 25 years ago she is still very fondly remembered in Leeds and also in Normanton.

Alice was fortunate locally to work with incredibly well-respected MPs who were of the same political persuasion as she was. Former Leeds West MP Charles Pannell referred to the Leeds quad of Gaitskell (Leeds South), Healey (Leeds East), Bacon and himself as 'Leeds United'. Alice's oldest political friend from Leeds was Denis Healey, her parliamentary neighbour who would go on to serve as Chancellor, Defence Secretary and deputy leader. Healey remembers Alice in his own biography and wrote and spoke to me about Alice, also reminiscing fondly about how they worked as a team of Leeds MPs. Pannell, in his autobiography, remembers 'Leeds Labour MPs stood like a rock behind the leader ... The four of us (Gaitskell, Bacon, Healey and Pannell) were not only Party colleagues but close personal friends.' And Alice helped protect the positions of her friends and colleagues. Healey remembers how Alice was instrumental in weeding out hard-left entryists in the party in the 1950s and 1960s, helping Healey (who described Alice as the 'Terror of the Trotskyites'), and many others too, hold on to their seats when under challenge from the left.

Alice's importance to other MPs on the right of the party was a key part of her influence and contribution to post-war Labour politics. As a member of the party's influential NEC from 1941 to 1970, and its chair in 1950–1, Alice was crucial in instilling discipline in the party, through expulsions, but also by travelling around the country, addressing rallies and stirring the party faithful and activist base to support the leadership of the party – particularly for Gaitskell, through good and bad times. Alice was never active in the Gaitskellite group, the CDS, but she was important to them. Lord Bernard Donoughue remembers Alice both from when he was secretary of the Gaitskellite CDS and then as Wilson's Policy Director at Number 10 Downing Street. The CDS was a rather intellectual group, not really Alice's scene. But Donoughue remembers Gaitskell's huge reliance on Alice to stay connected not just with Leeds but also the grass roots of the party more generally and the party's NEC. And the CDS felt they could rely on Alice and knew that she could reach parts of the Labour Party and movement where their more theoretical social-democratic thought might not resonate so well. Donoughue also remembers Wilson's respect for Alice – despite their politics being different, their Yorkshire roots and then later the work they did on modernising the Labour Party's communications (when Alice chaired the NEC subgroup on Communication and Political Education) gave them a shared understanding.

In Parliament, Alice's closest political friend was Hugh Gaitskell. Alice first met Gaitskell, before either of them was an MP, at a socialist conference in Geneva. They were soon parliamentary neighbours in Leeds with Gaitskell representing Leeds South. Herbert Morrison, and then Gaitskell, were mentors to Alice and Alice in turn was incredibly loyal and supportive to them.

In one of the most personal interviews for this book, I visited Julia McNeal, daughter of Hugh Gaitskell, and her husband Peter, and had lunch at their house, which had been the Gaitskell's family home in Frognal, Hampstead. Julia talked about being the daughter of the Labour leader, of walks on Hampstead Heath with her father, and she also remembered fondly visits to Leeds. Like Donoughue, McNeal remembers her father being very reliant on Alice. She wasn't a competitor to Gaitskell as some MPs with the same politics as Gaitskell were; she was always loyal and always looked out for her neighbouring MP in Leeds South and her great friend and mentor. Alice was one of only four MPs (alongside the Prime Minister, Harold Macmillan, interim Labour leader, George Brown and Liberal leader, Jeremy Thorpe) chosen to pay tribute to Gaitskell in the House of Commons debate following his death in 1963, at the age of 56. Alice visited him in hospital shortly before he died and talked in the Commons chamber of 'curtains [being] drawn in the small houses in the streets of South Leeds, not just for a Member of Parliament but for a very dear friend whom they knew and loved'. In her contribution about Gaitskell to the *Leeds Weekly Citizen* you can almost feel their closeness and her sorrow:

I shall miss him most in our small Committees of the National Executive, and in his room at the House of Commons where he and I have talked so frequently about his plans and hopes for the future, and where he has trusted me with some of his inner most thoughts about politics and people.

Gaitskell's death was a big blow to Alice both personally and politically. Alice wanted to see Gaitskell as Prime Minister and worked hard in Leeds, on the NEC and as a shadow minister to achieve that. She admired Gaitskell and respected him, but most of all he was a friend, and Alice lost a bit of her zeal the night he died.

Over the last few years I have spoken or corresponded with former MPs Tony Benn, Tam Dalyell, Bill Rodgers, Roy Hattersley, Jack Straw and David Clark as well as Baroness Shirley Williams, Lord David Steel, Baroness Betty Boothroyd, Baroness Joyce Gould, Lord Geoffrey Lofthouse, Lord Anthony Lester, and former Labour General Secretary Tom Sawyer as well as many others. It has been an immense privilege to speak to all these people – all of whom have made a huge contribution to British political life in the last 50 or so years. Each of the interviews has helped to piece together the life of the remarkable and fascinating woman Alice Bacon.

In writing this biography it has often been the personal reflections, the small things and the details that leave the strongest impression of what sort of woman, what sort of politician, Alice was. Most of all, she was loyal. Loyal to those she followed, most notably Gaitskell; loyal to her constituents, to whom she was a dedicated servant. And perhaps most of all loyal to her party. As Denis Healey noted, this Jane Eyre never found her Mr Rochester. But she loved the Labour Party and devoted herself loyally to it. Alice served as an MP under three leaders – Attlee, Gaitskell and Wilson. Although her politics were closest to Gaitskell's, she served Wilson without hesitation and without ever criticising him. As the Labour Party drifted to the left in the 1970s and into the 1980s, Alice remained loyal to it. In an interview with the BBC in the mid-1980s, she expressed her disappointment in the MPs who had left the party to form the Social Democratic Party. 'These people', as she saw it, 'owed every-thing to the party', and yet had left it and walked away. Alice – and this is backed up by interviews with Shirley Williams and others – never even considered leaving the Labour Party, despite being seen as on the right of the party. Alice was Labour before she was of any faction.

But, beyond the personal, Alice has left her mark on politics and policy: as a member of Labour's National Executive Committee for 30 years, as Minister of State at the Home Office and then the same role at the Department for Education. On Labour's NEC she was accused by *Tribune* of being on a witch-hunt against leftists, and she had notoriously poor relations with fellow long-standing MPs and NEC members Nye Bevan and Dick Crossman. Along with fellow Yorkshire-woman and one-time National Agent for the Labour Party, Sara Barker, Alice helped protect sitting MPs from deselection and helped to modernise the party – and along with Tony Benn, she helped take the Labour Party into the era of professional party political broadcasters and advertising in the 1960s.

At the Home Office, she was number two under Home Secretary Roy Jenkins. While she was a Home Office minister, the death penalty was all but abolished, and homosexuality and abortion legalised. It was a period of huge social change, if not all led by Harold Wilson's government, then at the very least given parliamentary time and support. On abortion, David Steel says the Labour government's support was 'tacit but crucial' to reform. On the death penalty and abortion in particular, Alice played a key role in winning the trust of the party, including more conservative elements, as well as working in the background on committees to see through these often controversial and groundbreaking reforms. Although Britain needed politicians like Roy Jenkins to make the principled case for social reform, and charismatic and determined backbench MPs like David Steel and Leo Abse to almost obsessively drive forward the change that happened on abortion and homosexuality, it also required practical politicians like Alice to help steer reform. Alice played her part in making Britain a more socially liberal country.

Alice's last job in government was where her heart was. Alice went to a grammar school in the 1920s, but despite the opportunities this had given her – to go on to college and to later study for a university degree – she had been an early advocate of comprehensive education. Your life-chances, Alice argued, should not depend on your performance in a test at the age of 10 or 11, nor less on your parents' income. In the 1940s and 1950s, Alice spoke in Parliament about comprehensive education more than any other MP. She had also lobbied education secretaries under Attlee, Macmillan and Eden relentlessly on the need for educational reform and investment and had been influential in changing Labour Party policy on selection in education. In the 1945–51 Labour government there was little appetite for such reform. However, by 1965, after sustained pressure and evidence from Alice and others, and under the leadership of Anthony Crosland at the Department for Education and with Wilson as Prime Minister, there was the prospect of real reform. By 1967, when Alice moved from the Home Office to Education, Crosland had started education policy on a journey that not even Margaret Thatcher could stop. Alice had the chance to put Crosland's initiatives into practice as Minister for Education between 1967 and 1970. By the time of the 1970 general election, when Alice stood down as an MP, nearly one-third of children were at comprehensive schools, a figure that rose to almost two-thirds four years later. With the issue of comprehensive education, she had the opportunity as a minister to put into practice the cause she had steadily argued for all her political life. Shirley Williams served as a minister with Alice at the Department for Education and remembers Alice as an 'administrator not an innovator'. That may be true, and is consistent with other accounts and with how Alice tried to create change. But it isn't necessarily a criticism. Politics needs innovators and inspiration. But government and party politics also require administrators. People who can see through change, know how to make things happen, and are willing to sit on committees, at times make compromises, and support others rather than drive change or be the leader of change themselves. That was the sort of politician Alice was, and it were those skills that she used to help create social and educational reforms as well to help win the internal party battles she fought.

*   *   *   *   *

I first heard of Alice just over six years ago and over that time I have gradually pieced together the story of her life and her contribution to the Labour Party and to policy and politics, especially as a minister for six years in the 1960s.

Alice did not write books or diaries, and nor was she part of a set or group in Parliament. But it would be a shame if the lives of pioneering women like Alice were forgotten. It is almost 110 years since Alice was born and more than 20 since she died. The number of people who knew Alice is dwindling and I am pleased to have been able to draw together the stories and memories of those people – as well as, I believe, read all of the speeches and interviews she gave, and articles she wrote. Because of women like Alice, being a woman MP is a little bit less unusual. But Alice was at pains to point out she was an MP, not a woman MP. And her contribution is more than to have increased the representation of women in Parliament. Alice played her part, for 25 years in the House of Commons and a further 23 in the House of Lords, arguing and steering through both social change and educational reforms that have helped make this country a fairer and more tolerant place.

I am pleased, along with Richard Carr, with whom I have been privileged to work, to have been able to write this biography so this Yorkshire-woman, miner's daughter, parliamentary pioneer, reforming minister and Labour loyalist is not forgotten.

∞ 1 ∞

FROM THE WEST RIDING OF
YORKSHIRE (1909–45)

Boots for Bairns

In 1929, a young boy called Geoffrey was taken on the back of his teacher's bike round to the house of Benjamin Bacon in Normanton. Miss Ada Oakley, a teacher at North Featherstone Primary School and Alice's aunt, must have noticed that her pupil's boots were in a very tattered condition. Benjamin Bacon, miner, West Yorkshire County Councillor, and local Miner's Federation president, ran a fund that provided boots for children in need – Boots for Bairns. Geoffrey Lofthouse's father had died that year and his mother was chronically disabled through rheumatoid arthritis, so Geoffrey was certainly a child in need. Benjamin, not being at home that day, was ably represented by a young Alice Bacon. That day a lifelong friendship was formed between the future MP for Pontefract and later Lord Lofthouse, and the future Leeds MP and later Baroness Bacon.

This was Alice's hinterland. Normanton, in the West Riding of Yorkshire. Rooted in her community, Alice was a miner's daughter, a campaigner, a practical politician – certain of her values and determined to put them in to practice. Sixteen years after helping her father with Boots for Bairns, on 10 October 1945 Alice stood to deliver her maiden address in the House of Commons. As Alice Bacon began, she was speaking of those formative years. 'I have always lived among miners', she told the House, 'and my home has always been one to which men have come with their difficulties and troubles.'[1] A politician's origins, as Ben Pimlott noted of Harold Wilson, are often a useful rhetorical weapon, and readily deployed as such.[2] Yet as with the future Prime Minister in

Huddersfield, there is little doubt that Alice's experiences growing up in Normanton were humble, and that these early years had a significant effect on her politics.

Alice Martha Bacon was born on 10 September 1909 at 346 Castleford Road, Normanton, seven months after her parents had married. The 1911 Census records eight residents at that address (almost double the then national average of 4.3 people per household).[3] Aside from their young daughter, Benjamin (1882–1958) and Charlotte – Lottie – Bacon (1888–1953) lived with Lottie's parents George and Alice (who also passed on her middle name Martha to the future MP). Lottie's two siblings, Alice's maternal uncle and aunt, Joseph and Sarah Handley, also lived there along with a boarder named Arthur Lee.[4]

The house, both literally and metaphorically, was built on coal. Benjamin, George, Joseph and Arthur Lee were all employed in the mines. And underneath the house lay a pillar of coal, making certain that the home never ran short of heat – or soot.[5] Bernard Atha, a Leeds councillor who knew Alice for almost the entirety of her parliamentary career, remembers Alice Bacon's father Benjamin as 'an old-fashioned socialist, with a flat cap on his head, and a very sharp and bright politician'. Indeed, when he first watched Marlon Brando in *The Godfather*, he remembers noticing the similarities between Alice's father and Don Corleone. Though Benjamin Bacon avoided the more sinister aspects of the character, Atha was struck by how people would come to Benjamin for advice – be it regarding a union dispute, housing, or virtually any political or social issue.[6] As Alice said in 1986 in an interview with the BBC:

everybody would come to our house for various things. Some would come to pay their union money if they hadn't been able to get to work. Some would come for the little pension that was paid to the miners from the union. At one time I remember we had a room full of 'boots for bairns', after one of the strikes.[7]

The house was a local hub. It was where Alice learnt her trade.

Benjamin Bacon was Alice's early political guiding light. Later she would have parliamentary mentors in the shape of Herbert Morrison and Hugh Gaitskell, but it was her father who stimulated Alice's interest in politics and the world around her. In later life, she would often speak of how proud she was of him, and how she had only advanced so far thanks to his efforts to guide, educate and encourage her.[8] 'When I was only twelve years old', Alice told her fellow MPs in her maiden Commons speech, 'I went down the mine into its inner workings and almost terrifying darkness.' This was almost certainly her father's doing: a desire to instil within his only child – for there would be no son to carry on his politics – a lifelong sympathy with the working man and a true understanding of their working conditions. As secretary of the Whitwood branch of the MFGB with 3,500 members, and an urban district and West Riding County Councillor, Benjamin was a man not just grumbling about the working-class lot, but willing to do something about it.[9] Benjamin was first elected in 1929 and returned in every election thereafter. In 1950 Normanton Urban Council paid him the tribute of calling a new street of council houses Bacon Avenue after his long period of distinguished service.[10]

Locally, rather unusually in the coal industry in the 1920s and 1930s, Benjamin Bacon was sometimes kicking against an open door: Whitwood Colliery (sunk in 1874) was a mine which utilised a profit-sharing scheme, and had employed the internationally recognised architect, Charles Voysey, to design housing for its workforce.[11] Yet, although conditions were significantly better than at other pits, it was tough and dangerous work. This was something Alice understood from an early age.

Bacon was a big figure in the union movement. The MFGB had been formed in 1889 to challenge what it saw as a cartel of government and the mine owners – with the former unwilling to meaningfully regulate the latter save for the odd political gestures after much-publicised tragedies. Membership of the union grew quickly and by the early 1890s it had 250,000 members. By 1912, with a membership of over 600,000, the MFGB instigated a six-week-long strike to secure a minimum wage. This was eventually unsuccessful (the then Liberal government introducing a bill that saw the strike called off whilst not, in the end, compelling mine owners to meet a specific wage). During World War I the government – after hostile and sometimes hysterical reaction from the conservative press about the supposed treachery of going on strike – partially acquiesced to two pay demands from the MFGB. A further call for a six-hour day and 30 per cent wage increase in 1919 was met by the setting up of a commission under Lord Sankey, which subsequently recommended nationalisation of the mines, and both wages and working hours to move in the direction the MFGB demanded. However, having promised to meet the Sankey commission's recommendations, Prime Minister Lloyd George subsequently reneged. Problems over the issues of pay and working conditions resurfaced in the 1920s, and particularly in 1926 with the General Strike. This must have reinforced to Ben and Alice Bacon the notion that only Labour was likely to translate kind words into meaningful action.

The pits of Normanton and Whitwood were mostly a product of the 1860s and 1870s, and added to those already surrounding the town. This produced a large rise in Normanton's population from scarcely over 500 in 1861 to almost 3,500 a decade later, and to over 12,000 by the turn of the century. A significant amount of this growth came from immigration from Ireland, Scotland and Wales. This also produced a rise in the construction of poor quality terraced housing, often resulting in problems with the water supply and sewage. Amidst such an environment the aristocrats of this town were highly regarded miners such as Benjamin Bacon.

Alice's father was solidly Labour, as was the town which returned a Lib-Lab Member of Parliament from 1885 to 1909, and Labour MPs ever since. This did not mean the area was devoid of political debate. The Liberal Party had organised in the town since the 1860s, and the Conservative Party maintained a permanent, if somewhat forlorn, presence locally.[12] But in the 1800s this was a small 'l' labour hinterland waiting for a big 'L' Labour Party to represent its interests.

From 1885 until his death in 1904, Normanton had former miner Benjamin Pickard as their parliamentary representative. Pickard was a local MP but also a representative of the mining community. He spoke regularly and passionately about the working conditions endured in the pits, including in this contribution in 1902 (seven years before Alice was born), on the continued and commonplace existence of child labour:

> We have in our mines today more than 47,000 boys under sixteen years of age working under these terrible conditions. In Scotland there are 6,400, in Northumberland 2,300, in Durham 6,700, in Yorkshire 6,000, in Staffordshire 1,100, in Lancashire 4,300, and in South Wales and Monmouthshire 11,000.[13]

Pickard served as President of the Miners Federation of Great Britain from 1889 to his death, and spoke, as would Alice, of both the dangers involved in mining and, because they were never expected to be destined for anything except life at the coalface, the terrible levels of illiteracy amongst young men in mining areas:

If you look at the number of lads who are injured in our mines, the conclusion is inevitable that something must be done for the boys. In some cases, boys have to crawl through passages ranging from twelve inches to two feet three inches in height, with the result that they constantly suffer from sore backs ... Since I have been a Member of Parliament. I have [also] had brought under my notice the cases of large numbers of illiterate men who when they go into the polling booth are compelled to put a cross against their names. I want that to be a thing of the past.

Pickard campaigned on this platform all his life, and two generations of Bacons – Ben and Alice – would continue the struggle.

Alice started school during World War I at Featherstone Infants School (she was just four when war broke out), where her aunt Ada Oakley had been a teacher. Since coal mining was essential for the war effort, it was a busy time for her father Benjamin. After the outbreak of hostilities in July 1914 and the realisation that it would not 'all be over by Christmas', the unions and the government sat round the negotiating table and hammered out an agreement. In March 1915 the unions agreed that for the duration of hostilities they would not go on strike, and would accept government arbitration in any disputes over pay and conditions. The Factory Acts which had restricted the employment of women and the young were relaxed, as was legislation related to the length of the working week. Arthur Henderson, later Foreign Secretary, became Labour's first Cabinet minister as President of the Board of Education from May 1915 – as a coalition government was forged for the duration of the conflict. There were still disagreements with the administration – 8,000 engineers went on strike at the beginning of 1915, and a Leeds meeting of June 1917 saw Ramsay MacDonald extend 'absolutely unstinted and unqualified' congratulations to the revolutionaries in Russia (not the government line) – but the party political truce broadly managed to hold.

Leeds, about ten miles from Alice in Normanton, was profoundly affected by the Great War in a number of ways. Two hundred Leeds football fans were enlisted in the early weeks of the war through a recruiting session at Elland Road (at half time of a Leeds United game). By March 1915 approaching 1 in 15 of all fighting-aged men in Leeds had joined up, higher than the 1 in 25 level seen in Bradford. But attitudes towards the war were more nuanced than this demonstration of patriotism suggests. For instance, the Leeds local tribunal set up to examine potential exemptions from military service (conscription being introduced in 1916) was one of the busiest in the country. The tribunal sat 435 times, held over 55,000 hearings involving 27,000 individuals (indicating that many appealed against the decision to compel them to fight, and more than once). The war memorial in Leeds reflects this ambiguity towards the conflict – the 'figure of victory, rather than brandishing a sword over its head, held the sword in front of it as a cross'.[14]

This ambiguity must have been true of Normanton too. In Alice's birthplace of Castleford Road, 16 young men would not return home having made the ultimate sacrifice. They are buried in places as diverse as Ypres and Baghdad. One of these men, Private Bertie Beedle, was killed just nine days before the armistice in November 1918, when Alice was 9 years old.[15] Throughout the war many Normanton young men made the trip to Wakefield – the regional recruiting centre – to enlist to fight for King and Country. In November 1915 the *Yorkshire Evening Post* did, however, note that there was a natural cap on recruitment since the men were needed elsewhere:

> the workers are practically all colliers, and the miner being almost as indispensable as the shell turner, he is not required in the Army. This fact accounts for such a large percentage of the men in Wakefield and Normanton Parliamentary Divisions being, starred (as necessary reserve workers).[16]

Morale amongst such workers was important and dissent was punished. Earlier in 1915 two workers at Sharlston Colliery – about five miles from Benjamin Bacon's colliery of Whitwood – were summoned to an industrial tribunal for absenting themselves without permission. The prosecutor:

> said that 500 men from the colliery had joined the [armed services], and one would have thought that those who were left would have realised their duty to attend regularly to their work in order that coal could be supplied for making the necessary munitions of war.[17]

The case was upheld and the appropriate wages docked. For the most part, the miners remained in work during the conflict – but there were sporadic strikes over pay and conditions. In August 1918, for instance, Benjamin Bacon took part in a short strike affecting the Castleford, Pontefract and Normanton districts. The Conservative-sympathetic press claimed it would 'probably be a lesson to the men not to take things lightly in the future' and that 'very few, if any, had any heart in the strike'.[18]

Away from the war and the world of work we can discern that Alice's parents were ambitious for their only child. Clearly, Alice was a bright girl. At the age of 10 she sat the grammar school entry exam and, being successful, started at Normanton Girls' High School in 1920.[19] This in itself was impressive – only 17 per cent of 14–17-year-olds went to secondary school at this time[20] and the grammar school opened up opportunities for higher clerical work, joining the railway companies, and, particularly for girls, teaching. Normanton Girls' High School even sent the odd pupil to Cambridge and Oxford (unusual since only 6 per cent of the tiny secondary school population would go on to university in the late 1920s – and only around a quarter of this already small number were girls).[21] On the other hand, for those who did not attend the grammar school, the future looked less comfortable. Almost certainly for young boys in the area this meant the pit, which remained, as Benjamin Pickard MP argued, a tough profession. For young girls the 1931 census shows that, without attending the grammar school, Alice could have expected to become a domestic servant (as did 21 per cent of women in employment), or to have worked in clothing (9.4 per cent) or textile (11.1 per cent) industries.[22] Eighty per cent of the girls in Bradford, where Barbara Castle was growing up at the same time as Alice, would go to work in the mill at 14.[23] To seek, much less achieve, another lot in life took great ability – and it also took imagination and guts.

Bravery to challenge established patterns of thought or not, much still however depended on a test taken at age 10. Alice was one of the lucky few who had new horizons opened up to her. Addressing the House of Lords in 1976, three years before Margaret Thatcher became Prime Minister, Alice reflected on the impact of receiving – and not receiving – a grammar school education:

> Mrs. Thatcher is fond of telling us that she is the product of a grammar school—and anything which produced Mrs. Thatcher must be preserved. I am the product of a grammar school, too, and a great many of my noble friends on this side of the House are products of grammar schools. But we were the lucky few, the few who got through, and I know that in my small mining town (and I can assure the noble Lord, Lord Elton, that I live among ordinary people—miners and railwaymen) there were a great

many boys and girls of my age who ought to have gone to the grammar school and receive a grammar school education, but there was not the opportunity for them to do so.[24]

It was precisely this guilt and knowledge of how lucky she was, and, within an otherwise demonstrably working-class environment, a feeling of *noblesse oblige*, that spurred Alice on to make a difference in people's lives, and to expand their opportunities. It was what she saw, what she knew of poverty and life-chances, even from a young age that motivated Alice as an MP and later as Minister for Education. Here she was building on the tradition of university-educated Yorkshiremen who ran evening classes in economics, history and philosophy – to open up horizons, broaden the mind and ensure that the opportunities available to the more privileged might also be opened up to working men and women.

At this time, grammar schools came with fees often prohibitive for working-class parents. Fees varied – but costs of between £6 and £12 per annum were not atypical. According to the sociologist Seebohm Rowntree (famous for his surveys of the poverty in Victorian York), the minimum wage to keep a family in basic subsistence around this time was 53 shillings a week (£2 13s – about £137 each year). Nearly half of the population was probably not earning even this meagre amount – in 1929 it was estimated that almost 12 million out of a working population of 20 million were earning under £125 a year, whilst in 1935 the Fabian writers G.D.H and Margaret Cole estimated those earning under 55s a week to constitute 47 per cent of adult male workers. To take one pertinent profession, Harold Macmillan's tract *The Middle Way* has the average adult male miner's week at 47 hours long and at a wage of 53s 4d. Given saving this 4d surplus was not even close to funding £6 worth of grammar school fees (it comes to just over £1 in old money), this meant that miners would simply not have been able to afford a grammar school education for their children without a scholarship.

Working-class families often did not have the means to change their lot. As Keir Hardie put it in Bradford in 1914, government policy had long been determined by:

cruel, heartless dogmas, backed up by quotations from Jeremy Bentham, Malthus, and Herbert Spencer, and by a bogus interpretation of Darwin's theory of evolution, [which] were accepted as part of the unalterable laws of nature, sacred and inviolable, and were maintained by statesmen, town councillors, [and] ministers of the Gospel.[25]

Talking to an audience which included many such workers, he continued:

[in the Victorian era] safety regulations in mines and factories were taboo. They interfered with the 'freedom of the individual'. As for such proposals as an eight-hour day, a minimum wage, the right to work, and municipal houses, any serious mention of such classed a man as a fool.[26]

There were a few benevolent paternalist exceptions – such as Harold Macmillan's later call for a minimum wage (possibly motivated by similar experiences of interwar poverty in his Stockton-on-Tees constituency) – but for the most part the Hardie vision of what the world should be like was not even remotely to come to pass for several decades.[27] In the meantime Labour at least continued to push for change, as and where it could exercise influence. In 1919 Poplar's Labour-led council pressed for far-reaching social reform and poor relief, and brought in equal pay for women and a minimum salary for municipal workers. The 1929 Labour government under MacDonald legislated for price controls in the coal industry (to ensure wages would not drop). When MacDonald famously resigned from office in 1931, it was part because of his colleagues' refusal to cut the salaries of teachers. As the 1931 party election manifesto put it, Labour would always 'place the needs of the workers before the demands of the rich'. But the tide could only be held back so much in an era of Conservative dominance at Westminster.

Alice's schooling, family finances and her experience of going down the pit were all part of what made her politics. So too was her time in working-men's clubs – the hub of the community in most mining places. Apart from the barmaid, women were not really to be seen inside these clubs, except on family days or perhaps for big public meetings. But the Bacons were exceptions. Alice's mother, Lottie, would lay on sandwiches at the club and her daughter would help in the kitchen. With her mum in the kitchen and her dad as a local union leader, Alice increasingly spent much of her own free time in the clubs – playing dominoes, darts and cards with the miners. But it was her father again who ensured that Alice saw the harsher side of the industry and community that she was born into. And, being educated, Alice was a real asset to the miners. After school and at weekends, Alice would help men complete their forms for insurance claims for industrial accidents and diseases[28] – a foretaste of the constituency casework that Alice would become so highly regarded for after 1945.

It was not a surprise then that in 1925, at the age of 16, Alice joined the Labour Party. Her father was her inspiration, and she said later that 'there was never a time when I decided to join the Labour Party – I was born in to politics'. Shortly after joining, she made her first political speech at the Railwaymen's Institute at Normanton. It proved Alice could think on her feet, and win over an audience:

> It was a council election in Normanton and a friend of my father's was standing for the council, and he said 'what about Alice making a speech?' So I prepared a speech all about local government. It was very, very learned and then I went to the meeting, and looked around at the audience and realised this speech wouldn't do at all. I had been telling my father, mother and aunt what I was going to say. They were in the audience and I decided 'no, I must make another speech out of my head'. I got up and my mother said, 'oh, Ben, she's forgotten it all!' They went out and walked around the little hall until they heard the applause. And that was my first speech.[29]

Alice was proving herself as a practical politician, rooted in her community and its challenges but also able to articulate what she knew and saw in words and speeches.

The 1920s were heady times for organised trade unionism in Britain, and Benjamin Bacon, as a local MFGB leader, was at the centre of things. Having come together in 1914 to form the 'Triple Alliance' – the National Transport Workers' Federation, the National Union of Railwaymen and the Mine Workers – the trade union movement was rocked in April 1921 by the refusal of two of its members, the transport and rail unions, to support further strike action by the miners over wage reductions.

That the young Alice was led down the coal mines at this time was surely no coincidence. Conditions were, although improving, very poor. Silicosis – severe respiratory problems such as shortness of breath, coughing, fever and bluish skin (due to a lack of oxygen) – was a common affliction for the interwar miner.[30] Mines were also infested with vermin – in a study of a South Yorkshire mine in the 1950s it was observed that 'numerous reports exist of [workers'] food being eaten from the pockets of jackets laid on machinery, and rats have been seen to approach and take scraps thrown down less than 6ft from the feet of sitting men'.[31] It would be a long way from here to the benches of Parliament.

Parliament itself was heavily Conservative-dominated between the wars. Indeed, few of those who legislated from the government benches for most of the 1920s would have had even the young Alice's experience of the mines. After the collapse of the Lloyd George coalition in 1922, the Conservative Party secured sizeable election victories in the general elections of 1924, 1931 and 1935. Though not all Conservative politicians were 'hard faced men who had done well out of the war' – to borrow Keynes' phrase – a significant proportion, and particularly the party's upper reaches, clearly had no meaningful connection with the working class. Stanley Baldwin's 1924 21-man (and it was only men) Cabinet contained eight peers and eight knights of the realm, hardly the best representation of a 1920s Britain where unemployment was perpetually over 10 per cent of the labour force. Whilst Labour formed short-lived minority governments in 1924 and 1929, led by the gradualist Ramsay MacDonald, they lacked a parliamentary majority for meaningful action. Later, MacDonald's decision to lead a Conservative-dominated National Government from 1931, implementing far-reaching spending cuts designed to balance the budget, caused him to become a hate figure in the Labour Party – and across significant areas of the country. Delivering a socialist majority government would henceforth be the goal of all the left, and Alice would take part in that historic achievement come 1945.

A Conservative-dominated era was certainly challenging for industrial relations. In May 1926, a year after Alice joined the Labour Party, there was the General Strike. Again faced by wage reductions of between 10 and 25 per cent, and a lengthening of working hours, the MFGB famously declared 'not a penny off the pay, not a minute on the day'. This time the trade unions stood together. Railwaymen, transport workers, printers, dockers, ironworkers and steelworkers downed tools in solidarity with the miners. On 5 May in Leeds there were reports of 'ugly scenes' involving 'several thousand strikers' attacking an emergency tramcar with lumps of coal, then rushing another, before the police intervened. After a police charge attempted to disperse them, two more tramcars were attacked.[32] West Yorkshire, particularly its Labour leadership, stood shoulder to shoulder with the miners – whatever the views of Ramsay MacDonald or his former (and future) Chancellor Philip Snowden.[33] These protests, and most of all, their impacts on the mining community of which she was a part, had a big effect on Alice – and on her politics. As she later recalled:

I do remember the Yorkshire miners' demonstrations when my father would get the banner and bring it home to my mother. She would stitch the banner and make it all ready for the next day and then the band would set off with the banner at the head. During the strike of 1926, my father had an arrangement with a fishmonger to deliver fish to our house twice a week, and there was a little queue outside in the garden to buy it at about a penny a pound. So that twice a week he saw that all his members at least had a good meal of fish.[34]

The strike ended on 12 May with a climb-down by the trade unions. The conservative press – most prominently the Churchill-edited *British Gazette* with its headlines of 'organised attempt to starve the nation', 'dissolve the T[rade] U[nions] C[ongress]!' and 'assault on the rights of the nation' – had, albeit through base, negative tactics, won the day.[35] Emboldened, the Conservatives subsequently passed the 1927 Trade Disputes and Trade Unions Act which had the effect of cutting the political levy paid by union members to the Labour Party, and banned civil service unions from affiliating to the TUC. The 1929 minority Labour government unsuccessfully attempted to overturn this legislation, but it would be Alice and over 300 of her colleagues who eventually repealed it in April 1946.

This period must have settled Alice on her anti-Conservative politics, but she may also have developed something of an anti-communist position – and would not have been the only one. Speaking in Normanton in 1929, the miners' leader A. J. Cook declared himself resolved to fight the communists, who had begun to infiltrate the trade unions and Labour Party, and as Cook put it 'raised the standard against Labour' – as an enemy of the broad labour movement. One suspects Alice would have agreed.[36] In the 1920s some 23 local constituency Labour parties were disaffiliated at one time or another due to local communist sympathies. Alice must have heard of this – and she would lead similar activities, of suspending members of local constituency parties, on behalf of the Labour Party machine three decades later.[37]

In the Classroom

By 1927, aged 18, Alice had finished at Normanton High School and had her own future to think of. A working-class young woman, even with a grammar school education, had limited choices, but Alice took both the route that best suited her and one that gave her time to continue her political journey. From school she went to Stockwell College in South London, to train as a teacher.

On returning from her training, Alice began teaching at Featherstone Junior School, back in Normanton, from where her aunt Ada Oakley had brought a young Lord Lofthouse to get his boots a few years before. Though she had seen poverty before, there were new depths to uncover:

> I went to Featherstone at the height of the depression in the early 1930s, teaching boys of 11, and while I was there the medical officer came and reported that 73% of the boys at that school were suffering from malnutrition. And there was no school dinners then, no school meals at all. So the council decided to open what was more or less a soup kitchen – we only served soup. Featherstone has one very, very long lane called Station Lane at the top of which is the miners' welfare hall and the other end is the school where I was teaching and we had to take the children every lunchtime along this long lane to the miners' welfare hall for them to have soup and bread. And it was then that, although I'd been in politics as a child, it was then I realised that something was very wrong. And that I must do something that could help to relieve this kind of thing.[38]

Alice later moved to Queen Street Elementary School in Normanton, from where she transferred, with the senior pupils, to the new Normanton Modern School in 1937. Shirley Williams' comment that 'she would have made an ideal schoolmistress' is reflected in Alice's own reminiscences.[39] A reference from her headmaster at Queen Street also provides some insight into her abilities:

> her work throughout has been of a high standard, for she has real teaching ability and possesses a proper appreciation of the child's mind ... Quiet and dignified in manner, she is particularly suited for work with older children, and I have no hesitation in recommending her for a post where a practical teacher with organising ability is required.[40]

Although Alice was an education reformer and involved in banning corporal punishment, like other teachers at the time – including the future MP Jennie Lee, who was teaching in Cowdenbeath in Scotland – she used the cane to enforce discipline, as former pupils have testified.

If Alice's grammar school days had imbued a sense that others were not so fortunate, her teaching career provided a firsthand taste of life in an interwar secondary modern. Her later advocacy of comprehensive education, Alice said, 'had nothing whatever to do with my politics. It was due to the fact that … I was a teacher in the secondary modern school, and saw the unfairness of the eleven plus system and the separation of children between secondary modern and grammar schools.'[41]

As might be expected of the daughter of a union official, Alice joined the National Union of Teachers as soon as she became a teacher. Alice shared the NUT's views on comprehensive education, dilapidated school buildings, class sizes and the school leaving age, and would become one of their lead members – outside, and inside, Westminster.

An insight into the average secondary modern is given by the demands of the 1935 NUT conference in Scarborough. The NUT executive committee noted that 'they were not prepared to tolerate the continued existence of antiquated buildings which were a disgrace to the twentieth century'. Successive governments, they argued, had essentially condoned a 'sardine tin policy' of cramming children – sometimes 50 at a time – into classes. Even if the interwar secondary modern was far from ideal, leaving at 14 (the school leaving age at the time) was not the best solution. Instead, they wanted the school leaving age to be increased to 16. Increases in juvenile delinquency were put down to the 'premature precipitation of young people into commerce and industry' by the NUT, and motions to raise the school age were also passed by their conference.[42] Martin Pugh has recently suggested the explosion of the interwar gambling market – betting being illegal everywhere but on a race course since 1906 – owed its existence in part to 14-year-old boys ferrying bets between bookmakers and their customers – often in pubs or outside labour exchanges. Better for 14-year-olds to be at school! Smoking at such ages was almost expected, despite again being illegal for under-16s since 1906.[43] Alice would not have tolerated such behaviour from her pupils, but once they had left school there was little that could be done.

Alice used these experiences in the Chamber of the House of Commons for years afterwards. Facing the Conservative parliamentary benches in 1954, she doubted 'whether many of them ever have been in a council school except to speak at General Election meetings'. However, she did not lack such experience: 'I know what it is like to try to concentrate on arithmetic when the class next door, which is separated by a thin partition, is having a lesson in music'. She was by then:

a politician but, I taught children from the ages of 11 to 15 for some years before I came [to the Commons], and my belief in the comprehensive school is derived, not from my membership of the Labour Party, but from my experience with children.[44]

Leo Abse (Labour MP for Pontypool between 1958 and 1983) said that Alice had been elected at too young an age (35), and argued that teaching was all she had to talk about. Yet her commitment to such issues was real, sustained and well-informed. Certainly well over a decade in the classroom was not bad preparation for the parliamentary debates to come.

Beyond her strong views on comprehensives, the issue of space and the dilapidation of many schools also motivated Alice. The experience of teaching maths with a temporary partition between classes was one concern, yet the terrible state of so many school buildings was also a huge problem in the secondary moderns. Later references to 'dark, dreary, airless [schools] … badly equipped and full of old furniture' was a typical interwar experience. Her assertion, addressing Winston Churchill, that 'I doubt whether the Prime Minister would have passed the common entrance selection test if he had not gone to Harrow' was not so much an indictment of the (by then old) man's intelligence, but an acknowledgment of the difference to children that a good education – in decent buildings, with smaller class sizes and better facilities – could make.[45] Yet with the government in the 1930s, as again after 1951, Conservative led, ministers resisted such costs. Six hundred schools condemned as unfit for use in 1925 were still in use in 1953.[46] It was a disgrace and Alice knew it was holding back young people – in places like Normanton – from meeting their potential.

Pent-up demand for new school buildings produced strains on class sizes. As part of her teacher training, Alice taught in an infants' school: 'during that time I knew what it was like to have to teach a class of 30, 40 or more'. Whilst 40 for primary and 30 for secondary schools were the recommended limits as set out by the Ministry of Education in the early 1950s, Alice knew the difficulties of getting 40 infants to concentrate at any one time: 'we might consider whether it would be better to have smaller classes for the smaller children and perhaps slightly larger classes for the[ir] elders'.[47] These issues would form a key part of Bacon's political agenda in the early 1950s, and her zeal in attempting to fund new school buildings as a minister in the late 1960s owes a clear debt to her formative experiences. Abse may have poured scorn on Alice's intellectual abilities, but the point is that her politics were not academic in both senses of the word. Alice didn't dress up her views in flowery or intellectual language; instead her politics was always grounded in practical experience.

As well as giving Alice a cause and a story, teaching furthered her trade union links. As she had done with her father in the working-men's clubs, Alice worked as a trade unionist in the staff-room, organising the teachers at Featherstone, Queen Street, Normanton Modern School and in time across the West Yorkshire district. The 1943 NUT Annual Report lists her as a vice president of its West Yorkshire division (prior to her succeeding to the presidency the next year), and as one of 16 NUT members teaching at Normanton Modern School.[48]

On 8 April 1942 Alice was elected to the National Executive Committee of the NALT as its northern delegate, a position she held for two years.[49] Though few specific minutes survive from the period, we do know that the executive committee of NALT unanimously passed a resolution urging the government to set a definitive date for raising the school leaving age to 16. A motion encouraging the Communist Party to affiliate with Labour was passed, but not without some abstentions. Though the record does not exist it is almost certain, given her views, that the abstentions included Alice. Alice received support from the teaching unions while they got some prestige from their young protégé. The NALT supported Alice in her election campaigns for the NEC of the Labour Party. And all MPs elected in 1945 with NALT membership were offered a vice presidency of the group (which most, including Alice, accepted), with the understanding that – as expressed at a 1945 executive committee meeting – 'if the Association was to continue it should now seek to work very closely with the Labour Members of Parliament, particularly the group of ex-teacher MPs'.[50] Alice continued to be lobbied by the NALT in the 1960s even when she was both a Home Office and Education minister.

As well as maintaining links with the teaching unions, Alice kept in touch with former colleagues. Mary Goodall, who had taught alongside Alice in Normanton, remembers Alice being a popular teacher who 'didn't mind when others didn't share her politics' and who was always willing to help out a teacher – with cups of tea on bus-strike days for example, or a fellow pupil – especially if she knew the pupil had problems at home. Even once Alice was in Parliament, Mary and other teacher friends were invited down to Parliament by Alice, and put up at the Strand Hotel by their former school teacher friend.

League of Youth

That a miner's daughter with a desire to become a teacher should join the Labour Party was hardly surprising: it was 'as natural as breathing', to borrow Anne Symonds' assessment of Alice.[51] It is, however, worth noting that her early politics were hardly typical. The Abse critique suggested a 'spinster' – his word – whose experience might have made for a useful member of the NUT, but who understood little of the wider, more complex political scene.[52] This view though was wrong. Alice had roots, yet she was more than just her father's daughter, and took a keen interest in broader socialist politics both at home and abroad.

At home there was the LOY – an organisation designed to get the young involved in the mechanics (including campaigning, writing political pamphlets and making speeches) of socialist politics. The LOY's purpose, as far as the party was concerned, was 'to enrol large numbers of young people, and by a social life of its own, provide opportunities for young people to study party policy and give loyal support to the party'.[53] In reality, the LOY seems to have served as a hub for small groups of already committed Labour supporters, many of whom had an eye on future political engagement. As Michelle Webb has noted, 'by 1935, most members of the League of Youth were active in electioneering whilst many had been endorsed as party candidates or members of borough councils'.[54] In 1933 indeed, it is estimated that 300 branches of the LOY had a core of around 20 members each. From a pool of around 15 million young people, this, as Webb states, was rather 'paltry'.[55]

The letters to Alice from Jack Prichard, the LOY's organising secretary, indicate that reaching beyond the committed core could prove tough. Attempting to enlist Alice to campaign in Cross Gates and Temple Newsam in Leeds with the LOY in 1939, Prichard commented:

> We have, of course, run such campaigns before, but the response in the last three years has been so meagre that it was only with considerable trepidation that it was agreed that you should be invited to assist us in this campaign. I was, therefore, instructed to acquaint you with the possibility of failure and to invite you, if you felt you could spare some of your valuable time despite the risk of failure, to address ... a League meeting.[56]

If crowds were small Alice was clearly an important figure. When Ted (later Lord) Willis joined the LOY in the early 1930s, he described it as being largely dominated by George Brown (later Labour Party deputy leader from 1960), Alice, and Will Nally (MP for Wolverhampton from 1945) – all of whom tended to adopt 'a position of outright hostility towards the growing left-wing feeling of the rank and file'. Alice's speech to the 1936 Party Conference seems to conform to such a view. Urging the party to invest in the LOY, she offered a warning against certain elements within it. Labour Party time and money, she argued, should concentrate on the ordinary members of the league and not the 'irresponsible people who are inside the League of Youth not to advance the Labour Party, but to advance points of view and -isms which they cannot get across inside the Labour Party itself'. As with communists in the 1950s, Alice always feared the potential for fifth columnists. In 1955, partly through lack of funds, partly through poor organisation, it would fall to Alice to partially dissolve the very organisation that had helped launch her, with LOY activities being passed back to local constituency organisations.[57]

Alice's involvement in the League of Youth also helped her travel abroad for the first time. Commenting on Harold Wilson's reshuffle in 1967, *The Times* described Alice as '"a young looking 55" [sic]'. Probably more pertinent, however, was its claim that she represented 'one of the most travelled members of the government'.[58] This did not start with ministerial or parliamentary delegations, but had significant pre-1945 precedent. Her first meeting with Hugh Gaitskell, who became a dear and not merely a political friend, came not in Leeds or Westminster as MPs, but in Geneva 'at a Summer School for Young Members of the Labour Party' a full decade earlier. In her warm obituary to Gaitskell in 1963, she recalled that in the Geneva summit 'Hugh was one of the lecturers … the first conversation I remember having with him, he told me I was a clever girl.'[59] The 'clever girl' was to become a close confidante and a parliamentary neighbour in Leeds. It was the start of an important relationship, for both Alice and Hugh Gaitskell.

Having reached the upper age limit of 25 for the Labour LOY in 1934, Alice became increasingly active in the Socialist Youth International, serving as the British delegate to its European conferences in Copenhagen in 1935 and in Brussels a year later. It was necessary, she told fellow delegates in Copenhagen, 'for democratic countries to show that democracy could be more successful than any other form of government, and in that way to give hope to the peoples suffering under Fascism'.[60] In domestic terms this provided an introduction to Hugh Dalton, at the time serving as the chairman of the International Sub-Committee of Labour's NEC, but who later took Alice under his wing after the budget leak of 1947 forced his resignation as Chancellor of the Exchequer.[61] It also gave her a wider exposure to European politics than her later domestic ministerial portfolios would allow. Aside from high-minded, if accurate, resolutions regarding 'the imminent danger of war', the Brussels conference in 1936 included discussions over 'the international exchange of ideas between national committees of young people from 14 to 16', the running of educational camps, and the creation of a body called the Red Pioneers to oversee such operations.[62]

These platforms, and Alice's contacts, gave her the opportunity to speak for Labour on the issues of the day around the country. In August 1937 the *Berwick Advertiser* records 'the well known orator' Alice Bacon giving a 'forceful address' to an audience mainly composed of holiday-makers on introducing paid holiday leave from work. Alice spoke for all those 'denied an annual holiday with wages, and of the two million industrial workers who had just secured this benefit mainly through agreements by their Trade Unions'. In order to vote through such changes which could bring 'health, efficiency, and social well being [for] the workers', however, Alice would need a seat in Parliament. As it turned out, she was soon to take a step closer to this.

Parliamentary Candidate

As the 1930s unfolded, unemployment rose, industrial disputes increased and the political atmosphere soured. In Normanton unemployment rose from 392 in 1930 to 876 by 1934 – the highest proportional increase in the West Riding.[63] This was a fact not always raised in Parliament for one procedural reason – Frederick Hall, the Liberal (1905–9) turned Labour MP (1909–33) for the town was, as a party whip, largely silent in the Commons for the entirety of his tenure. But his successor from 1933, Tom Smith, was much more vocal – speaking on unemployment insurance, profits in the mining industry and regularly on industrial compensation – the latter the theme of Alice's maiden speech a decade later.

Even as the British economy began to recover – not least due to the stimulus of sorts provided by the need to rearm for an impending conflict with Nazi Germany in the late 1930s – there were massive regional disparities. The 1935 Conservative-led National Government manifesto had boasted of 'cheap money' having 'facilitated enterprise and stimulated industrial expansion'. New industries, they claimed, were flowing into the 'special areas' – that euphemism for areas of mass deprivation. By balancing the budget, lowering interest rates to 2 per cent, and bringing the exchange rate down, the National Government claimed its monetarist strategy had worked. Yet Alice knew through her own experience that if this had indeed applied a jolt to the economy this was at once regionally specific and limited in scale. Factories moved to London (some 85 per cent of total factory moves in 1933 were to the capital, and still as high as 70 per cent by 1937) with over 50 major businesses leaving less prosperous areas of the country in the mid-1930s. By contrast, fewer than 20 factories moved to the north-east between 1932 and 1938. Similarly, once people living outside the south lost their jobs they tended to stay unemployed: 6 per cent of London's unemployed in 1938 had been out of work for 12 months or more, a figure dwarfed by 30 per cent of those made unemployed in the north, Scotland and Wales. As a result of all this, total employment in Britain did not exceed its 1920 peak until 1938.[64] Interwar Conservatism was not working for too many people.

George Lansbury, Labour leader after the electoral collapse of 1931, turned to a former Conservative to sum up the contemporary situation:

> Disraeli's 'two nations' no longer live together. So far as they can, the employing and land-owning classes live right away from the workers. 'What the eye doesn't see the heart doesn't grieve', and the rich have settled their consciences over the question of poverty by going away where they cannot see it, and only occasionally visit the districts from which their wealth is drawn.[65]

Part of this was about jobs, but there was also the lack of state provision in several areas. And such fears were not solely the preserve of the left. As Harold Macmillan wrote in 1938:

> The protective blanket of social care extends over the whole area, and the casual person with an aridly logical mind might well ask – what more do you want? But the picture is not so rosy when we look at it more closely. Admirable as it is – our system of public health, environmental and social services, falls very far short of providing an adequate basis of physical well-being and security.[66]

Responding to the pre-war conditions and the post-war hopefulness, William Beveridge predicated his famous 1942 report dealing with the 'five giant evils' of squalor, ignorance, want, idleness and disease. In July 1943 Beveridge addressed a group of Leeds businessmen and remarked that whilst unemployment in the south had dropped to 5 per cent by 1937, he was primarily concerned with joblessness in other parts of the country. The conditions of war solved this in part – with hundreds of young Yorkshiremen being sent down the pits as 'Bevin Boys' and then later through enlisting and conscription into the armed forces. But a post-war evolution in industrial and social policy was needed if poverty and unemployment were to be banished, and opportunity and prosperity more fairly shared. A step-change was needed, but the options were limited. Lloyd George had been 'the man who won the war' in 1918, but he had virtually eliminated the Liberal Party's prospects of forming a government on its own thereafter. Even with the sporadic protest of the younger generation of politicians such as Harold Macmillan, the Tories had presided over two decades of high unemployment. Only Labour seemed to offer a plausible programme for action.

To help shape this agenda Alice needed to be in Parliament, and her own professional and political careers were taking shape in the 1930s. In April 1933 Alice contested the West Riding Urban District Council election in Normanton, but with only 265 votes she failed to reach the 457 votes of the lowest elected councillor in a then multi-member ward.[67] This unsuccessful campaign did, however, launch her into local political prominence. The local press reported that:

> an interesting possibility at Normanton is that the new Council may possess the youngest woman member of any local authority in the country. Among the candidates was Miss Alice Bacon, a 23-years-old school teacher, whose father, Mr B. Bacon, is already on the Council. Miss Bacon is an experienced and fluent public speaker, particularly on political matters.[68]

Despite not being elected to the council, by the late 1930s Alice had acquired a reputation for competence, having in 1937 secured a degree in public administration from the University of London – as an external candidate while still teaching. Her academic success again made the local paper, which detailed the subjects she had taken (economics, social and political theory, statistics and social administration) and the fact that she 'was the only woman who passed'.[69] Getting a degree while also working full-time was a tremendous achievement and one that caused great pride in the Bacon household, Alice was the first in her family to achieve such high academic success. In Labour circles Alice was also moving up. The League of Youth, Socialist Youth, as well as the NALT and NUT were platforms from which to build, and she adeptly combined her teaching and political roles.

Soon after receiving her degree, Alice successfully fought for the nomination to be Labour prospective parliamentary candidate in Leeds North East in 1938, her second attempt to secure a parliamentary selection. Though the records of this decision do not survive, the publicity surrounding her addition to the list of potential Labour parliamentary candidates give something of a clue as to how she secured this position. The *Yorkshire Post* had previously noted that she:

> has done considerable public work locally, and has been President of Normanton and Altofts Association of the National Union of Teachers. Last year she was a member of a Labour group who visited Geneva to study the League of Nations in relation to Labour's foreign policy.[70]

This was an incredible achievement for a young woman of 29, at a time when fewer than 40 women had ever been elected to Parliament before. Lena Jeger, later MP for Holborn and St Pancras South, spoke powerfully of what young women were up against in parliamentary selections:

> Local committees, confronted by a young woman, wonder if she will get pregnant and neglect her duties. If she has children she is often asked, with obvious disapproval, how she proposes to care for them. 'Not a good mother' the worthy matrons will mutter. But I have never heard of a man being asked how he proposes to combine Parliamentary life with conscientious fatherhood. If she waits until, say over the age of 40, the selection conference will instead choose some pushing young man, although at this stage in a woman's life she has perhaps the maximum contribution to make in wisdom and experience to the mother of parliaments.[71]

One wonders whether Alice faced such questions, and indeed how she responded. The future MP for Manchester Gorton, Gerald Kaufman was born in Leeds and became an active member of the Labour Party there as a boy in the 1940s. He notes that 'women MPs were quite extraordinary during Alice's time. They had to fight to become candidates. Alice was elected for a very safe Conservative seat that, at the time, there seemed no possibility of Labour winning.' This was also true, he argues, of Alice's rival and fellow MP Barbara Castle. 'Barbara', Gerald argues, 'got the candidature in Blackburn, then a two member constituency, on the basis that they might as well choose her because she wasn't going to get elected.'[72] If Kaufman is right, then the Labour landslide of 1945, as was true of Labour's second landslide in 1997, brought into Parliament an army of women MPs by accident. But these were accidents that shook up politics and put on to the political agenda issues that previously had not had champions, including in the post-war period equal pay, women's pensions, class sizes and abortion law reform.

The notion of women's seriousness and capability for political office has receded through time, although it persists still today. An undated newspaper clipping from the 1930s in Barbara Castle's archive at Oxford illustrates that even when women had achieved public office – in this case in local government – they were often treated in a patronising manner. Castle, then using her maiden name of Betts, was however not one to take such treatment without challenge, as the albeit sympathetic article showed:

> We sympathise with Miss Barbara Betts' protest against the flattery of the St. Pancras alderman who referred to her as 'the charming lady' and a 'thorough born aristocrat in appearance'. 'Before you flatter a man so grossly to his face', said Dr Johnson to Hannah More, 'you should consider whether your flattery is worth having'. But we fear Miss Betts is fighting a losing battle. It is very difficult to persuade men that women do not like flattery. They like it so much themselves. The sequel of this St Pancras incident illustrates the fact. 'Apparently', said the chairman, coming gallantly to the lady's rescue, 'this lady does not like to be flattered'. 'Apparently', observe. He did not really believe it.[73]

This low level of everyday sexism that was sometimes dished out is illustrative of the challenges women faced to ensure they were heard as well as seen.

No woman had successfully contested a parliamentary seat in Yorkshire before, but Alice reflected in a Yorkshire Television interview in 1991 (subsequently documented by John Grayson in 'Solid Labour') that her gender was irrelevant – it was a question of 'upbringing', not sex, that mattered, with Alice convinced that her years spent in Normanton working-men's clubs were the best preparation for the selection meeting at a working-men's club in industrial Leeds. Yet, despite Alice's own protests, her age and sex made her stand out. In the wartime Parliament fewer than 3 per cent of the Parliamentary Labour Party were women and only 24 of Labour's over 160 MPs were under the age of 50, with 45 of them being over the age of 65.[74] At this time Alice was in her early thirties and about to enter an (older) man's world.

Leeds North East did not feel like a Labour stronghold at the time of Alice's selection (with a majority of nearly 12,000 for the Tory John Birchall in 1935). But, by 1945, conventional political wisdoms were being turned on their head. The election campaign itself was far from a regular campaigning experience – the decision to extend the lifetime of the 1935 Parliament until the conclusion of World War II left MPs otherwise on the way out rather marooned in office, and kept a generation of parliamentary candidates waiting for up to a decade.

Though Labour was destroyed nationally in 1931 and, albeit to a lesser degree, 1935 general elections, the party had retained influence at a local level in Yorkshire. Leeds Council was won by Labour in 1933–5, as was Rotherham (1933) and Wakefield (1934–8). Ten Labour MPs were returned in Yorkshire in 1935, compared to a single MP four years earlier. Labour was on the up in Leeds and Yorkshire when Alice was selected to fight Leeds North East. So, when the Conservative MP for Leeds North East, John Birchall, retired in 1940 it could have been Alice's moment. A by-election was called and Alice had been the prospective parliamentary candidate for the Labour Party in that constituency for two years already. But the parliamentary truce throughout the war between the parties in the National Government meant there was no chance of election to Parliament without jettisoning the Labour Party (something Alice would never countenance). Candidates from Sir Richard Acland's (a former Liberal MP) Common Wealth Party did win three by-elections during the war – only to see its members gradually drift to Labour after the 1945 election – but this was never an option to which Alice gave any thought. In the end the Conservative Party candidate, John Craik-Henderson, a university professor, won the by-election with 97.1 per cent of the vote opposed only by Oswald Mosley's British Union of Fascists. Alice would have to wait another five years to fight and win a parliamentary election. But, during those five years, Alice became a more experienced and confident politician, and, by the end of the war, people were looking for change.

The war was challenging for the mining areas of Yorkshire in which

Alice had grown up. When war began in September 1939 the government had permitted experienced coal miners to register for the armed services and other, higher paid work in reserve occupations. The intention was that relatively depressed areas of the country still had large pools of unemployed labour which would fill the gaps left by these departing miners. But it was not to be and by mid-1943 there was a shortfall of over 40,000 miners needed to maintain production. By December 1943 some estimates claimed Britain was scarcely more than a fortnight from running out of coal altogether. In response Ernest Bevin started his so-called 'Bevin Boys' scheme whereby 48,000 young men were conscripted to go down the mines and get production back on track.

On Christmas Eve 1943 the new recruits found out their placements and on 18 January 1944 the *Yorkshire Post* reported that 600 youths were 'settling down in the unaccustomed atmosphere of [Yorkshire] coal mining towns'. Some Leeds-based Bevin Boys interviewed by the local newspaper (travelling to their new work in Pontefract) declared they would rather have been placed on active service in one of the armed services, but all resolved to get on with their new work to the best of their ability.

As for Alice's new political home, Leeds had not been hit as badly by bombing raids as cities such as London, Coventry and Hull, but there were still German attacks on the city. On 14 and 15 March 1941 around 40 Luftwaffe planes dropped incendiary and high-explosive bombs with targets including the town hall, the main railway station, and the new social housing in and around the Quarry Hill flats. More than 60 people were killed in the raid, 100 houses were destroyed and almost 5,000 damaged. The limited stock of social housing in interwar Leeds was only exacerbated by Hitler's bombing raids.

Not being able to stand for election, with World War II looking like it would continue even longer than the first, it must have been difficult for Alice to keep ploughing on as a prospective parliamentary candidate. Local membership in Yorkshire Labour parties collapsed during the early years of the conflict – in Sheffield Brightside a pre-war membership of 1,000 dropped to just 280 by 1943, albeit to recover somewhat by the end of the war. Keeping a meaningful constituency presence, particularly given her role on NUT and NALT committees – as well as her teaching which she kept up until becoming an MP – cannot have been easy. In 1945 she would get her reward.

Despite her age and her sex, Alice was becoming a national presence before becoming an MP. In 1941 she was elected to the National

Executive Committee (NEC) of the Labour Party through the women's section. Throughout the conflict, the NEC debated issues such as the future borders of a new, democratic Germany, how socialist parties had been eradicated completely or sent into exile across Europe, and the various candidate selection processes prior to the general election. William Beveridge was invited to outline his proposals for reforming the social services before Alice and the NEC, and the body debated various schemes of post-war reconstruction and social policy, including the Butler Act with regard to education. Alice's interventions often appear largely procedural in these wartime minutes – for example on 14 April 1942 she raised the issue of women members of the NEC attending a Standing Joint Committee with 'Working Women's Organisations'. But she was now in the corridors of power – debating the future of the Labour Party with luminaries such as Ellen Wilkinson, Hugh Dalton, Morgan Phillips and Harold Laski.

The NEC gave Alice a national voice for the first time, but her teaching background gave her the cause. Speaking in Blackpool in May 1945 from the party's executive, she told the Party Conference that the Tory Education Secretary Rab Butler's recently passed Education Act was only a step in the right direction: too many of the provisions were only in 'the offing, and not yet in the bag. There must be priority for school buildings and the training of teachers.'[75] She would soon get her chance to help put this agenda into practice. The day before this speech, the Labour conference made it clear they would no longer continue with the wartime coalition, and Churchill formed his short-lived caretaker administration. The 1945 general election, Attlee's triumph and Alice's route into Westminster, was imminent.

∞ 2 ∞

PICKING YOUR BATTLES
(1945–64)

In six years in office, the Labour government, under Attlee, transformed Britain's social security policy, introduced the NHS and built substantial new council housing. But, just under the surface were bubbling intra-party struggles between the left and right, and between the personalities of that government. These splits became more pronounced once Labour moved into opposition. Alice was involved in the series of battles that shaped the British left. This chapter considers Alice Bacon the political operator. Put simply, nothing was handed to Alice. She had to fight as a woman MP to be taken seriously, sought to cultivate alliances with like-minded MPs to ensure Labour remained in the electoral game throughout the 1950s, and took difficult steps within the overall battle of 'left' and 'right' that contributed to both these ends. Alice also had a significant role in shaping Labour's relationship with the Co-operative Movement, in her position on the National Executive Committee proved steadfast in the face of Trotskyite infiltration of the Labour Party, and was loyal to her friend, mentor and leader Gaitskell, whom she supported in Leeds and Westminster. Finally, as well as being a 'local MP', she also travelled widely – including to the Soviet Union, where she witnessed a totalitarian regime of the extreme left at close quarters. Here again, as we will see, her views were far from predictable. We start, though, with an issue that shaped her political career even before she entered Parliament: her gender.

A Woman MP

In 1945 Alice was one of 15 women elected as Labour MPs for the first time – a group also including Barbara Castle and Bessie Braddock. The general election also saw Jennie Lee return to Parliament for the first time since 1931. Labour now had 21 women MPs, significantly higher than the single individual the Conservatives and Liberals had each managed, and a total no party would better until Labour returned 37 women in 1992. The Conservative Party has only exceeded this total twice (2010, 2015) since women first stood for Parliament in 1918. And only in 1997 did women first exceed 10 per cent of the parliamentary chamber.[1] Alice may have overcome the odds to reach Westminster in the first place, but challenges remained.

Whilst Alice was not unique in being a female MP, she was rare. Of the 15 women MPs first elected in 1945 for Labour, only three – including Alice – were unmarried. She was also just one of three to make it to ministerial rank – Barbara Castle and Margaret Herbison, who had a tenure as Minister for Social Security, being the others from this cohort. Ellen Wilkinson at Education, Jennie Lee for the Arts and the Open University, and Edith Summerskill as Minister for Social Security would all make significant post-1945 contributions, but had been first elected to Parliament before World War II. Of this 1945 generation, Alice's service in the Commons was also only exceeded by two of her contemporaries, Freda Corbert and Barbara Castle – who remains the longest serving female Labour MP in the House of Commons. And whilst 80 per cent of her contemporaries had a husband to serve as emotional (and indeed, in many cases, including Castle's, logistical) support, Alice would have to do it – the help of friends aside – alone. Even for those who were married, there were still sacrifices to be made. Not having children would be one of Barbara Castle's greatest regrets in later life. Marrying, having children, and achieving a successful parliamentary career was a balance that few achieved. As Lena Jeger noted in the early 1970s:

> This timetable is very difficult combined with married life – especially in a family with young children. Unless you live very near the House you must let somebody else put the children to bed, read their stories. This sort of help is increasingly hard to get. Few husbands would expect to be baby-sitters almost every night. During this parliament at least two of the younger women MPs have had their marriages break up. Though nobody

can totally blame Parliamentary life, it certainly puts a strain on many marriages.[2]

Despite breaking with the normal conventions of the day and not getting married, Alice in other ways did what was expected of her. To Martin Pugh, the defeminised woman – of which he cites Alice as an example – resulted in 'little challenge being offered to the dominant masculine culture of the labour movement'.[3] As the academics Amy Black and Stephen Brooke have shown, gender did indeed represent a real problem for Labour in the road back to a stable parliamentary majority in the 1951–66 period.[4] Most obviously, women were not voting Labour in sufficient numbers – only in two elections (1945 and 1966) in the quarter-century after the end of World War II did Labour enjoy leads among female voters, giving the Conservatives a possible advantage of up to 1.2 million votes (in 1951 women made up approximately 54 per cent of voters).[5]

In any event, the different status of women MPs in the 1940s and 1950s compared to their male counterparts could be seen, literally, in the corridors of Parliament. Quite aside from the usual hustle and bustle of such areas, during Alice's early parliamentary years it was quite likely that she, Barbara Castle or any of the female MPs could be found with their papers sprawled on a bench or even the floor, carrying out their everyday work. The Lady Members' room – 'small, cramped, just seven desks to work on' – often led to the migration of women members to the library or various benches across the parliamentary estate.[6] Though women were now in the corridors of power, for the purposes of work they were relegated to its floor. Then, as now, glass ceilings remained to be broken.

Alice was certainly aware of this second-class status, but essentially took the same line as that given by Barbara Castle in her own parliamentary selection meeting – 'I am no feminist, I want you to judge me only as a socialist.'[7] 'A woman MP', proclaimed Alice in 1961, 'would be a failure if she just regarded herself as a women's MP. She has got to be prepared to do all the jobs that a man does.'[8] If Alice was at pains to stress she remained a representative of her constituents of both genders over and above any trailblazing of the feminist cause, almost inevitably – if only as a product of the quite staggering statistics – being a female MP clearly brought its own unique challenges. Women represented only 323 (3.1 per cent) of the 10,312 candidates at general elections between 1918 and 1945. They were often selected for hopeless seats: in six interwar general elections, they received on average only four-fifths of the male candidate's vote. The interwar peak of female MPs at any given point was just 15 (in 1931), 2.3 per cent of the chamber as a whole, and only 38 women in total became MPs during those 21 years (of these, 15 were unmarried at election – eight Labour, five Conservative, one Liberal, one Independent – and 23 were married or widowed). So Alice, along with the other 14 Labour women elected in 1945 for the first time, was the joint thirty-ninth woman to be elected to Parliament. And just eight women had paved the way for Alice – in entering the Labour parliamentary benches as an unmarried Labour woman.

Of her female predecessors, a number were there because of their husbands. Indeed, 'male equivalence' – the notion that a woman could plausibly be representing a man – played a key role in the election of several key figures. Whilst Lady Cynthia (Cimmie) Mosley provided little beyond a mouthpiece for her husband's politics, and Ruth Dalton entered Parliament as something of a stop-gap (to keep Bishop Auckland warm for her husband Hugh, who was looking to move to that seat at the general election of 1929 only to see the incumbent die, and trigger a by-election, a few months early), there were substantive contributions from women MPs in the interwar era from all sides of the house. Though she had entered the Commons upon the elevation of her husband to a peerage in 1919, Nancy Astor provided a clear – albeit increasingly Hitler-sympathetic – voice from the Tory benches as the 1930s wore on. More palatably, Jennie Lee and Ellen Wilkinson provided trenchant criticisms of the impact of capitalism which Yorkshire, amongst many areas, was experiencing in the early part of that decade. Other women represented or campaigned on specific causes: the Duchess of Atholl (appeasement) and the Countess of Iveagh (Indian self-governance) making important contributions albeit, again, not without controversy. In no year did women contribute more than 4 per cent of the speeches in Parliament, and their average for the 1918–45 period was only 1.9 per cent. Yet in debating contribution per head women exceeded their male counterparts in 16 years of the 25 between 1920 and 1944: the fewer women there were, the more they felt obliged to speak. Yet, it is obviously the case that a woman's voice was still rare in Parliament in 1945, and indeed, is still much rarer than a man's even today.

Women's rhetorical space was limited compared to the men. Welfare (incorporating education, public health, housing, unemployment and labour restrictions) accounted for 49 per cent of women MPs' total debating contribution from 1919 to 1945, with foreign and defence policy

(14 per cent) lagging well behind. Of real importance is what women avoided discussing, particularly moral issues (alcohol, sexual morality, betting and religious issues) which represented only 3 per cent of speech time. Questions relating specifically to women made up around 13 per cent of speeches. But, as Barbara Castle and Alice would probably both have understood and had sympathy with, party loyalty trumped gender – on crucial issues such as the Beveridge Report women divided along party lines when it came to the vote.[9] Moral issues – albeit ones where a party whip was often not used – like birth control were avoided: only three women MPs (including Nancy Astor and Mavis Tate) said anything on the topic. Alice Bacon was therefore stepping into a Westminster pond where women had dipped a toe, but had been careful to stay within prescribed limits. When Lena Jeger entered the Commons in 1953, a conversation she had with Herbert Morrison indicated that attitudes took a while to shift. Morrison told her to 'stick to women's problems. "When I made my maiden speech", Jeger recalled, "in a foreign affairs debate, about the need for international peace, he was furious with me."'[10]

Within the Labour Party there were also questions being asked as to whether the ghettoising of women into groups such as the Women's Labour League and Women's Luncheon Club (which Alice regularly addressed) was harming the female cause within the party. By the 1960s many women had become self-conscious about their subordinate role in the party hierarchy – and when Lena Jeger highlighted the condescending nature of the man who would 'pat you on the shoulders and say you are a "splendid little woman"', one wonders if Alice recalled her first meeting with Hugh Gaitskell, and his comment that she was a 'clever girl'.[11]

There was a real dilemma here. By using the women-only structures in the party, women could advance and build alliances, but those structures might also stunt you if you became pigeon-holed within them. Alice used those structures particularly to get elected, and stay elected on the party's NEC. Women who stood for the NEC (in the constituency ballot) against men stood a far smaller chance of getting elected and a far greater chance of losing their position even were they to be initially successful: Barbara Castle was the only woman on the 27-strong body to win a position contested against men between the Party Conferences of 1963 and 1967. There was thus a distinct chance of missing out on the policy-making process altogether, without using the women's section. Charles Morris (MP for Manchester Openshaw 1963–83) was a fan of Alice's parliamentary work, but values 'equally significantly the contribution she made over such a long period of time to the proceedings of the Labour NEC'.[12] For a right-wing Labour MP such as Alice, particularly with the leftwards drift in the composition of the NEC in the early 1950s, it is very unlikely she could have maintained such longevity and influence had she contested any other ballot but the women's section. It is worth adding that even Barbara Castle, in later life, recognised the importance of Labour's women-only institutions:

> I was against it [the women's section] on the grounds that as long as there's a women's section the men will say, 'Oh well, they're women and they're in there' you see. 'You don't need to fight for women for Constituency Party Section'. So I was always against – anyway I found them dead boring. Then I began mellowing with the years. I remember coming back from one Labour Women's Conference and being surprised how, I hadn't been for ages – quite a lot of young women came to the rostrum … I thought, 'jolly good', and on the way back at York Station one of the young women came and sat next to me and I was saying to her what did she feel about the Women's conference. 'Oh, don't let them abolish it Barbara, it's a training ground for us we can't get anywhere else'.[13]

There remains 'tremendous admiration' to this day amongst her former colleagues for what Alice achieved on her own stead, 'without any social engineering'.[14] She was clearly unflappable: indeed, one veteran Labour warhorse recalls the day that disaster struck in a House of Commons lift. 'Suddenly, Alice's knicker elastic snapped. This voluminous pair of flannelette drawers fell to the floor. With a cheery smile, Alice just stepped out of them, picked them up, and popped them in her handbag.'[15] Likewise, she clearly did not lack a sense of humour, even if sometimes at the expense of her fellow women MPs. An article appeared in the *Sunday Express* suggesting Bessie Braddock and Edith Summerskill had slept in a room in the House of Commons fitted with two beds, 'stretched out on them and both snoring'. Braddock's biographer, Millie Toole, wrote of the evening:

> Alice Bacon said that the four occupants of the room were Mrs Ford and herself, occupying chairs, and Dr Edith Summerskill and Lady Davidson on the couches. 'It is a particularly unobservant person who would mistake [the larger] Mrs Braddock for Lady Davidson', said Miss Bacon amid laughter.[16]

Such banter between fellow travellers of the Labour right was presumably acceptable stuff – but relations were not always so cordial with those on the left.

It was Barbara Castle, as Shirley Williams notes, who changed the face of female politics in Britain. Pre-Castle 'women were very tediously respectable', a phenomenon typified by the 'knickers over knees' brand of interwar politician like Margaret Bondfield who were serious at all costs.[17] The post-1945 generation were the first to be able to hold high office more or less independent of their husbands' careers, and into the political sphere entered a new type of man – the male political spouse (of whom Denis Thatcher would arguably become the most famous). Lena Jeger highlighted the left's own version:

> I often wish I had a wife. Even if a woman is married with a sympathetic husband (lucky Barbara Castle – Ted is the ideal husband of all MP husbands) he cannot somehow take the same sort of consort role as an MP's wife. I mean he can't do the tea parties and accept the bouquet at the hospital fair.[18]

Alice did not have a husband to compare to the political wife. But a woman like Alice was in some ways representative of an old-fashioned type of female MP: a childless 'spinster', who was married to politics and the Labour Party. A new breed of women like Barbara Castle, Shirley Williams and later Margaret Thatcher, Harriet Harman and Yvette Cooper were taking their place in politics and at the Cabinet table.

What is undoubtedly true though is that issues that were once not debated in Parliament were becoming hot political topics – not least, from the 1950s up until today, the issue of equal pay. Although Castle is rightly credited with steering through the Equal Pay Act and meeting the women from Dagenham's Ford factory, Alice also entered the debate – specifically, in 1952, on equal pay in the Civil Service. Speaking in a parliamentary debate, Alice pointed out the absurdity of the contemporary situation:

> On 25th July 1945, I was a teacher. On the next day, 26th July, I became a Member of Parliament. In both cases I held the same responsible position as my male colleagues, but up to 25th July 1945, I was paid four-fifths of the men's rate, and since I became a Member of Parliament I have received equal pay with my men colleagues. I cannot say that on any

occasions I did any less work or had any less responsibility than the men with whom I worked.[19]

This position was tacitly agreed by all parties. A Royal Commission had reported in 1946 recommending equal pay but, with the then Labour government baulking at the extra expenditure, nothing was done. The attitude of the public was more ambiguous; having lost significant swathes of their female support in 1945, the Conservative Party took soundings on the issue of equal pay when in opposition. The findings were hard to read – on the one hand people supported the principle of equal pay, but traditional views of a woman's place in society had not shifted. Both parties went into the 1950 election promising to look into the issue, and to implement equal pay when economic circumstance allowed – a political fudge. But precisely because both parties had adopted so similar a fudge, cross-party cooperation on the backbenches became possible. Irene Ward, now Conservative MP for Tynemouth, returned in 1950 after losing her seat in Wallsend in 1945, refloat the equal pay issue in November 1950, the first parliamentary intervention on the matter in 30 years.

Ward's intervention elicited very different responses from Alice Bacon and Barbara Castle. Speaking during a May 1952 debate on Equal Pay in the Civil Service, Castle argued that women were sick of rhetoric, and demanded concrete policy. The Commons resolved itself in favour of pay equality. Castle had, however, been working behind the scenes alongside Irene Ward to ensure consensus across the aisles. This, to Alice Bacon, was disgraceful and even if she agreed with equal pay, collaborating with Tory backbenchers to deliver it was not something she was prepared to countenance. But progress was made in the post-war years. Equal pay in the Civil Service was introduced by Rab Butler in 1955, coming fully into force in 1961. In 1970 Barbara Castle steered through the Equal Pay Act, broadening the previous legislation's scope to the private sector, with Castle again taking the opportunity to praise individual Tories for their role in passing the Act of 1955. Alice's friend, the Leeds West MP Charles Pannell praised both her and Castle in the 1970 debate on equal pay, but Alice, as a junior minister, had no opportunity to comment.[20]

On top of their tactical differences, Castle was the antithesis of Alice more generally: glamorous, married, and fully prepared to take men on. Perhaps this is why mentions of Bacon in Castle's diary are so sparse, for their personalities certainly clashed. As Shirley Williams remembers, 'you never saw the littlest bit of flirting in Alice. Barbara Castle was brilliant at it.'[21] A more serious manifestation of the divide can be found in the diaries of Tony Benn. Attending a ball at the 1963 Party Conference, Benn and his wife Caroline encountered the future First Secretary of State:

> We met Barbara Castle who was almost in tears because Alice Bacon had been given a major speech and she had not … She was outraged that Shirley Williams should have been put on the presentation team. It was almost hysterical and reflected the great uncertainty of the Left at Harold's success (in becoming leader).[22]

Left/right politics were clearly part of Castle's concern (with Alice and Shirley Williams on the right of the party). Castle's claim that 'Harold was good on the machinery but always sold the left down the river' was certainly not just bad grace.[23] When Castle was promoted to First Secretary of State in 1968, she received no letter of congratulation from Alice (or, alternatively, did not feel enough affection to keep it).[24] But it was not just about high politics – the interplay between Labour women mattered. Here were two women living radically different lifestyles competing for the spotlight at times. Leo Abse, less charitably than Benn, wrote of 'the group of intelligent hysterics who make up an uncomfortable quota of women MPs'.[25] Many, this Freudian implied, suffered from penis envy. Such comments, while laughable or cringe-worthy today, also tell you something about the way women in politics were viewed. If Tony Benn's early diaries tell of continual stress and strain in order to achieve his goals long mapped-out, women like Alice were forging anew in an often hostile environment.

For Barbara Castle – glamorous, attractive and confident – there was also the continued prospect of propositions from leading Labour figures. In the late 1930s when visiting Nye Bevan's Bloomsbury flat, Castle found him halfway through a bottle of white wine (at 11 in the morning) with Beethoven playing on the gramophone, and soon had to spurn his advances. Harold Wilson would give her a 'fumbling kiss' on a Board of Trade trip to Canada in the late 1940s, again leading to much embarrassment on Barbara's part. According to Michael Foot, he and Castle had a brief affair on a holiday the pair took to France in October 1938 – a story he repeated regularly at Party Conference in later years with the punchline, seemingly borrowed from some stand-up act, 'more than an asthma attack happened that night!'[26]

Alice was not glamorous and remained single for her whole life. But perhaps such attitudes explain why she occasionally took refuge in the non-threatening environment of the Leeds Women's Luncheon Club. The group was set up in 1960 'to promote educational, social and cultural facilities for members and friends of the Labour Party'. Dora, Hugh Gaitskell's wife, was its first president, with Alice and Edna Healey amongst the vice presidents. This, certainly, was an odd position for a politician serving on her party's front bench, but presumably Alice welcomed the chance to be close to the Gaitskells, as well as to build her own political base. She invited luncheon club members to the House of Commons in June 1961 where she told them that 'the difference between a man MP and a woman MP is that a woman MP does all the work that a man does – plus a little bit extra'. She also hosted a party in Leeds at the Metropole Hotel in December 1963, almost a year since the death of her closest political ally, Hugh Gaitskell. She told the women present that she had no idea when the general election would take place. It was a non-threatening audience in which to spread the Labour gospel and energise the party's base, with the general election that would see her become a minister less than a year away.

In some sense, these functions represented the usual cultivation of a local political grouping that MPs often prioritise. Certainly Alice would never have seen herself as simply appealing to narrow interests. Sex mattered, but so did class. As she told Melanie Phillips in 1980, 'there are no longer any working-class young men or women MPs. They have lost touch with the working-class population, and in many ways it's a retrograde step that they are now all well-educated, middle-class MPs.' If she campaigned on specific issues such as clothing rationing in the 1940s and helped legislate on abortion in the 1960s, her main political concerns were not specifically with women, but were about the universal: comprehensive education, good quality housing and employment. Class not sex was her political motivation but cultivating the support of women for the Labour Party was, as she saw it, part of her role.

Hugh Gaitskell and Leeds United

Although a woman MP, her closest friendship within the parliamentary party was undoubtedly with a man, Hugh Gaitskell. The papers of George Murray, the secretary of the South Leeds Labour Party, where Gaitskell was MP, are filled with references to Alice and Gaitskell. This is important because Gaitskell's diaries did not always portray the warmth of the man: 'solid discussion' and 'effective' are the type of business-like descriptions he gives of Alice there.[27] The Gaitskell–Murray letters indicate just how useful Alice was to her leader. When campaigning in November 1955 ahead of the impending party leadership contest, a stalwart of the Leeds Labour movement suddenly died. This was clearly difficult for Gaitskell – how to maintain both local and national presence – but he had an effective compromise: 'I cannot get away from the House. But Alice, I am glad to say, is going to be there, and I have asked her to represent me personally.' This, to Murray, was acceptable enough for the locals: 'as Alice is going to be present and will represent you [then] that is all right'.[28]

Alice kept Gaitskell, as party leader and local MP, in touch with the Leeds and Yorkshire scene. Partly this was logistical:

> Miss Bacon has shown me a very useful document which she possesses – a list showing the streets in the various constituencies in Leeds – which I gathered she obtained from the town clerk. I wonder if I could possibly obtain a copy from her.

Likewise, one catches reference to comments such as 'as you know from Alice we have been invited to the Westfield ward social evening'.[29] Alice also acted as a source of information and advice for Gaitskell's London secretary, Beryl Skelly to bounce diary invitations off, as this letter from Alice to the leader's office shows:

> Your letter was waiting for me when I reached home at the weekend – hence the delay. I have received an identical letter. They are not asking us to give them our views about Greyhound tracks – they are merely asking us to go to the dogs one night and have dinner! (not a dog's dinner I hope). I've only just realised that he wanted us to go during the recess. I shall write to say I couldn't manage during the recess, but if any Sat evening in the future, I can manage it etc – without being too specific. Tell Mr Gaitskell it looks as though we're both going to the dogs! I think they're rather nice people and won't press us too much about policy.[30]

Even on policy matters however, things were friendly and chatty. Beryl asked Alice where things were on the 1960 Licensing Act – which dealt with proposals related to Sunday afternoon opening of pubs – and was told that:

we have not yet discussed the Licensing Bill in detail, but there is a general opinion on matters like this, that we have a free vote and it is left to the individual conscience of everyone. I would not, therefore, presume to speak for Mr Gaitskell's conscience! I am afraid on this he must make up his own mind with regard to licensing hours and drink!![31]

The point was that the Bacon–Gaitskell relationship had both a professional and personal dimension. Alice, as on 1 March 1953, would often accompany Gaitskell to meetings and then drive him to her home in Normanton for tea.[32] The regular, almost mundane, nature of this pattern is best reflected in two documents.

10 October 1958, Gaitskell to Murray:

I have asked Alice to meet us. The train gets into Leeds from Manchester at 11.13am, so that we can go with her to the Civic Hall and no doubt she will drop us at the station afterwards.

26 May 1960, Gaitskell to Murray:

I shall be coming up to Sheffield tomorrow for a meeting of the University Labour Society. I shall be coming on to Leeds that night and the present plan is that I am due to arrive at Leeds City at 9.37pm, although I believe Alice has it in mind to drive over to Sheffield and take me to Leeds by road.[33]

It is the expectation here that grabs one. Here was Alice Bacon, by 1960 a shadow minister, ferrying around Hugh Gaitskell. There is little question that Gaitskell was imposing (although certainly no more than on the Murrays, with whom he often stayed at their house in Thorpe Mount, in South Leeds). Alice, as the following letter from Gaitskell to Murray in 1956 reveals, seems to have gone out of her way to make her leader and friend feel at home:

I will come up on the Saturday morning as usual and make my way to Cambrian Terrace. Alice Bacon has suggested that she drives me off to Featherstone after the interviews in search of my ancestors, some of whom apparently came from that neighbourhood many years ago! I understand that she is going to give me tea at her house in Normanton and then return me to Leeds. Can I impose myself upon Mattie and yourself again?

If this is all right and I do not see you [beforehand], Alice will no doubt return me – I should imagine round 8 to 9pm. We could then either go off to another Club or just stay at home.[34]

For Gaitskell's part, his harshest tone towards Alice seems to have been his request that she kept quiet whilst, when staying at the Murrays, Alice had been shown in to see him as he was watching a film (a western) on the television.[35] As he was relaxing after the stresses of the 1960 Party Conference at Scarborough, this was probably fair enough. His continual positive references to his parliamentary neighbour – 'it was good of Alice to help', 'I should hope to go to Normanton to see Alice on Saturday' – indicate the close links between the pair.[36]

It was not only Alice in Leeds who stood behind the party leader and MP for Leeds South. Charles Pannell, MP for Leeds West, noted that 'Leeds Labour MPs stood like a rock behind the leader ... The four of us (Gaitskell, Bacon, Healey and Pannell) were not only Party colleagues but close personal friends.'[37]

Pannell wrote in 1960:

I'm glad I play for 'Leeds United', which is a better parliamentary team than the football team I saw play this afternoon and lose 1-0 to Stoke City. At Westminster, Leeds has Hugh Gaitskell as our leader, Denis Healey our No.1 on Foreign Affairs and Alice Bacon the leading woman of the left.[38]

Pannell was perhaps overestimating the credentials of his friend – Barbara Castle and Jennie Lee would have been more obvious candidates for such a title – and, as Alice herself admitted (albeit overly modestly), her first exposure to frontline politics was helped by her relationship with the leader. Speaking to Melanie Phillips in 1980, she commented that:

I was a great friend of Hugh Gaitskell, who was my next-door neighbour. When Labour lost the election in 1959 he knew I was feeling miserable, so he invited me to help Patrick Gordon Walker shadow home affairs. I told him I knew nothing about it, but he knew it would take my mind off the defeat – and it worked, because I became engrossed.[39]

To Phillips this represented a wider pattern regarding 'luck'. 'The advantage of knowing the right people', she concluded, 'seems to have played a large part in the careers of most of the women I spoke to who had held office.'[40] Perhaps so, but this was hardly a distinctly female trend. Healey's association with Gaitskell presumably did not harm his career, nor had it a plethora of Conservative statesmen throughout the centuries (the phrase 'Bob's your uncle', for example, originating from the 1902 succession of Prime Minister Lord (Robert) Salisbury by his nephew, Arthur Balfour, to the premiership). But the Home Office was an odd choice for someone who had spent so much time campaigning for comprehensive education. Yet almost two decades on the NEC together with her knowledge of the crime the slums could sometimes harbour was hardly the worst intro-duction to Alice's shadow ministerial role at the Home Office.

In any case, during this stage of his leadership, Gaitskell certainly needed friends, both politically and personally. Following Labour's third successive defeat in 1959 (and the fact that 1945 remained the only time in its history that the party had gained a stable majority) Gaitskell looked to significantly reposition the party – away from Clause IV nationalisation and an anti-nuclear stance. He supported the Macmillan administration's decision to buy the US-made Skybolt defence system, and earned the ire of the left in doing so. Importantly, the left would not shy away from raising the issue at Party Conference where Gaitskell's leadership was very much under threat.

Alice's role in supporting Gaitskell was as much through emotional and practical support as it was being a conventional political ally. It is true that Tony Crosland's correspondence to Gaitskell during the foundation of the Campaign for Democratic Socialism (CDS) reveals no mention of Alice. But, ideologically, she was in agreement with its aims. Draft notes for CDS speakers instructed their advocates to argue that:

> All the 'old Left' can offer are the protests and slogans of the 1930s. These sound 'old hat' and meaningless to voters under 40 – so they think the Labour Party has no answers to their problems ... Whatever the rights and wrongs of the clause four question, the debate showed a depressing reluctance to think about the world we live in today and its real problems – and a widespread willingness in one noisy group to stay in opposition till 1964, 1974, 1984 ...[41]

The CDS had been set up to provide political support for Gaitskell's leadership. While the Labour Party Conference passed resolutions in favour of unilateralism (Britain giving up its nuclear deterrent to encourage others to follow), Gaitskell had no intention of pursuing such a course of action if elected Prime Minister. CDS campaigned within the party for more moderate policies but also tried to convey a sense of Gaitskellite Labour as opposed to the Labour of the Party Conference. One of the key figures in building up the CDS was Bill Rodgers, who served as Secretary until he became the MP for Stockton-on-Tees in 1962. Rodgers' replacement as Secretary was Bernard Donoughue, who later became head of the Number 10 Policy Unit for Harold Wilson and then Jim Callaghan. Supportive MPs included Roy Jenkins, Denis Healey and of course Crosland. CDS was also supported by many other figures on the right of the Labour Party, including, outside Parliament, Phillip Williams (later Gaitskell's biographer) and Nuffield College's Hugh Clegg, grandfather of the future Liberal Democrat leader and Deputy Prime Minister, Nick Clegg.[42] In that sense, the CDS was always a slightly academic affair – not Alice's natural environment.

The CDS adopted a ruthless plan to 'establish absolute control ... [and then go] back to revisionism and moderation'. Part of this was reflected in Crosland's comment that 'every selection for a Labour seat must now be treated as a major operation'.[43] Hugh Gaitskell's daughter Julia McNeal remembers her father being 'hugely' reliant on Alice, for support in the party both locally and nationally. McNeal recalls that Alice, while not an intellectual agitator for Gaitskell or the CDS, was more reliable and less egotistical, than, say, Anthony Crosland or Roy Jenkins. She was loyal to her leader, giving him a bedrock of support that others – who were thinking of their own careers too – could not, or did not, provide.

It was, however, the personal touch that mattered most. When delivering his famous speech against unilateralism at the 1960 Party Conference, and pledging to 'fight, and fight, and fight again to save the party I love', Gaitskell sat down to loud applause and kind words from the woman to his right.[44] This was, of course, Alice Bacon. Two years later, after an argument with George Brown, Gaitskell confided to Alice that he was thinking of quitting politics. Ever the caring friend, Alice gained access to his diary and crossed out all the trivial engagements. If, by then, 'his weariness was becoming obvious', he could still rely on Alice for support.[45]

In 1960 Gaitskell really needed this support. With the left contending that Gaitskell was defying the will of conference over his decision to reject unilateralism, Tony Greenwood resigned from the Shadow Cabinet and announced his decision to challenge for the leadership. He subsequently stood aside for a candidate of the left he felt offered a broader appeal: Harold Wilson. And so, on 3 November 1960, in a Committee

Room of the House of Commons, Labour MPs gathered to hear the result of the leadership ballot. Under a picture on the wall of the Battle of Hastings, the numbers were read out: Gaitskell 166 votes, Wilson 81. Alice, delighted at her friend's victory, and glancing over at the picture on the wall, cried: 'The defeat of Harold! The defeat of Harold!' She would, of course, have to work with Wilson, not Gaitskell, as Prime Minister, but for now her great ally had fought off a significant challenge.

Alice respected Hugh Gaitskell's mind, and saw him as being a strong voice in the field of economics, where she herself felt a little lacking – according to Shirley Williams.[46] This, as Bernard Atha points out, was something of a trend – whether she personally liked (Hugh Dalton) or disliked (Jennie Lee) intellectuals within the party, she was usually prepared to acknowledge the brainy.[47] Merlyn Rees (Gaitskell's successor as MP for Leeds South) thought Alice 'was suspicious of many middle-class intellectuals' and that 'Hugh Gaitskell was the exception'.[48] And with Gaitskell there was clearly an added dimension. 'As a single woman', Shirley Williams contends, 'she was rather in love [with him].' Baroness Gould agrees. Whether or not that was true, the relationship certainly went beyond party leader and MP. Denis Healey mirrors Shirley Williams on this matter – '[Alice] was besotted'.[49] Yet, despite Alice's strong feelings for Gaitskell, it seems unlikely that their relationship was ever romantic.

Their key connection and reason for them becoming close was local and practical. As well as occasional chauffeur, Leeds deputy and local organiser, Alice was also useful to Gaitskell in his role of party leader. As Denis Healey pointed out, Alice was 'immensely valuable to [Gaitskell] since she was ... a member of the women's section of the National Executive Committee'. This was not merely an issue of Gaitskell seeking votes to see off the Bevanites. As Ralph Miliband noted, by being members of the NEC and having to work with figures like Alice Bacon (arguing the cause and helping to block alternative positions), the left found it difficult to articulate a separate, credible message to the status quo of which they were now a part.[50] Alice's obituary in *The Times* recorded her 'on the move constantly throughout the constituencies, with Ray Gunter and Sara Barker ... smoking out heresy and recommending expulsions'.[51]

Sara Barker, a key ally of Alice's and a future National Agent for the Labour Party, played a key role in the left/right battles of the 1950s. In 1945, Barker had just taken on her first full-time political job when she beat 134 applicants (all men) for the post of secretary and agent of the Halifax Labour Party. Though later described in a *Queen* magazine article as 'quiet, calm, efficient and (important in the Labour Party) soothing', she was clearly quite a tough character.[52] As Gerald Kaufman recalls, 'I knew Sara because of later working for Harold [Wilson]. Alice and Sara were very close. A tough cookie, then again, to get that job as a woman she had to be.'[53] Although she later moved down to London to assume a job at Transport House, she was a natural ally – being both local, and of the right – to the new MP in Leeds North East.

Alice and Sara Barker were referenced regularly in *Tribune*, *The Spectator* and other political journals for their work maintaining discipline in the party. For instance, *The Spectator* in 1966 ran a piece about:

> the steely inquisitors of Transport House [the Labour Party's headquarters], single-minded heresy-hunters such as Miss Alice Bacon, Mrs. Bessie Braddock and Miss Sara Barker, both 'validate' a nomination for a seat and endorse the final selection. Thus undesirables (though chiefly, it must be added, supposed undesirables of the left) are kept out at the beginning. Afterwards, when the candidate becomes an MP, he is made subject to much more stringent discipline than any Conservative. So, in a sense, the local parties' repressive work is done for them, both by Transport House and by the Whips.[54]

Alice evidently continued this type of faithful service, as she would have seen it, even after her friend's death. And in that sense her friendship with Gaitskell was quite symbolic, containing as it did Leeds, Transport House and Westminster dimensions.

That said, Alice was capable of challenging her great friend. During a visit in 1956, addressing Labour's NEC in the Commons, the Soviet leader Nikita Khrushchev made a blundering speech rejecting the idea of disarmament controls in the divided Germany. Having asked the premier about the conditions of Jews in Russia as per NEC instruction, Alice was angry that Khrushchev had said nothing regarding recently imprisoned social democrats in the Soviet Union. Passing a note along to Gaitskell whilst Khrushchev was still talking, Alice told him 'I think you will have to reply to this at once'. Gaitskell did so, as he later noted, in his own words, in a 'conciliatory' manner, only to be met by a 'silly speech' – after Khrushchev had left – from Alice. Leader and backbencher were certainly close, but Alice was never without her own mind or opinion.[55]

But the personal dimension was most obviously seen at moments of personal difficulty, particularly when Alice was hospitalised in November

1961. Shortly after returning from a gathering of the Socialist International in Rome, Alice suffered a minor heart attack. Out of the public eye for months – she did not speak in the Commons again until 29 March 1962 – her spirits were lifted by the visits of her friend Hugh Gaitskell. Though she was released from Clayton Hospital in Wakefield on 23 December, full recovery took a while longer, and the support of her friend mattered dearly.[56] As she later noted:

> Over a year ago, when I was critically ill in Yorkshire, he did not hesitate to cancel all his engagements, leave his Parliamentary work, and dash 200 miles by the first train he could get. He knew that the knowledge he had done that might help me pull through. He was right, for one of the doctors had said his visit was a morale booster which did me a lot of good at a critical time. But that was Hugh and he would have done it for any of his friends.[57]

And Alice was there for Hugh when he collapsed and then died a little over a year later. In December 1962, Alice visited Gaitskell in Manor House Hospital, and she was charged with delivering his Christmas presents to party officials, and to let them know he would soon be back to work.[58] He died a few weeks later.

Alice gave a moving tribute in the House of Commons, commenting on the 'curtains [being] drawn in the small houses in the streets of South Leeds, not just for a Member of Parliament but for a very dear friend whom they knew and loved'. 'Those of us', Alice later wrote, 'who knew him best mourn the loss of a dear friend. Hugh was warm-hearted and emotional, and his friends, loyal, trusted friends, meant a great deal to him.'[59] Hugh Gaitskell's successor as MP for Leeds South, Merlyn Rees – for whom Alice helped secure the seat – recalls her words 'reaching the heart of that hard-bitten audience'. But it is perhaps her contribution to the *Leeds Weekly Citizen* that most resonates:

> I shall miss him most in our small Committees of the National Executive, and in his room at the House of Commons where he and I have talked so frequently about his plans and hopes for the future, and where he has trusted me with some of his inner most thoughts about politics and people.[60]

Although Alice mourned greatly for her loss when Hugh Gaitskell died, she was also instrumental in securing the selection and election of

Gaitskell's successor. Merlyn Rees remembers retiring to Alice's house in Normanton for supper after his successful selection as the Labour Party candidate – along with party agent Sara Barker. And then in the days that followed Rees recalls that whilst 'touring the streets it was Alice's voice through the loudspeaker that brought out the women. She did not talk down to them, or dress down for them but she did understand the aspirations of ordinary people and expressed them in political terms.'

Was Alice merely her master's voice on the NEC? Certainly she was, as Bernard Atha noted, 'Gaitskell's strongest supporter'. Tam Dalyell also recalls her being 'ferociously pro Hugh'.[61] Her precise position is difficult to gauge, and whilst Bill Rodgers' view that 'she was not part of Gaitskell's inner circle' might have held true in terms of holding a determining influence on Labour policy, her friendship and familiarity with the party leader was beyond doubt.[62] But this was not sycophancy. As well as Alice being useful to Gaitskell she used her connections with him to expand her own power base into several areas. Education was a natural such avenue for the former teacher. But it also played out in terms of the internal battles then overwhelming the Labour movement.

Left versus Right

Labour was seriously divided in the 1950s and Alice Bacon, for one, had firmly picked her side. Descriptions of Alice include 'right wing and tough' (from Lord Tom Sawyer, former General Secretary of the Labour Party from 1994 to 1998), and 'very hard-line right' (according to Baroness Joyce Gould). Others included 'predictable right wing loyalist', 'ferociously loyal to Hugh [Gaitskell]', and 'good with the "right wing" trade union leaders, less good to Frank Cousins and Jack Jones'. Alice's supposed comment that left- and right-wingers should use different lifts at Labour's HQ, Transport House, might have been tongue-in-cheek, but it was broadly indicative of the attitudes of the time. On nuclear weapons, the welfare state, and Labour's commitment to nationalisation under Clause IV of its 1918 constitution, the party appeared ideologically incoherent and divided. As in 1931 and then later in 1983, the Labour Party in 1951 was tearing itself apart after defeat, and so perhaps unsurprisingly failed to make much headway with the British electorate in the 1950s.

Alice was to the right of most of her local activists in Leeds. Bernard Atha, speaking of the nomination process for parliamentary candidates in 1955, recalls that 'it was my job to make sure we didn't select Alice'. The two would soon get on very well – Bernard often popping round to see Alice and her parents on a Saturday afternoon in Normanton – but such strength of opinion was symptomatic of the intra-party divide.[63] Such divides could often be symbolic, and played out to establish one's own personal political authority. Clause IV provided the ultimate example – only a small minority of its defenders still believed in its literal application, but maintained the necessity of holding onto the general principle. In that regard, Harold Wilson's famous comment about attempting to revise it being akin to 'taking Genesis out of the Bible' was doubly important. Whilst his rather entrepreneurial form of government – Tony Benn used consultants from McKinsey whilst Postmaster General and the 'White Heat' of (predominantly private sector) technological advancement driving the economy forward – did not exactly suggest a doctrinal commitment to nationalisation, the fact that Wilson had maintained an anti-revisionist, leftist line on the principle of nationalisation reflected the fevered debate of the time: you had to pick a side.

Aneurin Bevan was at the epicentre of the conflict – a conflict that had been bubbling under even during Labour's period in power after 1945. To Herbert Morrison – who valued the role of Parliament in providing a chamber for spirited debate, but also believed he should be 'capable of having a drink with the chap afterwards in the smoking room' – Bevan significantly stepped over the line in 1948 when he famously described Conservatives as lower than vermin. This was not just about form, or the rights and wrongs of the comment, but Morrison felt such language had contributed to the loss of support in the country in 1950 and 1951:

> I deprecated the speech. The trouble with Nye was, he was a great orator – there was no doubt about that, and he'd got a vocabulary almost as extensive as Sir Winston Churchill's. I was told that Nye Bevan, instead of reading the newspaper at breakfast, he read a dictionary, and I can well believe it. Well, this was a silly thing to do. It wasn't true for one thing. But then supposing some prominent Conservative had called us vermin. I wish they had. It would have made people work six times as hard as they otherwise would, and that's what happened to the Conservatives ... it stimulated them, instead of those nice respectable suburban commuters quietly going to vote, they got mad. And they fetched a lot of people out to vote as well.[64]

Morrison was an important influence on Alice – particularly in the early 1950s. To recap his background Morrison had been instrumental in the development of the London Labour Party. First elected as MP for Hackney South in 1923, he was a parliamentarian whose humble background matched Alice's own – he left school at 14 to become an errand boy. Having served in Ramsay MacDonald's ill-fated 1929 administration he was appointed Home Secretary in Churchill's wartime coalition government in 1940. After the war he would become Deputy Prime Minister under Attlee, and, briefly, Foreign Secretary. He stood on the Labour right throughout his career – encouraging middle ground solutions such as state-owned monopolies run at arm's length from the government. His drive to create London Transport (he remained leader of the Labour Group on the London County Council until joining Churchill's government) was perhaps his most famous legacy.

The relationship between Alice and Morrison was close, and not just driven by a similarly practical politics. Morrison stayed with the Bacons whilst on a speaking tour of Yorkshire in March 1951, and a picture survives of Morrison, pipe in mouth, sitting in the Bacons' house whilst Alice's mother shows him the dinner she was preparing in a pot. Lottie Bacon, it should be said, was something of a party favourite and according to local press reports of the time was 'famous for her cooking'.[65] After staying with the Bacons whilst campaigning in Yorkshire, Herbert Morrison argued that 'the farther you live North from London the better time and the better food you have'. Once people saw these quotes this even led to Lottie Bacon being sent fanmail regarding her cooking technique and requests for the perfect Yorkshire pudding recipe.[66] And praise came from the Prime Minister's household itself. Violet Attlee wrote, via Alice, to Lottie saying 'what a wonderful cook you are!' after she had sent some homemade toffee and biscuits to 10 Downing Street.[67]

Alice was chair of the Labour Party's NEC, and by extension of the party, as the schisms grew in 1950–1. In 1951, Bevan resigned, along with a young Harold Wilson, from the Labour government – by then in its death throes – over the introduction of charges in the NHS by Gaitskell as Chancellor. It was this unwillingness to yield from the framework the 1945 government had created that characterised the Bevanites – those MPs who rallied to his side – throughout the early and mid-1950s. A *Tribune* article published the week before the party whip was withdrawn from Bevan at the height of the further split in the mid-1950s – and entitled 'Right wing showdown: Attlee under fire' – gives something of an idea of the heated debate:

> In 1951 Mr. Hugh Gaitskell, then Labour's Chancellor of the Exchequer, insisted on imposing charges on the Health Service. He did this to save £13 million in a Budget which later proved to be some £300 million awry in its calculations. He must have known that the result would be to split the Labour Cabinet. Yet still he was determined to get his way even at the price of such disunity. Since then unity within the Labour movement on this issue has been restored by the repudiation of Mr. Gaitskell's policy. That dispute is now shown up for what it truly was—a totally unnecessary quarrel provoked by Right-wing intransigence. In that same Budget Mr. Gaitskell also insisted that the arms programme of £4,700 million should be proceeded with, at great risk to Britain's economy and even though it could never be fulfilled in the time allotted. He was warned of the dangers both to the nation and the Labour movement. Now it is proved by events who was right and who was wrong.[68]

Thus whilst Bevan's own role in the creation of the National Health Service no doubt lent health policy a special place in the Bevanite cause, the divisions were further reaching in also demanding, for example, the renationalisation of the steel industry (going against many on the party's right) as well as in an innate scepticism of American foreign policy (by then increasingly anti-communist). In 1952 Bevan published his book *In Place of Fear*, which posed the question 'Where does power in Great Britain lie, and how can it be obtained by the workers?' The Labour leadership, he suggested, were not paying enough heed to the latter half of this question.

By this stage Alice was closely connected to the Labour Party leadership. Following Labour's defeat in 1951, Alice, as chair of the NEC and hence chair of the Labour Party, took charge of the annual Party Conference at Scarborough. The party was drifting leftwards, and conference typified this. In the elections to the constituency section of the NEC – in which Alice, as candidate for the women's section, never had to stand – the left's candidates Aneurin Bevan, Barbara Castle, Tom Driberg and Ian Mikardo all managed to get elected: a powerful swing to the left. The casualties of the left's gains were Alice's friends, Hugh Dalton and Herbert Morrison. Throughout the 1950s Bevanite left and reformist right wrestled for control of the party. Alice was firmly entrenched in these battles.

Increasingly, the divisions in the party centred on foreign policy. Bevan's disillusionment with Labour's foreign policy had two strands – opposing what he deemed the 'encirclement' of Russia and China, and a steadfast line against the proliferation of nuclear weapons. In April 1954 Bevan resigned again from the Shadow Cabinet over the creation of the South East Asian Treaty Organisation (SEATO) – a NATO of the Asian Pacific rim. Bevan saw Labour's line as scarcely distinguishable from the then Churchill–Eden position: 'if the Conservative government are prepared to follow the American lead in this matter, in my view the British Labour Party should stand steadfast against it.'[69]

A month after resigning from the Shadow Cabinet, Bevan made a speech in Leeds – Alice and Hugh Gaitskell's political fiefdom – extending his anti-American credentials, and declaring that Britain should make it clear that they would send no troops to help prop up the French colonial regime in Indo-China (now Vietnam). 'Why', he declared, 'should I fail to feel sympathy for the people of Indo-China who, having been denied self-government for so long, are now trying to get it?'[70] That same month Bevan supported an amendment by the Labour member for Uxbridge, Frank Beswick, demanding that nothing in the Atomic Energy Bill then being debated should authorise the production of a new hydrogen bomb without a vote in both Houses of Parliament. Bevan enlisted the support of 63 MPs, including three party whips, for the amendment on which George Strauss – speaking for the Labour opposition front bench – had urged Labour MPs to abstain.

This fissure between the Bevanites and the party leadership continued throughout 1954, and battle lines were really drawn by the decision of both Bevan and Gaitskell to go for the influential position of Labour Party Treasurer that summer.[71] This was an intensely personal as well as political rivalry. In July that year Gaitskell wrote to Leeds Labour stalwart Solly Pearce outlining the nature of the role and the antipathy it had engendered:

(a) this is not a sinecure, but an unpaid job which really needs doing by somebody who knows a little about finance.

(b) that A[neurin] B[evan] is obviously only doing this from spite, since clearly he could retain his seat on the Executive through the Constituency Parties' vote.[72]

Bevan lost that election, and was swiftly making enemies amongst the party hierarchy. One such enemy was Alice Bacon. In early 1955 Bevan again led a revolt (this time with 57 Labour MPs abstaining) on nuclear policy – and as a result the leadership promptly took action. Recalling the meeting which discussed the removal of the party whip from Nye Bevan for disloyalty, in March 1955, Hugh Dalton (Labour's former Chancellor) noted Alice's contribution:

> Alice Bacon asks Bevan whether he remembers [in 1947] taking her by the arm and walking her down the corridor and saying that Attlee was hopelessly weak and that they must have [Ernest] Bevin as PM. Bevan screams, 'That's a lie'.[73]

In Dalton's eyes and probably in Alice's too, Nye Bevan appeared almost manic. By a vote of 141 to 113 Labour MPs the party whip was (albeit only for a month) withdrawn from Bevan.

Gaitskell's election to the party leadership in December 1955 (defeating Bevan by 157 votes to 70, with Herbert Morrison gaining the support of 40 MPs) would eventually see something of a thawing of relations, with Bevan becoming Shadow Foreign Secretary and, to the dismay of many of his supporters such as Michael Foot who joined the CND, declaring that Britain needed to keep its nuclear deterrent. Yet, during the early 1950s, and only a few years after it seemed the party had eliminated the Conservatives as an electoral force for a generation, not only was the party out of office but it was beginning to tear itself apart. As Austen Albu, later a minister under Wilson, noted, 'intra-party bitterness ... effectively prevented the rational development of new policies to deal with a changing world'.[74]

Alice, ever composed, took all this in good humour most of the time. Speaking in 1955, she remarked that:

> according to the 'Manchester Evening Chronicle' of 7th April, one of the [local] councillors described comprehensive schools as Communist policy adopted by the Left wing of the Labour Party. That must be the first time I have been accused of being on the Left wing of the Labour Party, let alone adopting Communist policy.[75]

But debate was fierce. As Gerald Kaufman remembers:

there was a barrier dividing the Parliamentary Labour Party at this time –
that of right and left. People wouldn't even talk to each other on different
wings of the party. Harold Wilson appointed Alice to the government in
1964 partly as the leadership was under an obligation to cater to both
wings of the party. You could see this at conference too. The National
Executive committee was controlled by the right, through to the Bennite
era, and trade union bloc votes made sure that conference was controlled
by the right. Constituency and affiliated societies generally voted for the
left, but trade unions, for the most part, kept the right wing candidates
on the NEC.[76]

That included Alice, though things were a little hairy on occasion.

Behind the Scenes

Throughout the internal wrangling Alice was both a national and a
local figure. In the early 1950s, as Gaitskell began to position himself for
a leadership bid when, as expected, the elderly Clement Attlee retired,
Alice regularly liaised with the loyal George Murray, Gaitskell's constituency party agent in South Leeds. When it came to the party treasurer
election in 1954 Murray informed locals that a vote for his boss was a vote
for the type of candidate that would serve Labour well in future years: 'his
appointment would give great satisfaction and assurance to many people
in the country, and would undoubtedly bring many additional and vital
votes. For socialism to be effective we have to win an election.'
    In August 1954 Alice got involved too, and wrote to Gaitskell to tell
him that:

> my General Committee is meeting, after all, next Sunday, and I expect
> will nominate. We'll do the best we can, but it won't be easy. I understand
> one or two of the Trotsky people are even interrupting their holidays to be
> present! I wish everyone cared as much![77]

Gaitskell's reply reveals his closeness to Alice as much as it does his
concern at the potential outcome:

> Thank you so much for your note. I know you will do your best with all
> the difficulties. If there are any members of the Committee whom Solly
> knows and could influence, I am sure he would be very glad to help. I took

two Conferences on German rearmament at Edinburgh and Glasgow over the weekend, and was reasonably encouraged by the outcome. At the end of the week we go off on holiday to Pembrokeshire. I must say I shall be quite glad to get away from it all. I hope you too are sometime or other going to have a rest.[78]

After that rest Gaitskell eventually won both the South East Leeds vote and the treasurer's position itself. But it wasn't the end of the matter.

To the Labour left, figures such as Alice Bacon were 'haters' of their brand of politics; haters of true socialist politics.[79] Recalling a rally in Leeds, local activist Frank Pullan saw 'both Bevan and Bacon speaking. Alice spoke first and said the country needed a Labour Government. Bevan followed and said to Alice: We only need a Labour Government if it is a Socialist Government.'[80] Antagonism existed on both sides. Even after succeeding Gaitskell as party leader in 1963, Harold Wilson – 'whose later views', as Ben Pimlott noted, 'were hard to pin down' – was greeted with quiet 'contempt' by Alice for his previous resignation in April 1951 along with Bevan.[81] Whereas Bevan saw charges as 'the beginning of the destruction of those social services ... which were giving Britain the moral leadership of the world', Alice denounced such perceived disloyal elements as 'doing their best to succeed where the Tories have failed'.[82] Such grudges were long-standing, and Alice could be one to bear them. Certainly, according to Joyce Gould, Bevan 'hated Alice' and what he felt she represented.

At the more grandiose intellectual level, Croslandite revisionism, which Alice was sympathetic to, with its acceptance of the broad parameters of contemporary capitalism bumped up against the more left-wing leanings of Bevan, Foot and others. These battles were waged over pamphlet, the radio, and Party Conference. But the debate went beyond lecture theatre-style intellectualising. It had a practical, and very local, dimension in which figures like Alice Bacon played a key role. Denis Healey recalls how Alice used her position on the NEC to forward her agenda:

As Chairman of the Party's Organisation Sub-Committee, which was responsible for discipline, she and the National Agent, Sara Barker, another Yorkshire woman, were the terror of the Trotskyites. They expelled some members of my own constituency party during Gaitskell's most difficult period; at that time he could not visit Leeds without being assaulted by a crowd of students and university lecturers – I recall one of them actually spitting at him as he entered his hotel.[83]

Healey was of the right, and fully backed Alice's campaign against the radical left:

> the small attendance at constituency party meetings makes it easy for a tiny group who are well organised to capture the constituency as a whole, even when they belong to a body outside the Labour Party and hostile to its objectives. In my early years such groups were usually Communist, often from front organisations, such as the innumerable societies for peace and friendship with the Soviet Union or the satellite states. Following the Hungarian rising [in 1956], various Trotskyite organisations took their place. However, Alice Bacon and Sara Barker succeeded in getting rid of the external infiltrators.[84]

Despite Healey's leanings, this was not just the work of right-wing MPs trying to crush local, leftist dissent. Despite a revision of constituency boundaries affecting both their seats, Healey and Alice were both success-fully reselected as parliamentary candidates ahead of the 1955 general election. Healey moved to the new constituency of Leeds East, and Alice to his old seat, Leeds South East. However, Healey did face a challenge from Trotskyist and Bevanite groups, the timing made more difficult by the Parliamentary Labour Party's decision to withdraw the whip from Bevan the week before the selection meeting. Such debates were seen at council level too, particularly in Leeds. At a meeting of the City Labour Party in January 1960 Bernard Atha – by no means ideologically similar to Alice – weighed in on Clause IV: 'nationalisation [represents] only a means to an end. Labour may be returned to power but not if we propose to nationalise every activity of the people ... We need flexibility in methods of Public Ownership.'[85] Yet the meeting as a whole – backed by forthright contributions from the left-leaning Cllr Lloyd and Mrs Yelland (and by Cliff and Barbara Slaughter – the East Leeds organisers for the Trotskyite Socialist Labour League):

> reject[ed] any suggestion that the recent defeat in the election is any reason for the Labour Party to abandon its Socialist principles. It calls for new proposals for Social ownership which will make workers and consumers feel that they have a full share in its management and control of socialised industries.[86]

Despite such exceptions however, as John Grayson, author of *Solid Labour* notes, Yorkshire was right-wing during the Gaitskell/Bevan period, perhaps in part due to having Hugh Gaitskell, Denis Healey and Alice Bacon as local MPs, though equally the leanings of the city was arguably the reason these MPs were selected in the first place.[87] Left-wing MPs like Lance Mallalieu (Brigg), Henry George McGhee (Penistone) and George Craddock (Bradford South) were unable to offset a generally rightward drift of Yorkshire MPs within the PLP, particularly in Leeds. Karl Cohen (chair of the Housing Committee on Leeds City Council from 1955 to 1967) believed strongly that MPs in 'his city' should not interfere in local issues, but should do a national job, not least the job of supporting their leader, Hugh Gaitskell. A loyalty oath to the local party in Sheffield was implemented in the early 1950s. A similar oath was sent out by Leeds secretary Walter Preston in 1954 following a ruling by party General Secretary, Morgan Phillips (a Welsh former colliery worker who rose up through the Labour Party machine in the 1930s), on behalf of the NEC that 'Socialist Outlook' should be a proscribed organisation because of its Trotskyite tendencies. This was a decision backed by Alice – who answered for the NEC to conference on the decision at the Labour Party Conference in 1954 – but opposed vehemently by Jennie Lee, Bevan's wife and MP for Cannock Chase. The comment of Leeds West MP Charlie Pannell, 'show me a communist and I'll show you a crook', was indicative of the strength of feeling. Some from the left wing saw the dangers of expelling broadly sympathetic – and active – members of the wider Labour church. A Leeds councillor Lancelot Lake spoke at the 1955 Labour conference, and asked: 'Can we afford to go on thinning out the active workers in the party in this way? If we go on expelling various groups of left wingers, who will do the work?' In the end, attempts to deselect Alice Bacon and Denis Healey in 1955 – orchestrated by Trotskyites – met with resounding failure.[88]

Part of this was down to the machinery of party politics at the local level. The regional office of the Labour Party in Yorkshire had a reputation of being both for the right and a rigid enforcer of party discipline. The number of proscriptions and expulsions in Yorkshire was disproportionate, in part reflecting the legacy of the regional organiser, Sara Barker. Barker, who left Yorkshire in 1952 for a national role at Transport House and later became national agent, had a big impact on regional politics.[89] 'Social Democratic Centralism' as it was known was the dominant ideology in the regional party – with a premium on loyalty and discipline, learnt in the trade union roots of the local party and enforced by characters including Alice, Sara Barker, Len Williams (who preceded Barker as national agent between 1951 and 1962) and John Ansom (Labour's Yorkshire Regional Organiser after Barker). As Healey notes, Alice was right in the thick of things. In December 1954 *The Times* reported that she had resigned from the Labour Party's National Sub-Committee for Organisation after taking issue with a *Tribune* article labelling her the head of a 'travelling tribunal seeking out Trotskyites in the Constituency Labour Party' including in Norwood and Islington – and indeed in Leeds, where Alice expelled members including the Slaughters in East Leeds. *Tribune* (set up and controlled by the Bevanites, and edited from 1948 to 1952 and 1955 to 1960 by Bevan's protégé Michael Foot) had long been after Alice – labelling her activity in this area as 'one of the most disgraceful ever taken by the Labour movement'. After an intervention from Morgan Phillips – who stated that whilst Bacon and others might attend CLP meetings 'as the need arises', this would only follow the direct request of the local party in question – Alice was eventually coaxed back onto the sub-committee, and continued her work.[90]

Ideology might have been the battleground. There were certainly clear tensions between those feeling that 1950s Labour had 'sold out' to the forces of capitalism and American influence, and others arguing that not to adjust would simply guarantee Conservative electoral dominance and decades of Labour in the wilderness. Dick Taverne, Bill Rodgers and other up-and-coming future MPs on the right declared their view that:

> we are glad to see people better off, and have no patience with those who are comfortably-off themselves yet seem to resent the prosperity of others. Though profoundly critical of many defects in our affluent society, we much prefer it to the poverty-ridden society of the past; we want to reform it, not repudiate it.[91]

Alice, essentially, agreed.

Yet for all the proud ideological disputes, there were personal vendettas and battles too. A classic case was between Alice and Richard Crossman, MP for Coventry East, fellow NEC member and prominent Bevanite. On 24 March 1954, Clement Attlee led an NEC motion to keep all proceedings of their regular meetings a secret. Throughout the 1950s, however, stories were getting out to correspondents of various newspapers – particularly The *Manchester Guardian* and *Daily Mirror*. In 1955 this reached a climax when Jim Griffiths MP voted against delaying the prospect of German rearmament, information which no journalist should have had access to, but which subsequently appeared in the press. Alice Bacon – new co-chair, with Harold Wilson, of the party's publicity machine – launched a serious complaint against the leaks, and demanded to know the source.

The issue became live the following summer. Standing in the House of Commons lobby on 11 June 1956 Richard Crossman named Alice as 'the person from whom [the journalist] Hugh Massingham gets his stuff for the *Observer*', claiming that she was 'simple minded', and that he was the real expert on journalism, not her. Presumably he thought this would remain anonymous, yet Alice was tipped off. Writing to him, Alice took 'very serious objection to what you said' and demanded that he 'substantiate it, or withdraw it'. Crossman, tail between legs, took the latter option and withdrew 'what I said unreservedly as well as apologising for my rudeness'. Whilst 'whenever anyone says something to me in the heat of the moment, and afterwards apologises', Alice was 'always willing to accept the apology and say no more about it', this, apparently, was an exception. Having investigated further Alice learned that Crossman had made the same accusation months earlier, and even repeated it the previous week. 'Distressed to think how widely this gossip may have spread', Alice believed the only course was to 'put myself right with the National Executive Committee' – and the correspondence with Crossman was forwarded on to Party General Secretary Morgan Phillips, and circulated for the next meeting. Nothing more came of the incident, and Crossman was left to exasperate 'Why not accept my apology and forget it?'[92]

Very few MPs remained outside the divide that engulfed Labour in the 1950s. Alice was certainly not one to shirk a fight, particularly where she felt her integrity was being called into question. But it was hardly surprising that Labour spent more than a decade out of power when so much energy was spent attacking fellow party members.

It is a reflection of her success perhaps that she is remembered as a Labour Party fixer 50 years after her organising days were at their peak. Writing in 2000 in *Tribune*, Ian Aitken reflects on the failure of New Labour to organise – in this instance commenting on the Frank Dobson/ Ken Livingstone contest to be Mayor of London. Aitken writes that 'in all my 50-odd years as a card carrying member (of the Labour Party) I have never witnessed a cock-up on quite the scale of the row surrounding the London mayoralty'. He goes on to say:

of one thing I am certain: 'Old' Labour would never have engineered a cock-up on quite such a scale. In the early fifties, when I was starting out on *Tribune*, five giants were in charge of fixing elections in favour of the Gaitskellite Right wing. They were Morgan Phillips, Sara Barker, Ray Gunter, Alice Bacon and Jim Raisin … in terms of backstairs machinations they were the most frightful rogues. The point, however, is that they were master rogues. When they fixed something, it stayed fixed.

Much of Alice's work was behind the scenes, organising and controlling within the structures of the party. Although she was a tribal Labour loyalist, she worked hard to ensure that the party stayed on the centre, not on the hard left.

Staying on the NEC

The intra-party fighting of the 1950s did not cease with the victory that was Labour's in the general election in 1964. Indeed, despite being appointed a minister by Wilson, Alice's cherished place on the NEC which she held for almost 30 years came under threat. As Lewis Minkin comments:

> Nothing illustrates better the powers of the Right-Wing trade union leaders of the early 1950s than their determination to fill [the women's] section [of the NEC] with those whose political orientation was dependably and vehemently anti-left. Even a moderate enough figure like Eirene White [MP for Flint East, between 1950 and 1970] found that her possession of one of the seats was incompatible with the hard line demanded by the group of Trade Union leaders who had such a large part in deciding the elections for this section.[93]

Thus, even if the CLP section was more volatile – with notable left-wing successes (including Bevan and Ian Mikardo in 1952) – Alice was virtually guaranteed a seat at any NEC election in the 1950s. Yet if she had the right-wing unions more or less sown up, she was less effective with those on the left, and come the mid-1960s this posed a threat to her place on the NEC.

Convention had it that the big unions would vote for each other's candidates, all would vote for sitting candidates and thus, other than the odd name or two, the composition of the NEC would remain relatively constant. In 1965 an attempt by the left-wing unions to unseat Alice came very close to success – after the AEU threw their weight behind the more left-wing Lena Jeger (MP for Holborn and St Pancras South). It was only the unwillingness of the TGWU to do similar that kept Alice on the committee. With the view that Alice was seen, according to Minkin, 'as orthodox and right wing a Labour Government Minister as one was likely to find', she was always likely to be a target for those feeling Wilson's Labour Party was drifting too far to the right.

Alice was not the only Labour figure to occasionally cross swords with the unions. Shirley Williams later commented that 'this huge interest didn't really see itself as part of society, it saw itself as getting the most it could out of society. Both Harold Wilson and Ted Heath tried to bring trade union leaders into sharing responsibility.'[94] But this, Williams argues, was rather a losing battle. Clashes were likely, and common.

Through the course of the 1960s the unions were becoming more militant and more confrontational with their Labour Party colleagues. At the 1966 Party Conference in Brighton 500 car workers marched outside the conference hall protesting against redundancies and sackings. Whilst Jim Callaghan, then Chancellor, came down to speak to the protestors, they demanded to see Wilson. Eventually shop stewards were welcomed in for a beer with the Prime Minister – one of the more literal instances of 'beer and sandwiches' negotiations with union leaders that would mark his government. The unions' complaint, it should be noted, was often not that pay was not increasing enough, but that preferential treatment was being afforded to particular groups: whilst national pay policy allowed for increases of between 3 and 3.5 per cent, Wilson raised the pay of doctors and nurses by some 30 per cent in May 1966. While Alice survived on the NEC relatively easily in 1966, more was to come.

At the 1968 conference in Blackpool it was protests from the miners that most caught the news camera lenses. Initially lobbying ministers entering the hall with signs declaring 'coal not dole' and 'we support Labour, we ask Labour to support us', demonstrators eventually burst into the conference hall – to be calmed down by some soothing words from Jennie Lee, herself a miner's daughter like Alice. At that gathering the TGWU moved to the left and backed candidates like Lena Jeger over Alice (with the AEU continuing to be pro-Jeger). But with all the medium-sized unions remaining loyal, this was just enough to keep Alice on the National Executive once again. In 1970, Alice stood down from the NEC.

The Co-operative Party

Alice was a good facilitator, fixer and organiser, and a big part of this work in the 1940s and 1950s concerned helping manage Labour's relationship with the Co-operative Party and wider Co-operative Movement. Certainly this type of committee work was always something to which Alice was well suited. As Shirley Williams puts it: 'Alice was quite establishment. She was capable of taking decisions but not innovations.'[95] As numerous sub-committees on the Labour NEC found out, she was an adept manager. Part of this skill set – aside from her teaching background – was honed during her early parliamentary dealings with both the Acland Scholarship and the Co-operative Party.

The Acland Scholarship was set up to memorialise the Liberal politician (though, by the 1920s, Labour convert) and author Sir Arthur Herbert Dyke-Acland. The £10,000 bequest, which continues to operate today, funded four scholarships – two for the Labour Party and two for the Central Co-operative Board – to allow young men and women to travel abroad and to undertake research of value to either organisation: the 1939 competition, for example, encouraged entries on economic penetration of the low countries by Hitler's Reich, the labour movement in the Irish Free State, and the education system in France.[96] Alice Bacon took her place as an Acland Trustee, together with Labour's General Secretary Morgan Phillips, in August 1945.[97] Aside from additional access to Phillips, this gave her power over both which subjects and which people would make up the successful applicants. The 1949 application cycle is of particular interest. Having been sent the names of eight 'Class A' candidates who, presumably, were guaranteed short-listing for the awards, Alice commented that 'I think all those are very good (academically)'. Yet 'another point that arises is do we give the scholarships to those with the best qualifications?' She proposed an additional name be added: Olive Barstow, a teacher. 'In her case', she wrote to Phillips, 'I am particularly impressed by the fact that she is now a teacher and was a domestic worker.'[98] Though Barstow lost out in the final round, Alice Bacon's desire to give a hand up to a fellow young teacher was an interesting, and warm, gesture. It also later found some place in her parliamentary discourse – with her acknowledging that former teachers-turned-Conservative MPs with whom she profoundly disagreed could at least know 'what they were talking about'.[99]

Relations with the Co-operative Party were a little more complex. Initially, all was uncomplicated enough: Alice was invited to attend the

1945 Co-operative Party Conference in Scarborough as the Labour Party NEC delegate. Alice perhaps seems an odd choice at first glance – she tended to shun the wider left wing and labour movement (particularly the Fabian Society, in which she appears to have taken no interest, and the Communist Party, against which she held a deep suspicion) – but it was an interesting early brief for someone not yet an MP.[100] One question that both she and the Labour Party faced was what to do about an organisation which retained the capacity to opt out locally from affiliation to the party, but still demanded, as per a 1936 agreement, ready access to Labour ministers when matters of commercial interest to the Co-operative Movement arose. It was, read the 1936 document, the 'duty of Labour Ministers to consult with the appropriate representatives of the Co-operative Movement on issues directly affecting Co-operative trading matters'.[101] As Greg Rosen notes, with the Co-operative Movement lukewarm at best to aspects of nationalisation (particularly concerning the insurance industry), this was something of a tightrope to walk.[102]

Yet going into the 1945 Parliament the political relationship remained ambiguous too. In 1927 the so-called Cheltenham Agreement had allowed local Co-operative parties to affiliate to their Constituency Labour Party, and thus help select candidates for Parliament. As a result the 1935 election, for example, saw nine Co-operative MPs returned and the 1945 election returned 23. In part therefore the debates that would emerge, and in which Alice would take part, would see the Labour Party using the Co-op to set the scene for more important battles – particularly involving the trade unions in the 1960s. As Labour's tent became bigger, the potential for internal pressure groups to influence policy began to grow. The danger was that message discipline would become tricky.

To put all this into some context, in 1945 there were 2.4 million members of the Labour Party – of whom 420,000 (18 per cent) were individual members, with the balance holding membership through affiliate groups. Of these groups, however, 1.9 million (80 per cent of the total) were members of the trade unions with only 45,000 (2 per cent) joining via societies such as the Co-op.[103] Once the Attlee government had replaced the 'opt-in' mechanism of trade union membership of the Labour Party to an 'opt-out' relationship – i.e. trade union members would have to indicate they *did not* wish to be members of the party – the union hold on party membership increased to 87 per cent, a situation only radically altered under the leadership of John Smith in the early 1990s, and changed again by Ed Miliband in 2014.[104] The Co-op was small in and of itself, but it mattered because of the parallels with the trade union relationship.

The issue of what the exact relationship between the Labour and Co-operative parties should be dragged on through the 1950s, and eventually the Co-op snapped. On 29 March 1957 a meeting was held, which Alice attended, at Transport House to discuss the decision by the Co-op to tell the Labour Party that their previous agreement would no longer stand. Hugh Gaitskell commented that the trade unionists were beginning to feel threatened by the rise in the number of Co-op MPs. Harold Wilson complained 'about persons nominated for Parliamentary candidatures by the Co-operative Party who, obviously, had climbed on the ... bandwagon and ... had no background of Co-operative activity in the way that most Trade Union nominees had a record of Union activity'. Alice attended the Co-operative conference again in 1955, and arguably went the furthest: 'She expressed the concern at the character of a large body of the delegates who, obviously, were using the conference as a platform from which to advocate the policies opposed to those of the Labour Party.' The Co-operative delegates in the room, perhaps unsurprisingly, took umbrage and expressed 'firm opposition to any principle which would limit Co-operative political activity'. Alice's warning that decisions 'contrary to the PLP and Labour Party would be a cause of great embarrassment' went unheeded.[105]

As with her anti-Trotskyite activities in Leeds, Alice was fully in favour of wielding, and increasing, Transport House power. A table in the appendix outlines the various power blocs in the Parliamentary Labour Party, but the general story was one of declining trade union affiliation.[106]

In 1946 Alice had helped broker a new agreement between Labour and the Co-op to replace the 1927 Cheltenham Agreement. This maintained the provision for local Co-ops to affiliate to CLPs, but still made plain that 'the Co-operative party does not affiliate with the Labour Party nationally'.[107] This left the type of ambiguous tension Alice expressed concern about at the 1957 NEC meeting: if three-fifths of the Co-ops and four-fifths of members were affiliated with the party, that still left a significant proportion who were not, and thus with little direct reason not to embarrass the party should they wish.[108] The public, it was feared, would not get the nuance of radical, non-Labour elements within a predominately Labour-sympathetic organisation expressing doubts about the party. This was not a merely theoretical concern – with the London Co-operative Society (the biggest in the country) opposing increased military spending in the early 1950s and moving to outright opposition to nuclear weapons by the end of the decade, the notion that sectional interests within Labour could undermine the party's national message was hardly moot.[109] As with the loyalty oaths seen in CLPs across Yorkshire, Alice was in favour of a blunt policy here: though good relations should always be maintained, the Co-op was either in, or it was out.

In July 1957 the 1946 agreement was terminated. Co-operative members, it was asserted, should in no circumstances be exempt from the Standing Orders of the PLP. Without such arrangements, there was the 'the danger of a Party within a Party', which paid no national affiliation fee (unlike the trade unions). Whilst Labour 'had no desire to weaken the ties between [it] and the Co-operative Party' they demanded the Co-op become a pressure group (albeit one still able to back candidates): free to agitate for policy, but with no formal power to make it. So, essentially, does it stand today. Alice valued loyalty to Labour and its leadership – a battle that was played out on the NEC and in Constituency Labour Parties over several years.

To Russia from Ilkley Moor

Alice always actively disliked being considered as 'just' a woman MP. It was a misleading characterisation in any case. For one, the fact that she didn't have a husband and children meant that it was easier for Alice to pursue interests that many women MPs didn't or couldn't. In terms of practicalities, her time on the NEC helped define her politics more broadly, as did her extensive international travel. Though her early parliamentary remarks were mostly related to her own experiences – either direct or indirect – she soon branched out, both within the Labour Party and in national politics. To borrow the rather twee description used of her in a Pathé News report of 1946, the 'socialist go-getter' soon became much more than 'the member for Leeds North[-East]'.[110]

During the summer of 1944 Alice was invited to the USSR as part of a five-person delegation – also including Harold Laski, Percy Collick, William Gillies and Alfred Dobbs – with all travel facilities laid on by the British government, and with the express permission of Anthony Eden, the Foreign Secretary. This was an impressive crowd. The academic Laski would serve as chairman of the Labour Party (1945–6), whilst Collick, Gillies and Dobbs would all go on to be elected at the 1945 election (the latter, tragically, only serving as an MP for a single day before being killed in a road traffic accident). It is difficult to gauge whether Alice believed the delegation's pledge to impress upon Stalin that 'liberated peoples have the full right and freedom to determine their own form of democratic government' was likely to meet with any success. Most probably, as a right-leaning parliamentary candidate and trade unionist, she would have welcomed the assertion that 'the principle of non-interference in the internal affairs of the self-governing, democratic Socialist movements' should be maintained.[111] In August 1946, now an MP, she visited the Soviet Union for a second time, and met Stalin in a trip documented in a series of articles she penned for the *Yorkshire Evening News*. Though she did not reveal much about the conversation, spending two-and-a-quarter hours with the *Generalissimo* was quite an opportunity. Describing him, perhaps surprisingly, as 'considerate, friendly [and] polite', she expressed her interest in the fact that so many women were holding high office in the USSR, compared to Britain. Stalin, speaking in such low tones that he 'would have had difficulty in making himself heard in, say, the House of Commons', expressed his approval through continual chain smoking. At the end of the conversation, Alice asked him to scribble his autograph on a piece of paper, which he did in both Cyrillic and Roman letters. Alice visited the war-ravaged Leningrad, Moscow and Stalingrad during the trip.

In Russia she witnessed long queues – somewhat ironically, both for food and to visit Lenin's tomb – and much homelessness. Yet she skipped over any accusations of press censorship, and praised the fact that there was 'no sex barrier – to top jobs as well as the bottom ones'. Alice was a lifelong anti-communist, and yet surprisingly, was not uniformally critical of the USSR, as evidenced in her column in the *Yorkshire Evening News*.[112] Though she did not follow Barbara Castle – or, most famously, Beatrice and Sidney Webb's *Soviet Communism: A New Civilisation?* – in trying to explain away all Soviet ills, there was some real praise for the Stalinist regime. In the shops of Moscow 'prices are cheap, so that everybody gets something at a fair price'. On Stalin, she saw:

> something of the poet about him, yet with those stocky feet rooted in reality – in the streets of Moscow and the grim ruins of Stalingrad ... Without doubt a man who would want all the time to see his visions translated into actions and his dreams come true.[113]

Yet Alice's words were cloaked in ambiguity – on housing she conceded the war and German occupation of large swathes of Soviet territory had created problems for the regime, but also pointed out that 'overcrowding had existed before the war' too. Castle, on the other hand, wrote approvingly in 1937 of children being constantly reminded that they owed their happiness to Soviet rule and explained away Stalin making abortion illegal by pointing out that the regime also punished absent fathers. Michael Foot, in part referring to Castle's output amongst others, admitted that the USSR was *Tribune*'s Achilles' heel.[114] Alice's praise for the USSR was certainly less fulsome, but it was there.

In reality, it should have been difficult to sugar-coat some of the realities of the contemporary Russian experience. In 1947 the Russian life expectancy was just 40 (the UK's, for comparison, was 67 at the time).[115] Estimates vary widely, but it is generally accepted that between 8 and 20 million Russians had been killed during the war. For those who had managed to survive, many cities like Leningrad and Stalingrad had been shelled to utter destruction. An astonishing one-and-a-half million Russians had been killed during the defence of Leningrad alone, more than the combined British dead in both world wars. But nor was the rural experience much better. The policy of 'scorched earth' practised by Stalin as the Germans advanced towards Moscow in 1941–2 had meant destroying foodstocks, farms, buildings and other such basic infrastructure. And when the Soviets began to turn the tide from 1943 onwards, the Nazis promptly carried out many of the same tactics. Areas of the Soviet Union had been destroyed not just once, but twice.

Alice, for her part, attempted to call it as she saw it whilst providing a valuable insight into Soviet life for her readers. Her column in the *Yorkshire Evening News* offered much illustration on the lives of women in the Soviet Union:

> Some women wore smart wooden wedge-heeled sandals and fully fashioned silk stockings, but very many wore only light carpet slippers … Many women were dressed peasant-like with handkerchiefs on their heads and bundles on their backs. Moscow, you know, is very close to the country and you see many people of nomadic type. It is a common sight in the suburbs … to pass a woman leading a cow on a rope.

This therefore was a trip to learn as much about the Russian people as their leaders. For Alice, 'the greatest enemies of a real understanding [between the two countries were] those who continually assert that everything is right in the Soviet Union and everything is wrong in Britain'.

Alice wanted a warts-and-all impression, an illustration of her varied interests beyond party politics.[116]

Alice's travels were regular enough to give her a broader political knowledge: she was in Vienna in May 1948 to debate how women should be encouraged to be more interested in the political process after years of totalitarian government on the continent, and how democratic socialism should renew itself between communist left and free market right.[117] At the end of 1949 she travelled to Israel at the invitation of the General Federation of Jewish Labour, and, together with John Hynd and Jim Callaghan, had been a delegate for the first session of the Council of Europe in August that year.[118] Indeed, one of the surviving documents kept by the Bacon family details Churchill's invitation for her to attend the Consultative Assembly of the Council of Europe in 1951.[119]

Alice was not just a local MP. She represented the Labour Party nationally, had met and debated with politicians from sister parties across Europe from the 1930s, and had met Stalin and Khrushchev. Yet she never lost her huge pride in Yorkshire and the community she grew up in. And so it was only appropriate that, thousands of miles away from home, in the battlefields of southern Russia, she burst into song, with her fellow Labour delegates. Not the Red Flag (or even the Internationale), but *On Ilkla Moor, Baht'at*. As our next chapter will illustrate, this local pride was reflected in her work as a diligent constituency MP.

∽ 3 ∾

LEEDS AND WESTMINSTER
(1945–64)

Politics was never an abstract thing to Alice. Her politics were grounded in the practicalities of what she saw. Being a diligent constituency MP, much of her perspective and her priorities stemmed from what was going on in Leeds. Whilst frontline politicians have always had a dual role taking in both constituency and national briefs, there was a real sense that the former informed the latter with Alice. This chapter tries to connect those dots – to outline Alice's work in the constituency on the one hand, but also the type of issues being a Leeds MP in the post-war period put at the top of her agenda.

Red Rover

Even amongst those who viewed Alice with some misgivings politically, or for those who knew her little, Alice was regarded as a very good constituency MP. By tackling the physical deprivation of housing, education, industrial injury, health and pollution, she gained many fans. True to her roots in the working-men's clubs, Alice excelled in the day-to-day nature of the job as an MP. Local Leeds resident and Labour activist Frank Pullan remembers Alice well. Pullan recalls that 'her politics were not mine. But I always liked Alice. She never put on any airs or graces, and never forgot her roots.'[1] Frank had particular reason to thank Alice. In 1966, Frank appealed to Alice for help in getting his nephew called home from National Service to be with his father whose kidneys had failed and was in hospital. Alice phoned the War Office and Frank's nephew got to the hospital just before his father died. She would have done it for anyone, said Frank. Perhaps so, but not all MPs might have gone that extra yard.

Her local surgeries are fondly remembered even today in Leeds and were made much of at the time. Even in 1964, when Alice was about to enter government for the first time, her election leaflets reminded voters that 'as MP for Leeds Miss Bacon has made a great reputation in her constituency. Her regular monthly interviews, on the first Saturday of each month, at the Corn Exchange with constituents wanting advice have become well known.'[2] 'In the street', Pullan recalls, 'everyone called her Alice and referred to her as "Our Alice".' June Beecroft, a former constituent, also highlighted the down-to-earth nature of her dealings:

> Alice Bacon had a surgery in a small shop at the top of Bayswater Row, Harehills, where I was brought up. I remember my mother … used to take her hot drinks because there weren't any facilities in the shop. My friends and I used to do our bit by skipping on the pavement to the tune of [American Civil War anthem] Tramp, Tramp, Tramp the Boys are Marching, singing the words 'Vote, Vote, Vote for Alice Bacon, She fights for Labour evermore'.[3]

And she certainly did. But most of all, she fought for the people who put her in Parliament, her constituents. In five of the six elections from 1950 to 1966 Alice increased her percentage of the vote, and her majority was never less than 6,000 (in 1955 it was over double that).[4] In her election manifestos delivered across the constituency Alice advertised her surgeries as well as the huge number of election rallies and addresses – at Leeds Town Hall, the Western Cinema on Florence Street, and at schools and churches across her patch – that she held in the run-up to the vote.

Alice was always recognisable, even before she set foot on the pavement in Leeds, as she arrived in her red Rover. Whilst Hugh Gaitskell would get much use out of it, as Alice drove him to meetings and clubs across Leeds, it was her constituents who latched on to her choice of car the most. 'Alice liked convertible cars', Pullan notes, and bought one as soon as 'she could afford to get one'. The car became a trademark: first voters saw her in a Hillman, and later a maroon Rover. 'It was good for being seen in the constituency', and, as Bernard Atha remembers, whenever Alice would arrive at a meeting by some other means, voters would tease her 'Where's your car?'[5]

However, in 1953 there was a moment of tragedy involving the car. In early August that year, the Bacon family – Alice, Ben, Lottie and Alice's aunt Sarah – took a trip to Ilkley Moor. Shortly after their arrival Lottie collapsed at the scene, and died shortly after in Alice's car. According to the *Yorkshire Post*, by this time Lottie had been a 'semi-invalid' for two-and-a-half years, but this did not make the death any less upsetting for Alice. The many floral tributes at Lottie's funeral included one from Herbert Morrison – abroad at the time and thus unable to make the funeral itself. The Leeds Labour Party, NEC members as well as local faith leaders in Jewish and Christian communities were all at a well-attended gathering which included many constituents wanting to support Alice.[6]

Constituents certainly valued the work Alice was doing in Westminster – a process ably promoted by the output of the Labour-supporting *Leeds Weekly Citizen*. Some MPs in the post-war period never or rarely visited their constituencies. This is typified by the account Ferdinand Mount, later Margaret Thatcher's chief policy adviser, gives of the period. 'Quite a few MPs', Mount notes:

> rarely visited their constituencies at all. Duncan Sandys, who was Tory MP for Streatham and Norwood most of the time between 1935 and 1974 claimed that he visited the place, only a short hop across the river from Westminster, but once a year, to address his association's AGM. Most MPs were more assiduous, but not many of them regarded it as their sacred duty to hold a 'surgery' in their constituency once a fortnight or even once a month.[7]

That was not the case in Leeds according to Baroness Joyce Gould, who was a local party activist during this period. Despite the seniority of the Leeds MPs – Hugh Gaitskell, Dennis Healey, Charles Pannell and Alice Bacon all reached ministerial rank – these Members of Parliament were very much part of the thriving constituency parties. Alice probably attended more than the others, having her roots locally, but Gaitskell's daughter, Julia McNeal, also remembers visits to Leeds as a young girl. And there was a lot going on locally. Two hundred people would attend the monthly Leeds Labour Party meeting at the Trades Hall, just off the Headrow in Leeds city centre. All factions of the party were well organised – the socialist Labour Leagues of Bevanites, the Trotskyites, the women's groups, unions, Gaitskellites and the University group all planned and plotted ahead of meetings and battles were often fierce.

But the Labour Party in Leeds was about more than politics. Annual bazaars were held each November, taking over the whole of the ground floor of the Corn Exchange, the venue for Alice's surgeries. A banner was dropped across the entrance to the building – one of the grandest in Leeds. Baroness Gould remembers party members there being stunned by the news of President Kennedy's assassination while preparing for the bazaar in November 1963. Bazaars weren't just for the local activists or Christmas bargains – local members remember Hugh Gaitskell addressing the bazaar with great speeches to the faithful.

There was the Leeds Women's group too, of which Alice was vice chair. Every branch of the party had its own women's section, most of which were very active. Activities culminated with the annual Yorkshire women's rally (first set up by Sara Barker in 1948) which attracted upwards of 2,000 people to Leeds Town Hall, Filey (with perhaps as many as 4,500 in attendance, according to Baroness Betty Boothroyd who was a regular attendee), and other venues across the region.

Leeds had some history of promoting women through the party. Isabella Ford, who organised the Tailoresses union in Leeds, was a delegate to Labour Party Conference in 1904 and became the first woman to speak at conference the following year. The historian Keith Laybourn suggests that West Yorkshire was probably more successful in selecting women than, for example, South Yorkshire. The main industry in West Yorkshire was textiles – which was employing more women than men in the 1950s, and women (who were often at work) had fewer children than in the mining communities in South Yorkshire, where labour market participation among women was much lower.

It was in the party's women's section that a young Betty Boothroyd first came across Alice Bacon when she started attending the women's section with her mother who was a party stalwart in Dewsbury. Betty's first encounter with Alice was when Alice presented her with a signed copy of a book by Clement Attlee, for winning the rally's 'beauty contest'. Boothroyd remembers Alice being 'very much in demand' in the women's section and after a week in Westminster would spend weekends on the platform at meetings, rallies and bazaars touring the Yorkshire region and the country with sandwiches, a flask and a rallying speech. Boothroyd describes being 'weaned' in the women's section of the Labour Party where established MPs like Alice, along with Yorkshire women's section organiser, Sara Barker, would encourage and motivate the next generation of women in the party. Alice was 'quite a star' in the women's section, whose support and character Boothroyd still remembers today.[8]

Alice made her mark as an excellent constituency MP who knew the concerns of her voters and spoke to them in a language they could understand. She had forged links with the electorate, local Labour and trades union sections, and never forgot her teaching background. As a testament to her popularity in every election she contested she outperformed the national Labour swing. Even if we consider her stunning performance at the 1945 election as something of an outlier, the Alice Bacon factor was worth an average of 3 per cent in elections between 1950 and 1966.

Leeds and the New Jerusalem

Alice's parliamentary career began in the halcyon days of 1945. To Bernard Atha, the declaration of results on 26 July 1945 was a 'new dawn akin to the second coming'. His particular experience of the campaign, using a peashooter to try (unsuccessfully) to hit Winston Churchill on a visit to Leeds, was presumably not replicated by everyone (the *Yorkshire Evening Post* reported instead of a 'spontaneous demonstration of enthusiasm for the man'). Yet the feeling of jubilation at the election of a Labour government, and the defeat of the Tories, was certainly widespread.[9] In later life Barbara Castle would wistfully recall the happiness of this time and drew on Wordsworth to do so: 'Bliss was it in that dawn to be alive. But to be young was very heaven.'[10]

A new dawn had broken, had it not? The Labour manifesto in 1945, 'Let us Face the Future', was an inspirational document. Referring to the 'gallant men and women in the Fighting Services, in the Merchant Navy, Home Guard and Civil Defence, in the factories and in the bombed areas' it demanded that 'they deserve and must be assured a happier future than faced so many of them after the last war. Labour regards their welfare as a sacred trust.' Labour's diagnosis of what issues the incoming government should address was simple but effective:

> The nation wants food, work and homes. It wants more than that – it wants good food in plenty, useful work for all, and comfortable, labour-saving homes that take full advantage of the resources of modern science and productive industry. It wants a high and rising standard of living, security for all against a rainy day, an educational system that will give every boy and girl a chance to develop the best that is in them.[11]

Thus did the manifesto proclaim 'jobs for all, industry in the service of the nation', improving the 'health of the nation and its children', and providing 'social insurance against the rainy day'. This was a revolutionary moment in British politics, and Alice Bacon was about to play her part.

Gerald Kaufman met Alice for the first time during the 1945 election. He remembers her focus on housing and employment issues throughout that campaign, and the 'very good public meetings she held'. On the day of the results, Kaufman came down from grammar school on the tram. 'I went to the museum where all the results from the six Leeds constituencies were being counted. When I arrived five out of six had been counted, the last was the Tory Osbert Peake – the only [Conservative] to scrape home.'[12] There, Kaufman recalls that John Craik-Henderson, the Tory whom Alice had defeated, icily remarked to her that 'I hope you will enjoy your short stay in Westminster.' In the event Alice would stay in the Commons for 25 years, five times Craik-Henderson's own tenure (1940–5), and almost ten times longer including her service in the House of Lords.

As John Grayson wrote, 'a relatively safe Tory fiefdom' had become, in 1945, a Labour stronghold with one of the biggest swings in the country.[13] Alice's hard work of addressing busy street meetings (the dominant campaign activity in 1945), 'every afternoon and every evening in addition to addressing many workplace meetings', paid off with a 22.6 per cent swing to Labour from the Conservatives.[14] The buzz that had been seen in the Labour Committee Room in Cowper Street prior to polling day was fully justified. 'I hope you win Miss Bacon, you should – I voted for you eleven times', said one Irish voter outside the Labour office.[15] As well as the Irish, other immigrant community voters came out for Alice, with Gerald Kaufman believing that 'everyone who was Jewish voted for Alice. 100% of the Jews who had votes would have voted for Alice.' Aside from the Jewish communities that had been in Britain for generations, this number would have included some refugees who had escaped from Nazi tyranny in the 1930s, though this would have depended on their achieving naturalisation in time.

Despite the landslide victory, Labour candidates were nervous before polling day that either the Churchill factor, or massive movements of population that had occurred in the ten years since the 1935 election, would see opponents sneak home. Even Ellen Wilkinson in Jarrow, who would in the end secure 66 per cent of the vote against her Liberal National opponent (and an 11,000 majority), felt nervous enough to write to Ernest Bevin in March 1945 to request that he come and canvass in her constituency: 'I really do need a spot of help, as over 2,000 of my staunchest votes are outside the division – having been moved out to a new housing estate since the last election.' Despite Ellen Wilkinson's plea, Bevin could not attend – having already promised to attend a luncheon in Leeds, where he joined another nervous candidate, Alice Bacon, along with Sara Barker and other leading Yorkshire Labour figures.[16]

After 1945, there were 40 Labour MPs in Yorkshire, up from 26 a decade before. Leeds had five Labour MPs compared to a solitary Tory. Of these, with her 25 years of service, Alice would have by far the longest career in the Commons, with Tom Stamford (1949) and Hugh Gaitksell (1963) dying in office, and James Milner (1951) and George Porter (1955) being elevated to the House of Lords. Alice's long involvement in post-1945 Leeds parliamentary politics was unique.

The experience of 1945 was one Alice would never forget:

> It was the most exciting time. I don't think there will ever be another general election like that. The awful thing was because the forces were voting and we had to wait for the voting to come in, we had to wait three weeks between the election and the declaration of the results. And my wonderful agent Alf Hodges would ring me every day. One day he reckoned I would be in by a thousand, the next day he thought I would be out by a thousand, and we had to suffer this for three weeks. It was terrible. Then the count was in the morning, and my mother had serious heart trouble. We wondered if she could stand the count. A few days before the count of the people who were actually living in Leeds Alf Hodges had to go see the boxes emptied from the forces. He rang me up and said, 'tell your mother she can go to the count'.[17]

Alice, a young woman, a miner's daughter and teacher, was elected as a Member of Parliament at the age of 35. The first female MP in Leeds, the first (with Muriel Nichol) in fact in Yorkshire. An article by Alice in *The Labour Woman* reflected the great burden on Nichol, herself and others, as well as the joy of the time:

> My most moving memory of July 26th was of old people weeping unashamedly in the streets of Leeds. As one said, 'All my life I've worked for this and at last it's here!' Yes, at last we have a Labour Government of such strength and power that we can put into operation the policy which has for so long been a dream to those who have given their lives to the cause of Socialism. At the first meeting of Labour MPs it was a great thrill

for me to meet so many young people I had known in the League of Youth and had met at week-end and summer schools.

It so happens that it has fallen to the young men and women of my generation to translate into reality the hopes and visions of the pioneers of the Labour Party and to be the custodians of the future. This Parliament includes 24 women, 21 of them members of the Labour Party. No longer will a mere five or six be regarded as an oddity in the House of Commons, although even 21 is a small proportion compared to the men.

What are we going to do as women MPs? I believe it will be a mistake to consider ourselves as a group apart from the men merely to deal with women's questions (although our specialised knowledge on such subjects will be of great value). We were not elected to the House of Commons because we were women, but because we were Labour candidates believing in a Socialist policy, and I think that we shall pay the greatest service to the cause of sex equality if we take our place with the men irrespective of sex. A great work lies ahead. We have now to put into operation Labour Party policy at a time of great difficulty, but I am firmly convinced that men and women, old and young, will all pull together in order to achieve our ultimate aim as quickly as possible.[18]

Huge challenges confronted the incoming Labour government and its new MPs. Bernard Atha recalls that the deprivation of interwar Leeds 'was obvious even to a child'. Alice would soon set to work – this was her chance to change things.

Workers' Rights and the NHS

In later life Alice would again reflect on the happiness of 1945:

The first few months it was euphoric, it really was. And as a member of the National Executive of the Labour Party during the war years, I had been a member of the various committees that were producing our policy for the next election. It was so exciting to see these being put into operation. That really was a great thing – to have been on that committee and then to be in the House of Commons when that was put through. We ended the old Poor Law, there was the industrial injuries bill, there was nation-alisation of the mines. It was really terrific the amount that was done. I remember on one occasion the saying, 'we hadn't talked the bill through, we'd walked the bill through' because we'd walked all night through the division lobbies.[19]

Addressing the Commons with her maiden speech in October 1945, Alice spoke on behalf of her constituents first and foremost. The debate was one on which she was well equipped to speak. The National Insurance (Industrial Injuries) Bill took the previous rule of compensating those workers incapacitated on the job for their loss of labour, and added an additional sum for the injury itself – 20 shillings per week in the case of permanent incapacitation. 'Among the mining population', Alice told the House, 'workmen's compensation plays a very great part ... in mining towns and villages there is scarcely an adult man who has not at some time or another been subject to workmen's compensation.'

This knowledge came from personal experience, as her reaction to Clause 72 of the bill set out. Clause 72 gave 'the Minister power to make arrangements to secure maintenance, free of charge or at a reduced rate, of equipment ... for any person who, by reason of loss of limb, is in need of them'. Alice was reminded of cases of facial injuries she had seen, afflicting men who worked in the pits in and around Normanton. She told the house that 'I know a man who met with an accident so bad that one eye and the surrounding parts of his face were completely torn away'. Aware such sensibilities might offend her audience – ironic given the patronising chauvinism some treated her with, she acknowledged that 'such details are not very pleasant, but these things are happening every day in the coalfields'. Fitting a man with a glass eye and a mask made all the difference for someone in danger of 'slipping away from the world with people turning away from him in revulsion'.

Also speaking in the debate was Alice's Conservative neighbour in North Leeds, Osbert Peake, who told MPs that the bill was 'not socialism'. Alice responded that 'there may be differences of opinion about that, but there is one thing that it does – it removes some of the effects of capitalism'. The Liberal leader Clement Davies congratulated Alice as speaking with the 'deepest sincerity ... it was obviously delivered from a wealth of experience and deep humanity, both of which have had their effect upon the House'.[20] It was her experience and her human understanding of issues that formed the cornerstone of Alice's political and parliamentary contributions, from this her first speech in 1945 and throughout her career.

Industrial injury and compensation were close to Alice's heart, but the biggest transformation that the 1945 Labour government achieved was the creation of the National Health Service. In the 1946 bill to introduce the NHS Alice spoke, like so many other Labour MPs, with great passion drawing on Aneurin Bevan's claim that the NHS gave Britain 'the moral leadership of the world':

> the Bill, on the whole, is the greatest measure for human wellbeing ever introduced into this country. Some hon. Members opposite and some whom I shall describe as vested interests outside, have denounced this Bill as taking away the freedom of the individual, and introducing into our health services what they call a 'soulless bureaucratic machine'. What loss of freedom can there be in giving to everybody irrespective of any conditions whatsoever a free choice of doctor, free consultant services, free hospital services, and, in fact, free medical and surgical service of every kind? This Bill gives to thousands of people freedom which they have never before enjoyed, freedom to consult a doctor or specialist without thinking of the cost.[21]

Alice offered a forthright rebuttal of the critics of nationalisation and argued that private sector critics of the process were misguided, wrong or just representing selfish interests:

> They refer to the transfer of the hospitals and their endowments as 'taking away their hospitals and confiscating their property'. But whose property is it? Whose endowments are they? The money which belongs to the voluntary hospitals is the people's money, which has been contributed by workmen's contributions, flag days and charity concerts. This money, while being technically transferred, is to be used in a much more economical way than at present for the benefit of the people who contributed it.[22]

Her views were in part informed by the medical professionals she knew locally. As Alice noted, the NHS was not just to be about alleviating the consequences of mass deprivation (important as this indeed was), but a genuinely 'national' good:

> in the City of Leeds a part of which I represent, the branch of the British Medical Association has come out in support of nearly all of the proposals in the Bill, including the abolition of the sale and purchase

of practices, and the public ownership of all hospitals and their organisation on a regional basis. Leeds, I believe, has been regarded as one of the black spots of the British Medical Association, which is discovering that it has more black spots than it thought it had originally. The Bill will confer great advantages on all sections of the community, and particularly on the middle classes, who have always been outside every scheme of National Health Insurance. They will feel its benefits very much indeed.[23]

The support of the local Leeds BMA for the majority of the bill was unusual (a 'black spot'), with most doctors opposing the creation of the NHS. Support was won by the promise to maintain the privacy of the consulting room within the new health service. The Leeds BMA had certain caveats – including demands for regional rather than local authority oversight, and the setting up of a select committee on the NHS within five years – but their broad position was positive. This was certainly an easier ride than in nearby Bradford, where the local BMA 'emphatically oppose[d] state service' over the old model.[24]

Still, Alice continued with her critique of the BMA – particularly for pressing for the continuation of paid-for services alongside the public hospitals and private practice creaming off services that should be available for all. Alice was strongly in favour of a health system free at the point of use and blind to ability to pay, but she was worried about the continuation of a two-tier health system (engendered through the continuation of private practices) even after the creation of a National Health Service.

Politically, Alice looked beyond the poorest, including in the health service – a shrewd attitude she also took with regards to rationing. Whilst Labour had made significant inroads into the middle-class vote in 1945 (principally at the expense of the Liberals), issues such as rationing threatened that advance. Labour had succeeded in making rationing 'fair', in that better-off households were hit harder than the poorest, but middle-class families were beginning to feel the strain as rationing continued even once the war was won. By way of example, in 1936–7, the average middle-class person was consuming over 3,100 calories a day compared to 2,557 calories for their working-class equivalent. By 1950, these figures were almost even, with the middle-class intake of 2,506 calories a day barely exceeding the working-class average of 2,468. In one sense, this was clearly a success, but it allowed, as Zweiniger-Bargielowska notes, 'the Conservative Party to become the home for middle class dissent' as middle-class families felt a larger reduction in their living standards. To a woman like Alice who, unlike the majority of Labour MPs, took care of her own household's shopping, rationing had a direct effect. Rationing of clothes (1941–9) and bread (1946–8) were but two such examples, and both working- and middle-class consumption of meat, fish and vegetables dropped by at least a quarter in the five years after the war.[25] Readers of the *Yorkshire Evening Post* were even offered, in one 1946 advert, a rather unusual way of plugging this calorie gap: Jem Brand Black Beer 'which contains nearly 2,000 calories: that's food value for you!'[26]

However one tried to get around it – rationing was hard. The Tories stepped into this space – not peeling away significant swathes of the working-class vote, but securing enough former Liberal voters to secure a threadbare majority by 1951. An evolution in Labour's message was needed – not necessarily concerning the party's goals but the means to achieve them. This required a greater understanding of the electorate and a practical engagement with what they actually would and would not accept.

Alice Bacon was at the forefront of this. By 1952 Alice had turned her attentions to arguing for exemptions from the new purchase tax for everyday items of necessity such as bicycles, razor blades, combs, cutlery and umbrellas – dryly remarking with reference to the latter that 'I suppose it depends on where one lives, but it would be regarded as a necessity in Manchester'.[27] Similarly, in the pages of *The Labour Woman* she noted that her party – and notably Labour women – were standing up for housewives:

> Scathing things are sometimes written about women members, such as a recent remark that women MPs were 'seen and not heard'. This certainly does not apply to our Labour women, all of whom are active and vociferous, and doing a good job of work. It is significant that during the Finance Bill, when Labour women played a notable part in moving amendments to keep down the prices of clothes, footwear and household goods, no Tory woman raised her voice on behalf of the housewives whose friends they pretended to be before and during the last election.[28]

Alice was, from the outset, a practical politician, addressing issues of immediate concern to her constituents. Consistent with her writing in *The Labour Woman* she tabled questions on the availability of women's shoes, clothes rationing coupons, the 'down-pointing of women's outwear', and the bacon ration.[29] The textiles industry was a big employer in Leeds, and Alice was also mindful of the impact of rationing on the industry – including the issue that stocks of women's coats and suits among manufacturers were increasing in the late 1940s as women could not afford to buy them with the coupons allocated. The issue of women's clothing showed something interesting about contemporary attitudes too. The following exchange could be taken as knockabout parliamentary stuff, but one wonders whether the same disregard would have been shown towards a similar men's issue:

Miss Alice Bacon asked the President of the Board of Trade if he is aware of the increasing difficulty in obtaining women's outsize garments; and what steps he proposes to take to encourage manufacturers to increase their supplies.

Sir Stafford Cripps: discussions are proceeding with the trade associations concerned, and an announcement will shortly be made.

Mr Edward Keeling: Can the right hon. and learned Gentleman give any explanation of the fact that the women of North-East Leeds are so much larger than the women of Thirsk?[30]

When Alice told local constituents and campaigners in Leeds, such as Frank Pullan, that 'being a woman in a man's world had never been a problem or disability, [in fact] it had been an asset', instances such as these were probably not at the forefront of her mind.[31] Alice's strength in debates and in politics was that she understood the needs of her constituents because she was from that community. She may have always claimed it was 'an advantage' to be female but, to some parliamentarians such as Edward Keeling, the Conservative MP for Twickenham, her sex undermined any reputation for seriousness in a predominantly men's world.

Yet Keeling's trivialisation of such interventions was a mistake (and not one all within his party would make). These common concerns of women – and men – were increasingly becoming issues of electoral importance. The personal was political. Despite Labour winning a landslide in 1945, within just two or three years the Conservatives were looking optimistically towards the next election. The relentless continuation of rationing some years after VE Day, and stretching into the future, was taking its toll on a weary public and the lack of consumer goods was allowing the Conservatives to re-establish a political *raison d'être* after 1945 had seemingly wiped them out for a generation.[32] Alice seemed to understand this in a way that few other Labour politicians of the time did. Grinding austerity was wearing thin with an electorate who wanted something more after all the years of war and rationing. This was crystallised in the two parties' advertising slogans – whilst Labour used the phrase 'ask your dad', conjuring up a *Road to Wigan Pier* type image of mass interwar unemployment presided over by Baldwin-era Conservatism, the Tories responded 'ask your mum' – referring, as future Labour MP Austen Albu noted, to the days 'when there were no queues at the shops'.[33]

Given the widespread belief, certainly in later years, that Labour's drab austerity had cost it the 1951 general election (and also a workable majority in 1950), this certainly indicated that Alice understood the changing mood of the country. Not all Labour politicians – even on the right of the party – really 'got it'. Even in his memoirs many years after the events, Alice's friend Herbert Morrison declared that the electorate 'should have realised the situation, for the facts were clearly set out in our programme and constantly repeated by Labour's political leaders'. He did, however, concede that the 'party' needed to 'adapt itself to the radically different situation of the nation'.[34] Alice warned as such at the time and the Conservatives – looking to the end of austerity, and the beginning of the end of economic planning – won the general election in 1951. Labour's New Jerusalem had delivered so much in the way of national provision – change that has lasted well into the next century, but people also wanted greater freedom to spend the pounds in their pockets. Alice spotted this trend, warned her party of it, and raised it in Parliament. But the consumer society was not to be embraced by Labour just yet.

Advocate of the Comprehensive

As with household matters and the cost of living, Alice, like many, often spoke of which she knew. So, Alice took her knowledge of the interwar comprehensive, as well as her own experience of being 'lucky' enough to go to grammar school, into Parliament.

Like in Normanton, in her constituency of Leeds North East, luck played a big role in determining your future. For the lucky few – the grammar school and the world that opened up. For everyone else the secondary modern, and the limitations that it engendered.

The young Gerald Kaufman grew up in Leeds during the 1930s and 1940s and remembers that the inequalities in the education system were obvious. Going to grammar school, he notes, 'changed my life'. 'I never would have had the opportunities I had without going to grammar school, I was a lucky kid, and this fluke has governed my attitudes to education ever since.'[35] Kaufman attained a scholarship to go to Leeds Grammar School which allowed his parents – Polish immigrants with six other children – to provide an education that few had access to, and that certainly they could not have afforded without, as Kaufman put it, this bit of luck. Kaufman would become a key adviser to Harold Wilson in the 1960s, but Alice would get the chance to influence the debate on education policy at an earlier stage.

In the immediate post-war period, criticisms of the tripartite system of grammar, secondary modern (which local authorities were now under a statutory duty to provide) and technical schools (designed to 'raise the prestige of high manual skill' through occupational training) increased in the labour movement.[36] The wave of technical schools proposed in the 1944 (Butler) Education Act never materialised to any significant degree, so the vast majority of British children would have their future determined by the age of 10 or 11, on taking the test to determine whether they were allocated a place at a grammar or secondary modern school. For the lucky few, the grammar school and perhaps the prospect of university, to the unlucky majority the lottery of entering the local secondary modern.

Historian and peer Kenneth O. Morgan reflects that 'the National Association of Labour Teachers applied constant pressure, and in 1950 Alice Bacon, one of its less abrasive spokesmen, persuaded the national party executive to consider the question [of comprehensive education] by setting up a working party'. By 1951, albeit in the cloaked terms of calling for 'greater equality of opportunity in education', a commitment to comprehensive education was in the Labour Party manifesto.[37] Battles continued to rage throughout the 1950s and 1960s on the issue, but it was a big step, and one that Alice Bacon was instrumental in achieving. Her work, both within Westminster and outside, was of huge importance in establishing the comprehensive model in Britain. Harold Wilson might later describe the tripartite system as 'education apartheid', but it took the pioneering work of MPs like Alice to open up the political space for

him to make headway.[38] She did this in many ways – raising the comprehensive question more than any other member in the Commons.

The official government line through 1945 to 1951 remained a broad
commitment to the tripartite system. Ellen Wilkinson (1945–7) and
George Tomlinson (1947–51) at the Ministry of Education saw this model
of different types of school for different types of children as a good one.
Attitudes in the party, including the parliamentary party were changing,
though. As Martin Francis notes, 'it is important not to exaggerate the
Attlee government's negative attitude to comprehensives; it is best
characterised as a lack of enthusiasm rather than an active hostility'.[39]
Alice, for one, was an enthusiast for comprehensives but made her
argument, at least at this stage, in the context of 'variety' in school types.
In *The Labour Woman*, she wrote:

> We can expect nothing from the Tories. The White Paper issued before
> the 1944 Education Act envisaged a perpetuation of the system as we
> know it, and in doing so aroused opposition from the Socialist Movement
> generally and many educationalists … Once again we point the way. Not
> by dictatorial methods, because it would be wrong to impose a pattern
> of education upon local authorities. We want variety and there could be
> great variety between one comprehensive school and another.[40]

Alice also kept up the pressure in Parliament. Hansard records that
between 1950 and 1969 Alice was to use the phrase 'comprehensive
schools' 79 times, compared with 50 times for Michael Stewart (Wilson's
first Education Secretary), 50 times for Stephen Swingler (like Alice,
a long-term advocate of the comprehensive) and 64 times by Anthony
Crosland, Secretary of State for Education between 1965 and 1967. In
her first reference to the subject in November 1945, Alice queried the
grammar school structure whereby 25 per cent of places were free, 25
per cent allocated by the Local Education Authority, and half open to
fee-paying entrants, albeit who had to pass an exam. Was this 50 per
cent open to scholarship applicants? If, as the moderate Tory MP Hugh
Linstead claimed, such schools were 'valuable in narrowing the gap which
we all want to see in the educational field', one would assume they would
or should be. Yet rarely was it the case, so a grammar school education
was easier for rich and more affluent families to acquire than poorer ones.
Alice put it to the Commons in 1948 that 'the interests of the children'
demanded that '[comprehensive] schools should be definitely encouraged

and not just tolerated'. Brief experimentation had taken place (and/or was planned) in areas such as Middlesex, but Alice argued the time was ripe to roll the system out nationwide. As she told the Labour Party Conference in 1953:

> There is a great amount of luck regarding the education of our children, luck which to some extent is dependent upon where the child lives. For instance, a child who lives in Merioneth has eight times the chance of going to a grammar school as the child who lives in Gateshead, because in Merioneth they have got sufficient grammar school places for 64 per cent of the children, whereas in Gateshead they have only got sufficient places for 8 per cent.[41]

Support for comprehensive education had been Alice's position for some time, and her early interventions put her far in advance of many. 'Will my right honourable friend do everything he can', she beseeched the Labour Minister of Education George Tomlinson, 'to encourage these schools and so abolish the dreadful system of deciding, when a child is 10 years old, what its future shall be?' Tomlinson pledged that he would, but it would be left to Bacon herself to see the necessary reforms through two decades later. Alice's conference speeches, as a member of the party's NEC – such as those in 1950 and 1952 – were often on the comprehensive, but getting the party to change policy, and deliver change, was not easy.

For Alice, it was about improving the prospects and opportunities for all children. While critics of the comprehensive feared a levelling down of standards and curriculum, Alice saw it as a chance for 'levelling up'. Speaking in the House of Commons in 1955, Alice drew extensively on the work of Leicester University lecturer, Robin Pedley. Pedley's book, *Comprehensive Schools Today*, looked at the evidence from the first comprehensive schools in the UK. His conclusion, and certainly that of Alice, was that 'far from there being a levelling down, there has been a considerable levelling up. Many children ... who would not have passed the examination at 11 did exceedingly well afterwards.'

When Labour lost office in 1951, the overall battleground shifted. The Tories, unlikely to create a comprehensive system, needed to be held to account elsewhere. In 1953 Alice harangued Florence Horsbrugh – the first female Conservative Cabinet minister – on the issues of dilapidated school buildings and class sizes, another of Alice's crusades. The running theme here would be Alice Bacon asking the government to go further, and successive Tory ministers arguing that Labour had done little themselves between 1945 and 1951. Whilst the numbers did not directly disprove the Tory claim, there was not a level playing field here, as Alice pointed out:

> how can we compare 1952-3 – having been told that the building position has so improved that we can set the builders free and take off all the controls – with the years 1947-8, just at the end of the war, when we had so many shortages?[42]

Indeed, during the Labour government, the numbers of pupils per teacher fell year on year, only to increase under the early years of Conservative rule.

What comes across most of all from Alice's speeches is her passion and knowledge, and her frustration that the people in charge of the nation's education knew less than she did – and that was largely true whether Labour or the Conservatives were in office. At the conclusion of her 1953 speech in the House of Commons Alice summed it up thus:

> Meanwhile, we have the Government, who are content to leave everything to the Headmistress (Education Secretary Florence Horsbrugh) – rather like the old-fashioned school governors – provided that she does not spend too much. They do not care very much whether everything is right or wrong, because their children are not going to the school anyway.
>
> In short, the Minister is complacent, the Parliamentary Secretary is incompetent, and the government are indifferent. The tragedy is that these are the people who are in charge of six million of the nation's children – our most precious national asset. It is clear that the country cannot afford to tolerate them any longer, and that they ought to leave the charge of these six million children to people who really care about education.

Reading Alice's speeches, the 'people who really care' surely includes herself – that is, teachers and socialists who put education at the top of the list of priorities and resource schools accordingly.

The 1950 Labour manifesto, reflecting Alice's influence, was positive on school reform and improvement: 'Labour has placed the needs of our children in the forefront of national policy. Never before have our babies been so healthy; our youngsters so well fed, clothed and shod. Labour has raised the school leaving age. New schools are being built.'[43] All well and good, and it must be said that the Conservative manifesto that same year was pretty vague in its promises:

> Where necessary we intend to adopt simpler standards for school building. This will help the voluntary schools. A determined effort must be made to reduce the size of classes particularly in the primary schools. There is grave danger of education losing its meaning if what is happening in some areas is allowed to continue. We must be free to meet this challenge with fresh minds and active policies.[44]

Both parties would go on to downplay education policy in their 1951 manifestos, though the meaning of the new Tory government's 'fresh minds and active policies' soon became clear. The Department for Education under the minister Florence Horsbrugh issued Circular 245 in February 1952 – laying down the conditions under which local authorities could build schools. Circular 245, in the words of Labour MP Stephen Swingler:

> forbade building work for the purpose of relieving overcrowding and replacing blacklisted schools. It means the continuance of these schools in use. It means the continuance of 34,000 classes in each of which there are more than 40 pupils and the continuance of probably more than 1,000 classes in our schools, each of which has more than 50 pupils.

The reason for this circular, according to Swingler, was to effect a situation where the cutting of the school leaving age (to open up class space) became more palatable.

This issue of lowering the school leaving age back to 14 – after Labour had successfully increased it to 15, in accordance with the 1944 Education Act, in 1947 after many delays because of the impact of World War II – was continually raised in the early 1950s by Conservative MPs. Thomas Peart, Labour MP for Accrington, summarised such growing calls from the Conservative side in 1954 in the House of Commons:

> The hon. Member for Hampstead (Mr. H. Brooke, Conservative) talked about the Minister's critics. Many of those critics are members of the Conservative Party. The hon. Member referred to those who would have cut the school age. Surely he has read the Conservative pamphlet 'One

Nation', to which the Chancellor has written a preface, in which there is a suggestion that the difficulties facing the educational world should be met by a cut in the school age. Surely the hon. Member has read the speeches of his hon. Friend the Member for Ealing, South (Mr Angus Maude) who, in this House, advocated a cut in the school age. Surely hon. Members opposite remember Lord Waverley, when a leading figure in the Conservative Opposition, chiding the Labour Government for raising the school age. The critics have all along been members of the Conservative Party, and time and time again they have suggested that the Labour Government should not raise the school leaving age and they now advocate a cut in the school age in order to meet the difficulty of overcrowding in school.[45]

Money available for school building projects was carefully restricted by the Conservative government. With £88 million worth of buildings needed by 146 authorities 'to meet [the] bare minimum', Florence Horsbrugh began to reply to the first 75 of the applications from local authorities. To their request of £42 million, 'the right hon. Lady has cut the £42 to £24 million … it is quite clear that this sum is not sufficient to provide even the bare minimum'. For Nottingham this meant reducing a desire for four secondary schools and four primary schools to two of each. For Northumberland, a request for 12 schools was reduced to a bid for four. As Bacon pointed out:

> this sort of thing is happening all over the country. What I should like to impress upon the Minister is that the local authorities know the situation. They know the local problems. They see the children needing schools but know that they have no schools in which to put those children.

Alice felt 'strongly on this matter, because before I came to this House I spent my time in council schools'. 'This', she concluded, 'was a time to consider the whole question … of education in this country.'[46]

Such questions included the status of the private school – long a vexed question not least in the Labour Party. At the 1953 Party Conference in Margate Alice's friend and parliamentary neighbour Hugh Gaitskell (a former Winchester public school boy) would speak vehemently against the continuation of a fully separated private system of fee-paying schools. Gaitskell told conference that:

if we believe in genuine equality of opportunity, we really cannot go on with a system of education under which the parents of wealthy children are able to buy what they want and most people believe to be a better education for their children.

Gaitskell proposed not full-scale abolition but to 'throw [the] doors open' to a system whereby 'we could manage to offer, say, half the places at public school free as a start'. This position won the support of TGWU boss Arthur Deakin, but saw a temporary left/right united opposition from both Jennie Lee and Alice Bacon. Lee remarked that instead of opening up the private schools 'our party' should 'put all its enthusiasm and skill into comprehensive schools'.[47]

Alice's views on the matter saw her go against Hugh Gaitskell very directly, but they also show something of her practical politics. As she told conference, Labour:

> would be making a mistake in thinking that the problem of the public and private schools was the burning educational topic in our homes today. Mr and Mrs Brown, the ordinary parents of this country, do not feel aggrieved because their Tommy goes to a council school while little Lord Pontalduke goes to Eton, but what does grieve them is that Jimmy Jones over the road has a scholarship to a grammar school while their Tommy has to stay in the [secondary] modern school.

Alice's counter offer was to propose that local authorities stop subsidising the '£300, £400 or £500' scholarship fees of children at the 'minor public schools' – 'Why should we provide public money to bolster up a system with which we disagree?'[48] It was not until 1997 that such scholarships for assisted places were abolished by Tony Blair's Labour government. The money saved was used to reduce class sizes in infant schools – a measure Alice would certainly have approved of.

Alice led the battle for implementable, incremental reform both at conference and in the committee room. In March 1954 Alice chaired a Policy Committee on Education including both current and future MPs (such as David Ginsburg, later MP for Dewsbury and Edith Summerskill, MP for Fulham West) and members of the NALT. Requesting greater access to the policy making framework, the NALT stated that they 'had a wealth of experience in the educational field, but the [Labour

Party's] National Executive Committee were not making use of it'. The Committee itself noted that:

> most important to all was the question of whether the next Labour Government should give directives to local education authorities to set up comprehensive schools or whether it should be left on a voluntary basis, but attention should also be paid to issues raised by the so-called public schools and the question of church schools within the system of comprehensive secondary education.[49]

Alice offered specific ideas including introducing a specific grant from the Ministry of Education to schools, rather than giving a grant to the LEAs and allowing them discretion to determine which school received what grant – thereby alleviating a situation where, as Alice put it, 'some are mean and some are generous'.[50]

But the committee's deliberations would have to wait until a Labour government returned to office. Macmillan's government was returned to power in 1955 with the Prime Minister promising an 'Opportunity State', an earlier version of the Big Society. Two years later, Macmillan – in his famous Bedford speech – pointed to increased production in major industries such as steel and cars, telling his audience: 'let us be frank about it – most of our people have never had it so good'. Macmillan asked his audience to 'go around the country, go to the industrial towns, go to the farms and you will see a state of prosperity such as we have never had in my lifetime – nor indeed in the history of this country'. But it wasn't all rosy, as Macmillan himself acknowledged. A great problem remained over 'stop-go' economics – government spending could deliver growth and jobs, but also delivered inflation, which would undermine real wages and even employment.[51]

And the reality on the ground for children at school was rather different from the aspirational language of Bedford – especially in places like West Yorkshire. In April 1955 half of the six million children in British schools were being educated in classes the Ministry of Education considered too large. The Tories were governing, in many senses, an increasingly prosperous Britain, but had done comparatively little to improve schools: of the 1,384,000 school places provided by new buildings between 1945 and 1955, only 325,700 (23.5 per cent) had come from projects started since Labour left office, as Alice pointed out.[52] From 1945 to 1955, 2,395 new schools had been built, but only 24 per cent (582) of projects had been started after the 1951 election. The administration had rather rested on its laurels – content, as Alice noted, simply to cut the ribbons on buildings Labour had earmarked the funding for.

There were wider trends here. As the economist John Kenneth Galbraith argued, post-1945 America was an *Affluent Society* where the private sphere had become more prosperous whilst the public sector was living through austere times. In his 1960 Fabian pamphlet *Labour and the Affluent Society* – referencing, of course, Galbraith's work – future Cabinet minister Richard Crossman argued that American patterns were being replicated in Macmillan-era Britain:

> the inherent inability of the system to allocate sufficient resources for national defence is repeated in relation to education, scientific development, health and welfare services. The price which the modern, managed capitalism pays for avoiding the old-fashioned crisis of mass unemployment is the continuous sacrifice of public service, community welfare and national security to private profit.[53]

It would be wrong to say that Macmillan's government did not improve public infrastructure – most famously housebuilding in the greater south-cast. Likewise, it was reasonable for the Tories to claim that things were better than in the 1930s. Yet since that era had been one of failed appeasement and a failure to stimulate meaningful growth, this bar was rather low. The collective spirit Labour had carried over from the war to their New Jerusalem and 1945 government had been replaced by a more individualistic popular culture with, at the least, public service improvements not keeping pace with people's expectations of private wealth creation.

Leeds Slums

Poor conditions went beyond schools, and Leeds had been home to areas which successive governments had failed to improve. In a 1937 pamphlet *Leeds Toryism Exposed* the Labour Councillor George Brett (who engineered the selection of Hugh Gaitskell in Leeds South in 1937) railed against the Conservative led council that had governed the city between 1930 and 1933:[54]

> What kind of Government was it that preceded the return to power of a Labour majority? It was, of course, Tory, and of the most reactionary kind

... Every step they took was reactionary, from 1930 to 1933 the aged, the sick and the destitute all suffered at their hands. The Housing Act of 1930, which gave Local Authorities the power to deal with slums, was a dead letter in Leeds because the Tories took little or no steps to implement that great and visionary Labour Act of Parliament.[55]

Though the virtues of a property-owning démocracy were central to the Conservative Party philosophy since the early 1920s, by 1938 only one house in four was owner-occupied. Two-thirds of people rented privately, and only one in ten was in any form of local authority housing.[56] A 1933 report produced by the Labour opposition on Leeds Council declared that 30,000 houses in the city were not fit for habitation, and yet little happened. Part of the problem was vested interests – pressure from landlords, including letters to the Conservative press attacking the Labour Party for infringing the rights of free-born Englishman, i.e. themselves, to charge the rent they wished, resulted in a reluctance to act. In 1937 the Tory led council gave the go-ahead for the building of 1,102 homes with one hand, whilst scrapping Labour's Moortown development of 2,400 houses and flats with the other.[57]

All this was by no means unknown to the National Government that took office in Westminster in 1931. Edward Hilton Young, a former Liberal, turned Tory, MP, attracted to the Conservatives by Stanley Baldwin's soothing political demeanour, visited the Leeds slums in 1933 as Minister of Health. Reporting the trip, *The Times* seemed to express as much sympathy for the visiting minister having to view such conditions as for the people living in them. Confronted with the 'distressing spectacles' of back-to-back housing (of which there were 70,000 examples in the city) and 'a district in Holbeck which is a network of narrow streets, congested houses and sunless courts and alleys', Hilton Young engaged some of the locals in conversation. *The Times* told of one man informing the minister that his staircase was so narrow that he had to climb up sideways with the joke that 'it's a good job I am a teetotaller', to which Hilton Young replied: 'I should think it is the only possible thing to be for you.' A cheery old man told the Minister that he 'had never spent a penny piece in a doctors in 18 years' whilst living in the West Street District – one of the city's black spots. Yet flashes of the extent of deprivation got through even the journalist Geoffrey Dawson's notoriously pro-Conservative editorship: throughout the summer months, several residents reported, houses could be so infested with vermin that the occupants had been unable to sleep indoors.[58]

Despite such visits – and the interventions of the Archbishop of Canterbury Cosmo Lang (who, when serving his curacy in Leeds in the 1890s, had lived in a room so small that it was difficult to stand upright) – much was still to do when Alice Bacon became an MP in 1945.[59] The war had halted even the modest pick-up in levels of construction seen in the mid-1930s, and bombing from the Luftwaffe meant there was much work to do even on existing stock. As John Hynd, elected as an MP in nearby Sheffield Attercliffe, put it to his constituents in 1945: 'Attercliffe needs houses – not promises – a nation that can organise its resources for the production of tanks, guns and planes can, if it has the will, equally organise the building of homes.'[60] Such a message played well in Yorkshire, where poor-quality housing in heavily industrialised areas that had contributed greatly to the war effort left many asking for more from their government. The Conservatives had not delivered for many in West Yorkshire and other industrial areas and Labour in 1945 were promising a brighter future. The 'collective memory of the working class' – as Charles Pannell, MP for Leeds West remarked in 1964 – was long indeed.[61]

One witness to the housing situation in Leeds in the interwar period was Gerald Kaufman. Kaufman fondly remembers much family banter and conversations occurring in the kitchen of his parents' refitted house – but this room formed such a hub, as it did in many homes around this time, because there was no room in the house to gather anywhere else. Kaufman:

> grew up nine people in a house. It wasn't a back to back. There was a back yard, though not a back garden. And that was life for a family that had in many ways improved themselves. Buying a house, certainly, would have been considered an acme of wealth.[62]

When Kaufman and his siblings left the family home, his parents downsized to a more comfortable council flat. Housing was in short supply and the quality of housing in the private rented sector was very often poor.

Whilst people were gradually freed from wartime controls, freedom from deprivation had only come to a select few. As Alice succinctly put it: 'I know the party opposite have a slogan, "Let the builders build." We in Leeds have been wishing for a considerable time that the builders would come forward to build.'[63] Despite several small building programmes in West Yorkshire between 1945 and 1947, Halifax, Wakefield, Pudsey and Morley had all seen more houses built per person than Leeds – mostly due to the additional delays produced by the bombing of the German Luftwaffe.[64] There was a chronic demand for housing – in 1951 31 per cent of the houses in Leeds shared a toilet, a situation scarcely improved by the end of the 1950s, and 32 per cent shared a bath. The key question was supply. The Conservatives claimed at the 1955 general election that 'nowhere has the restoration of freedom had more of an impact than in the field of building', and Harold Macmillan's tenure as Minister of Housing did indeed spark a growth in the total number of houses in the UK from a figure of 13.9 million in 1951 to 16.2 million by 1960.[65]

This was some achievement. Yet there were massive regional dispar-ities: an affluent, increasingly property-owning south, compared with, as Alice pointed out, a north that remained poor – particularly in urban areas. In the mid-1950s Don Anthony, an academic at the University of Manchester, wrote to Barbara Castle that his:

> work in the north has shown me squalor which I thought could never exist in this country. I must say that this talk of 'underdeveloped areas of S[outh] E[ast] Asia' makes me laugh – I could show some incredibly backward areas within a few yards of this university.[66]

From Alice's perspective as a constituency MP, in 1959 'housing' was 'still the greatest single problem' in Leeds with Alice receiving 'more letters' on that topic 'than on every other subject put together'.[67]

In the 14 years from 1945 to 1959 Leeds completed 18,000 new dwellings, but 23,298 families remained on housing waiting lists. As Alice commented:

> anyone who thinks we have no housing problems today should go to the big cities where the surface of the problem has only been scratched ... Leeds is [but] an example of a city with an acute housing problem, and I am sure it is only typical of Manchester, Liverpool, Glasgow, Birmingham and all the other big cities.

Conservative reluctance to go further on the urban housing problem was not because of a lack of knowledge of the problem. Leeds had two Conservative MPs returned at the 1955 election to Labour's four. Other

1. Alice as a young girl, *c*.1917.

2. Alice teaching, *c*.1932. Alice's experiences in interwar secondary moderns informed her views on education. She came to publicly advocate the comprehensive system far earlier than other leading Labour lights.

3. Alice celebrates her victory in Leeds, 1945.

4. To the future Councillor Bernard Atha, the 1945 election result was a 'new dawn akin to the second coming'. Here a still-shocked Alice, with her mother Charlotte (Lottie) Bacon, takes in the margin of her victory.

5. Alice's mission was always to get Labour into government. Here she is with Prime Minister Clement Attlee in the late 1940s.

6. In 1945 Alice was one of fifteen Labour women MPs elected to Parliament for the first time.

7. Alice with Herbert Morrison (centre), c 1949. Morrison, active on the Labour right, was always a firm friend.

8. Alice with Herbert Morrison and her mother, c.1950. Morrison once remarked that 'the farther you live North from London the better time and the better food you have.' Here he had Alice's mother, Lottie Bacon (centre), very much in mind.

9. Alice's family was always proud of her achievements. Here her mother (right) inspects her CBE, awarded in 1953.

10. Elections needed organising and publicity. Morgan Phillips and Alice discuss both here in 1959.

11. The 1960 Labour Party Conference was fraught for Hugh Gaitskell (pictured here wearing dark glasses). At least he had his closest political confidant, Alice, sat to his right.

12. Leeds United. Leeds MPs Denis Healey, Alice Bacon, Hugh Gaitskell and Charlie Pannell (pictured left to right) were always close – both in terms of their politics and their constituencies.

13. Alice with Hugh Gaitskell, *c.*1960. Alice would dearly have loved to have seen a Gaitskell premiership. But she supported his successor, Harold Wilson, despite their differences.

14. Alice with Hugh Gaitskell c.1960.

15. Alice was a model constituency MP, as emphasised in her 1964 election leaflet.

16. Alice enters Downing Street for the first time after the Labour victory in 1964. Six years of ministerial office, and significant achievements at the Home Office and Education, would follow.

17. Membership of the National Executive Committee provided three decades of influence for Alice. Here she is speaking at the 1965 Party Conference in Blackpool.

18. The 1967 Party Conference in Scarborough saw Alice declare it 'absolutely unthinkable' that children should have their educational paths divided at the age of 11. She is flanked by Barbara Castle and Harold Wilson.

19. Alice meeting Queen Elizabeth II in November 1966. The miner's daughter had come a long way.

20. Alice with Harold Wilson, at the 1970 Labour Party Confrence.

21. Alice works from one of the ministerial red boxes at her home in Normanton, June 1970.

22. Alice, pictured here towards the end of her Commons career. To Bernard Donoughue she had been 'a fine Labour politician, whose main life commitments were to the Labour movement, to Leeds and to securing a more equal place for women in British political life.'

23. The House of Lords was never quite Alice's scene after she was elevated in 1970. But she was happy to join Dora, Baroness Gaitskell, and Michael Milner, another former Labour minister from Leeds, in the upper chamber.

cities also had significant Tory representation. Liverpool had three Labour to six Conservative MPs, with Glasgow eight Labour to seven Conservative, Sheffield four Labour to two Conservative and Manchester four of each. Certainly Tories were concentrated in the more affluent areas, but they cannot have been unaware of the problems facing urban Britain at this time.

As the letters to Alice Bacon suggest, city life was hard. One mother of five, 'lucky in some respects … in that she has two bedrooms, but … unlucky in that because she has two bedrooms she is not regarded as living in overcrowded conditions, and [therefore] stands scarcely any chance of getting on the general housing waiting list', wrote to Alice in 1959:

> I am writing this short letter pleading for your help. This house we are living in is getting on my nerves. It has two bedrooms and a box room, two ground floor rooms, and a basement. The basement cannot be lived in as the walls are all damp. My water supply is down there, and I have to carry all my water up 20 steps. My husband has just come out of hospital, he is being visited by the nurse, and there is no hot water supply of any kind.

As Alice knew – this was not the bottom of the social ladder, but something approaching normal. Between 1951 and 1959, eight years of Conservative government had reduced a 29,000-long council house waiting list (5,000 of which were classed as 'adequately housed') to a 23,298 list (2,350 of which were adequately housed).[68] This lack of progress was a direct consequence of the government's decision to reduce levels of local authority housebuilding by making it much more difficult for councils to build through a reduction in subsidies and an increase in interest rates; 30,000 fewer council homes were built in 1958 compared to 1951, and if the private sector picked up the slack elsewhere, it certainly failed to do so in Leeds. 'The test', as Alice pointed out, 'is not only how many houses are built, but who gets them.'[69]

The Conservative argument, rather foreshadowing Thatcher, was that the private sector boom would trickle down. As Viscount Hinchingbrooke – associated with the Tory Reform Committee during World War II, but a rather Hayekian free market Conservative – put it: 'So long as the houses are built, does it very much matter? When they are built for sale, the chances are that the person who buys them comes from a rented house and automatically releases more houses to let.' Leaving aside the time lag the invisible hand would necessarily involve – and the difficulties this would present for slum dwellers in the interim – the problem was that private contractors were building (understandably enough given their profit motive) the type of large house almost completely divorced from the slum dwellers' existence. 'I know perfectly well', noted Alice, 'that the 22,500 houses in Leeds that need demolition do not contain many people who would want (or, at least, could afford) one of these luxury houses for sale.'[70] State intervention was needed to plug this gap.

The construction boom that did occur was based, in large part, on the back of private capital. The PWLB rate, which had subsidised the building of council housing, was increased during the 1950s to an extent which meant that going to the markets was the cheapest way for councils to fund development. But the banks naturally wanted reasonable security that the money they lent would be paid back – and once central subsidy for council house rents was scaled back by the Tories in Westminster, southern authorities had a natural advantage. They could charge higher rents to a more affluent population in a position to afford them. This income stream could then be used to attract private capital for new construction (at likely cheaper rates given the higher future income stream they could evidence), and they could add to – rather than merely replace or improve – existing stock. By essentially removing state-backed cheaper borrowing from the PWLB from councils' finance options, the Conservative government had rigged the game. Borrowing to invest became a preserve of those authorities with capital assets (valuable existing stock) or the likelihood of future income (high rents).

These conditions were not true in the north. In most areas, units were all for the purposes of slum clearance – so there were no new net homes. By forcing councils to make the difficult choice between trying to help existing tenants on the one hand (by keeping rents affordable) and funding the construction of new stock on the other, while also contending with a withdrawal of government subsidy for housebuilding, this meant the low rent-charging north had little prospect of growing its total housing stock to any meaningful degree. With the removal of rent controls, by 1964 only one non-greater South East authority – Coventry – was in the top ten of highest council rents. Likewise, of the ten lowest charging authorities, only one – Norwich – was in a broadly defined south of England. Freedom from government did not necessarily mean construction across the board, even if the national statistics suggested things were on the move.[71] Money, to a large degree, flowed to the south.

Many people who Alice represented were becoming desperate for decent quality housing. Such desperation was part of the problem – for, as Alice highlighted, when government stood back from regulating the housing market unscrupulous private landlords had much to gain. Though the 1949 Landlord and Tenant (Rent Control) Act introduced by Labour attempted to curb landlords charging excessive rents, the 1957 Rent Act introduced by the Conservatives took away many of those controls. For a city such as Leeds, where demand – if not the actual ability to pay – far outstripped supply, this just resulted in the exploitation of tenants who had to live in squalor while the rents went up but with no alternative but to stay put. Though justified on the grounds that landlords needed extra finance to make necessary upgrades, Alice Bacon was not impressed:

> When we were considering the Rent Act we were told that rents had been allowed to be increased so that repairs could be done. In my constituency I have seen no rush by landlords to do those very necessary repairs. The position today seems to be no better than it was before the passing of the Rent Act … We have seen the Rent Act and we have seen what has happened with regard to decontrol. I hope that it will not be very long before this Government have no more opportunity of making housing conditions worse for the people of our country and that we shall have a Government that will really treat housing as a social service, which indeed it is.[72]

That landlords were not helping their tenants was borne out by the statistics:

> Although [Leeds] city council has gone out of its way to encourage landlords to take advantage of improvement grants, since 1949, in a city which has thousands of houses without water, thousands without baths and thousands without toilets of their own, only 634 applications have been granted. Of those, 459 have been granted to owner occupiers and only 175 to the landlords of tenanted property. I think that shows that, although they are encouraged, landlords are not going to make the necessary improvements to property. In the meantime, property is becoming much worse.[73]

Alice's constituents faced impossible decisions – as their MP found out:

I had a case of a man—a case with which I am now dealing—who was so desperate for a house that he paid £400 and did not realise that it was on the demolition list. So bad is the house that, although he still owes £400, he has written to me to see whether he can get the house condemned, so that he can get into a council house, knowing that he will get no compensation for the demolished house and will still have to repay £400. That is one of the problems which confronts us.[74]

With so few options for tenants, landlords possessed an enormous amount of power. Another constituent wrote to Alice to inform her that his landlord had threatened him with eviction in seven days and, with a pregnant wife, he had no option but to buy the house at way above market price (£400 for a c.£150–250 property). The house, he told Alice:

is no longer fit to live in and he has gone into debt trying to repair it … The roof is parting from the brickwork. It is raining into the bedroom. The living room floor is sinking from its level … Although he paid £400 for the house only two years before he wrote to me, he implored me to try to get the medical officer to condemn the house as unfit to live in.

Helping the man, albeit with little pleasure, to get the house condemned and be inadequately compensated, Alice saw that the house was closed and the family moved into a council house.[75]

Such legislation unleashed the ugly side of market capitalism. Without strict government regulation over the rental market, not only landlords but solicitors were getting in on the act. In 1956 Alice received a series of letters from a Mr Carney who had recently purchased a house in Ney Street for £180. Carney, 'an ordinary workman who came from the other side of the city … did not know that the area in which the house he was buying was scheduled for demolition in the very near future'. Buying the house through an estate agent, the agent informed him that he would need a solicitor, which they offered to provide. Only after the transaction was complete did the purchaser realise what had happened – the solicitor showed little remorse for not informing the buyer that his property was set to be condemned: 'You decided to buy the house before I came in. I was employed merely to do the conveyancing.'[76] Measures such as these were tolerated by a Conservative government who had relaxed the regulations which allowed much of this abuse to go on unchecked.

Alice took such local knowledge to the 1957 Party Conference when declaring that 'the Tories have produced a charter for the landlords. We hereby pledge that the Labour Party will produce a charter for the tenants.'[77] In her role on the publicity committee of the NEC Alice oversaw the production of 1.3 million leaflets outlining the problems of the Tory Rent Act. Alice took on the landlords in Leeds but it was the Conservatives who were her real enemy. It was a Conservative government which had fostered the conditions under which all this was possible, and it was a Labour government, she believed, which could deliver for the greater public good.

Mental Health, Clean Air, and Other Work of an Inner-City MP

Education reform and conditions in the slums took up much of Alice's work locally, but her interests were more diverse. One other passion was the fate of both workers and patients at what was then the Menston Mental Hospital, later High Royds Hospital. Mental health mattered to Alice – and she made some of her rare speeches in the Lords on the subject in the 1970s and 1980s. Other Labour politicians had previously highlighted the real problems that existed. For instance, the interwar leader George Lansbury had written in 1934:

> No-one who has not visited private and public mental institutions can imagine what terribly depressing places these can be. Whenever I have remonstrated and said that these grim and deterrent surroundings must hold back the patients' recovery I have been told by those who claimed to know and understand mental cases that people who are out of their minds do not see and appreciate their surroundings ... I do not accept those statements as true. I believe there is a huge sum of individual and collective misery in these places which few of us who remain sane can ever understand.[78]

As with housing, part of the issue at the hospital was overcrowding. At Menston 112 patients slept in only one ward. Broader issues of dignity existed too. After visiting Menston in 1952, Alice asked the Minister of Health Iain Macleod whether he realised that there were 'over 500 patients in the hospital over 65 years of age, many of them bedridden and not requiring any mental attention at all?'[79] Macleod answered, not without some irony, given the housing situation described above, that the solution was a 'large and expanding housing programme' to house such overflow. Alice kept up the pressure through the 1950s – arguing that the government's capital allocation to Leeds was 'totally inadequate for the needs of the area, particularly in regard to mental hospitals', and that a shortage of labour for such institutions could be reduced by recruiting more workers and paying their travel expenses.[80] It was the issue of mental health that would bring her closer to Menston's chairman Bernard Atha. As Atha notes, 'Alice viewed [mental health] as part of the health service as much as bumps and scrapes. Not everyone thought so.'[81] Even today mental health is too often the Cinderella service in the NHS and patients pay the price.

Other city issues that occupied the time of an MP who put her constituents first included pollution of different sorts. Alice supported the 1956 Clean Air Act which included measures to reduce dark smoke from chimneys, make new furnaces as smokeless as possible, and the imposition of smoke control areas. These were all important steps for an industrial city like Leeds (though a young Jack Straw still remembers a soot-covered town hall in the early 1960s in Leeds when he was a student at the university). Yet the Clean Air Act made some difference – Leeds in the 1950s was a city of dark (satanic) mills, factories and heavy industry. Tighter regulation made life a bit more pleasant for those living and working in the city.[82]

The other great irritant from the city's industry was noise. Though some may have uncharitably described Alice's voice in such terms, she informed the Commons in 1960 that 'there cannot be anything worse than having a pneumatic drill under one's window early in the morning. I always cringe, even during the daytime, when I go along a road when a pneumatic drill is operating.' The Leeds Corporation Bill of 1956, which Alice had played a part (along with her parliamentary neighbours such as Hugh Gaitskell) in securing, 'include[d] not only provisions on noise, but on vibration'. In Parliament, Alice remarked that 'everyone … who lives in industrialised parts of very big cities [knows] that vibration can be as bad, as big a nuisance and as prejudicial to health as noise itself'. Alice was successful in persuading Rupert Speir, the bill's Conservative mover, to introduce an amendment on this issue during the committee stage. A small measure perhaps – but one that brought a degree of comfort to inner-city lives blighted by 'dustbin lids which clatter in the morning' and, according to Alice 'youths who regard it as splendid to make their [motorcycle] engines roar … at 2 or 3 o'clock in the morning after a party which goes on into the small hours'.[83]

Spin Doctor

Alice discussed all these issues affecting Leeds with her friend, neighbouring MP and leader Hugh Gaitskell. With his death in 1963 Alice would lose her closest friend in politics and in some ways her mission – to see him as Prime Minister. But Gaitskell or no Gaitskell, by the early 1960s Alice had made herself an important cog in the Labour machine. Following Labour's defeat in 1955, Alice had been made chairman of the Publicity and Political Education Sub-Committee of the NEC. Part of its purpose was to address the need for an improvement in doorstep politics. Each Constituency Labour Party was therefore instructed to appoint a Political Education Officer who would be issued with instructions from the newly created central Political Education Office. Whilst Alice was 'at pains to emphasise that local activity is the basis of the scheme', officers would attend regional instructional conferences every few months, and a residential summer school annually. This, she believed, would contribute to the 'two way formation' of Labour politics.[84]

The Times was broadly sympathetic to the scheme. 'Its object is to improve the knowledge and dialectic of active party members, for both have surely declined since the days before 1945 when Labour was steadily building up its majority.' The 'inner party' activities such as these, much like Alice's anti-communist purges of local parties help explain why, despite being an MP for a quarter of a century, she has not resonated as a national figure. It was her back-room activities that in many ways mattered the most.

To Ralph Miliband, in 1964 Harold Wilson 'appeared to provide an answer to Labour's search for the kind of positive "message" which it had failed to find ever since the collapse of the Attlee Government in 1951'.[85] The word 'appeared' certainly indicates Miliband's scepticism regarding the 'renewal, modernisation and reform in every area of British life' which Wilson promised, but it also attests to the successful reinvention of the Labour brand.[86] Alice Bacon – in the words of a friend 'plain, dumpy, pudding faced, but not ugly' – does not immediately strike one as a latter-day slick media spin doctor. Yet she played a key part in being just this.

Throughout the 1950s, and even to some degree the 1960s, political parties were feeling their way with regard to the relatively new technology: television. Barbara Castle recalled Edith Summerskill having a particular, albeit presumably quite unique, gripe: 'I remember her being madly against television. I remember she would produce some extraordinary remarks when she said that you could get radiation sickness through sitting in front of the television too long.'[87] In terms of entertainment, she possibly was not missing much in political coverage. Until the general election in 1959 the BBC merely provided a dry list of the day's events as its election coverage. No analysis, no punditry, and no opinions of almost any sort. Once ITV took to the air in September 1955, and ratings became the order of the day (at the behest of, in Tony Benn's view, the 'vulgar, thrusting profit-rich tycoons'), coverage became a little more recognisable to a twenty-first-century audience.[88] Alice was to help Labour adapt to these new ways of doing things. In the run-up to the 1959 election, she briefed the NEC, for example, on progress on subjects such as 'party political broadcasting', 'broadcasting and T.V. staff' and 'newspaper advertising'.[89]

Hostility to change, and what it meant for how politics was conducted, ran deep. At a dinner during the 1959 Labour Party Conference where Nye Bevan, Jennie Lee, Bernard and Shirley Williams and Tony Benn (who had co-ordinated Labour's broadcasts at the 1959 election) were in attendance, Benn recalled Bevan turning on him. 'Nye turned on me most viciously at the beginning', recorded Benn (at the time a rather centrist figure), 'attacking the campaign, TV, and the idea of surveys of public opinion.'[90] Bevan, even to his critics, was a natural orator. For many, one suspects, the rise of television was a concern in that, if they were not deemed photogenic enough, their careers would founder for reasons of style rather than substance. Alice Bacon – 'braying' voice and all – was relegated to local addresses in Keighley in the run-up to the 1964 general election, whilst the more telegenic Shirley Williams gave the TV address on 'Family Problems and Social Plans', despite the fact that the vastly – at this stage – more senior Bacon was about to become a government minister.[91] By 1964 Wilson's pipe and easy manner had firmly replaced Clement Attlee's dull reliability when it came to electioneering.

As Bevan's comment reflected, Labour was reticent in its embrace of the new era of campaigning. In July 1960 Alice told the House of Commons that:

the Conservative Party [has placed] itself in the hands of an advertising agency, which produces the so-called image of the Tory Party by advertising methods. I believe that in doing this it introduces something into our political life which is alien to our British democracy. Do we want British politics to be like a battle between two Madison Avenue agencies?[92]

As incongruous as Alice mixing with *Mad Men* might be, by 1963 Labour had, to borrow a *Times* article headline, 'lost some of its sense of sin' when it came to advertising and promotion. In her role of spin doctor, Alice dispatched a new member of Transport House to Birmingham where an account was opened – for the first time – with a firm of PR consultants (T. Dan Smith Associates of Newcastle – the name here is important, as Smith would reappear in Alice's life during the Poulson Affair of 1970). A rumoured newspaper advertising budget of between £100,000 and £200,000 suggested a 'headlong' plunge into media management, and one in which Alice was fully signed up – even, as NEC minutes reveal, pressing the party to fund adverts for Labour alongside splashes for the other parties that she had been tipped off the press were going to run.[93] As *The Times* noted, 'there is still some coyness about the ... allocation of funds for [this account], probably in part for reasons of inter-party security but also in part because a rank and file steeped in the approved doctrine about capitalist waste on advertising might be outraged'.[94] By 1963, as the pollster Mark Abrams, the Managing Director of Research Services Ltd., pointed out, 'Miss Bacon was able to open six of the national daily newspapers and contemplate in each of them large display advertisements placed by the Labour Party'.[95]

Alice's conversion was not full-hearted, though.[96] It took Tony Benn to put Labour's public relations and advertising work on a more permanent basis. Attending a Joint NEC/Shadow Cabinet Broadcasting Committee meeting in March 1963, Benn presented his plans for the election broadcasts but 'then Alice Bacon simply proposed that our Advisory Committee should be wound up'. Benn explained the need for the broadcasting committee which he was to head – 'how necessary it was if our broadcasts were going to be serious and good in the next Election'. Wilson quietly sided with him. Alice does not appear to have protested against the issue – prepared to accept what was perhaps inevitable in the white heat of the technology era.

As well as the adverts there was a wider 'professionalisation' of Labour's election strategy in the early 1960s. Abrams was engaged by the party to carry out internal party polling as well as brief MPs and candidates on communicating with voters. In December 1963, at a talk to candidates, Abrams informed his audience that in a 60,000-person constituency, there would be 20,000 uncommitted voters, 8,000 parents, 4,000 old-age pensioners, 3,000 families 'desperate for a decent dwelling', 4,000 new voters, and the list went on. 'You will', Abrams urged, 'be very exceptional if you can afford to neglect any of these groups.' Part of this was about tone:

> when talking to parents of school children, the case for changing our educational system is best put in personal terms. ('Is your child trying to learn in an overcrowded class room?' 'Is the 11-plus going to condemn your child to a lifetime of drudgery and frustration?')[97]

Both of these points may well have emerged from Alice's input.

Alice took a lead on such occasions. In April 1963 she spoke to a gathering of several hundred activists at Transport House 'on the newspaper advertising campaign, which is an important part of the programme, [giving] the party advice ... not only on which national and local papers to use but which pages of those papers'.[98]

In terms of the content on those pages, there was a distinctly female edge to some of the advertising. One advert, with the election slogan 'Let's GO with LABOUR', showed a woman looking at her shopping basket in shock. 'Why', she asked, 'doesn't my money buy as much as it used to?' As for whom to vote for, 'it's no good the Conservatives wooing me now. I've not forgotten that under a Conservative government prices have risen fantastically – and go on rising ... And in the struggle to make ends meet who suffers most? We women do, of course.'[99]

The role of unofficial spin doctor also helped Alice build a relationship beyond the mostly formal, sometimes strained, dealings that had existed with Harold Wilson. Speaking in 1986, it seems that even if she distrusted Wilson and had not backed him for leader, she managed to form a productive working relationship:

> Harold and I were both Yorkshire people. There were difficulties at the time Hugh Gaitskell died. But I was Chairman of the Labour Party's Press and Publicity Committee and it meant at times I had to work sometimes closely with the publicity at Downing Street. I could see there were going to be difficulties about this and I asked to see Harold. I said, 'Oh Harold, I didn't vote for you'. His eyes twinkled and he said, 'I somehow didn't think you had'. So I said, 'but nevertheless, as far as I'm concerned, you are the leader of the Labour Party and while you are leader, you will never hear me utter one word of criticism. But now we've got to get this publicity thing straight'. We came to an agreement, and I must say that all the time that he was leader and Prime Minister, he never did anything

that in any way affected Labour Party publicity without talking to me. We got on like that. He would always say, and still would today, 'we understand each other, don't we?'[100]

Ultimately, Alice was Labour before she was of any faction. So, while she was on the right and was loyal to the leaders on the right – particularly Morrison and Gaitskell, she was absolutely loyal to the leadership, whoever the leader was. In 1964 as Labour returned to office, after 13 years in opposition, Alice, as a junior minister, and Harold Wilson, as Prime Minister, would get the chance to work together in government.

CR 4 CD

HOME AFFAIRS (1959–67)

By the early 1960s, the Conservative government – rather like the 1945–51 Labour administration before it – had run out of steam. Harold Macmillan, veteran of the Great War and married to the daughter of the 9th Duke of Devonshire, was not exactly symbolic of the bold new era of equality the 1960s looked set to usher in. It did not help that, across the Atlantic, John F. Kennedy's tragically truncated presidency seemed to combine youthful vigour with a genuinely progressive platform. When Macmillan had to retire on grounds of ill-health in 1963 the Conservative Party elected an even more aristocratic leader, Alec Douglas-Home – known, until he renounced his peerage to take office, as the Earl of Home. Still rocked by the Profumo affair – when John Profumo was forced to resign as Secretary of State for War after an affair (or rather because he subsequently lied in the Commons about the matter) with the reputed mistress of an alleged Soviet spy – the Conservative Party, under new leadership, went into the 1964 election facing an uphill struggle. In the end Labour only just scraped home with a majority of four, but would increase this to a 96-seat majority in March 1966.

Because the margins were thinner than the landslide of 1945, bills were more 'talked' at length in the chamber rather than easily 'walked' through the division lobbies, to paraphrase Alice's fond remembrance of the ease in which legislation had been passed under Attlee. But the period after 1964 was a good time to be Labour. Landmark reforms, particularly social reforms, driven through by a Labour government, were delivering genuine change in the country, as well as reflecting changing public opinion. Getting the train down from Leeds to London with Denis Healey, Merlyn Rees and Charlie

114

Pannell was a pleasure for Alice (though one wonders how often they ever shared a carriage with Keith Joseph, MP for Leeds North, who was already moving in the free market direction that saw him become Thatcher's philosophical guru). Walter Harrison (future Labour Party chief whip) was also elected for the first time in Wakefield, in 1964, meaning that Yorkshire – with Wilson from Huddersfield in Number 10 and Barbara Castle from Bradford in the Cabinet – was at the forefront of the new Britain.

As the historian Dominic Sandbrook has stated, for many 1964 was a new political dawn akin to Labour's victory in 1997. A meritocratic grammar school boy made good in Harold Wilson was soon mirrored by the Conservatives in their choice of leader in 1965 – Ted Heath. The two – fierce personal and political rivals – both went from interwar grammar schools to Oxford in the 1930s where, it is thought, Wilson heard Heath play the organ at Balliol on a few occasions. But despite outward similarities the two were rather different. Heath was from Kent whilst, according to Denis Healey, 'Yorkshire meant a lot to Harold as it has to me'. Wilson, to Shirley Williams, 'was deeply and naturally a man of the people. He wasn't trying to persuade the media that he was an ordinary man, he *was* an ordinary man.' Heath was always more austere and personally distant. Former colleagues attest to a dry sense of humour, but this did not always resonate with the public. Antipathy in the Commons was no mere political posing. Heath saw Wilson as 'gimmicky', whilst from the Labour benches, Roy Hattersley saw Heath as 'bland and pompous'. For a decade Wilson and Heath met each other across the dispatch box.[1]

The 1964 election, whilst not quite the revolution of 1945, did indeed seem to offer a brave new world. A post-election memorandum in the papers of Harold Wilson at Oxford outlined the general picture:

1. The public had at last become conscious of the deep-seated deficiencies in 'affluent Britain'.
2. They had been persuaded that these deficiencies were either caused by the Tories, neglected by them, or that the Tories were too tired and ineffective to cope with them.
3. They wanted a change and, especially the younger ones, saw in Labour leadership and policy a real chance of correcting the weaknesses they knew to exist.[2]

Whilst Macmillan-era Tories crowed about their unprecedented successes, in reality British growth had lagged behind that of her competitors throughout the 1950s. The British average rate of annual growth had been 2.7 per cent – stable enough, but lagging behind the US (3.3 per cent), France (4.3 per cent), Italy (5.9 per cent) and West Germany (7.6 per cent).[3] Indeed, you can see why many in Britain were increasingly keen on joining the European Economic Community, where the continental economies were growing faster than the domestic. The Labour manifesto of 1964, entitled 'Let's GO with Labour for a New Britain', showed a bullish confidence that the party could turn the tide:

> A New Britain – mobilising the resources of technology under a national plan; harnessing our national wealth in brains, our genius for scientific invention and medical discovery ... a new opportunity to equal, and if possible surpass, the roaring progress of other western powers.

Speaking to the concerns of MPs like Alice, it claimed that the Tory government had 'led to growing stagnation, unemployment, and under-employment in parts of the North, Scotland, Wales and Northern Ireland'. To help address these concerns Labour proposed a new DEA to plan Britain's economy over the medium to long term, the introduction of a new capital gains tax, and a crackdown on tax evasion. The responsibility for such measures would largely be the preserve of Benn, Callaghan and George Brown, but Alice was excited to take her part in an administration that promised so much.[4] After 19 years as an MP this was Alice's chance to help govern, and change, Britain.

The 1960s were a turbulent but also transformational time. In his assessment of the 1964–70 governments, Wilson's biographer Thomas Hennessey notes that 'after what, admittedly can be seen as serious policy errors Wilson set Britain on the road to recovery [including] restoring Britain's balance of payments position by 1970'.[5] The first major decision was to reject an early devaluation of the pound and, in practice, to commit vast sums of money to defending the rate of $2.80. In November 1964 the Wilson government hiked the Bank of England interest rate to 7 per cent (from 5 per cent), equalling the post-war high and far in excess of the 2 per cent rate Labour had left behind in 1951. The government was also forced to appeal directly to President Johnson to deliver $250 million of sterling purchases from the Federal Reserve and $250 million more from the US government itself, in addition to a further $100 million from Canada. The need to appease what Wilson called 'the Gnomes of Zurich' – international financiers – somewhat 'blunted the government's domestic policy', according to Hennessey. Alice was not in the Treasury but she could only act within the parameters it set out.

To walk this line between fiscal restraint and delivering important changes, the triumvirate of Wilson as Prime Minister, Callaghan at the Treasury, and George Brown at the new DEA agreed that 'it should be assumed for industrial planning and public presentation that gross domestic product (GDP) would increase by 25 per cent between 1964 and 1970 [whilst] the growth in public expenditure would be fixed at 4 per cent a year'.[6] Defence was to be the largest casualty of the austerity – with spending to be frozen at the 1964 level for the entire Parliament. The need to defend sterling and the difficulties in doing so produced a see-saw in policy making. In July 1965 Callaghan laid out plans to the Cabinet pledging an additional £240m of spending for 1969–70. But days later, as money had to be diverted to defend sterling, Wilson and Callaghan were soon forced to lay out cuts of £45m. Planning investment in the public services, which Alice knew needed improving, was not easy in this climate. With the election victory of 1966 safely secured, measures amounting to £500m of combined cuts and tax rises were laid out to try and avoid devalu- ation. But on 18 November 1967 that devaluation came, with a drop in the value of the pound of 40 cents, to $2.40 – a policy which Wilson famously remarked would not affect 'the pound in your pocket'.

These various volte-face led to problems with the unions, and almost had consequences for Alice's position on the Labour NEC. Though a prices and incomes concordat was brokered between representatives of the trade unions and leading industrialists, by 1967 the dockers had gone on strike for increased pay. The problem for Wilson and the Labour government was not that just that strikes were occurring, but that they were sometimes 'wildcat strikes'. These were unofficial instances of industrial action where negotiating with union leaders was no guarantee of a successful resolution. When then Employment Secretary Barbara Castle brought forward her White Paper 'In Place of Strife' – mandating the ballot of union members before a strike – the resistance from union leaders was immense, and saw Wilson accused of being a second Ramsay MacDonald, who would let down the workers as in 1931. Wilson was sympathetic to Castle's position – he knew it was necessary to deliver the sort of growth and investment he had promised – but was eventually persuaded by Callaghan and other colleagues to back down.

In this context the Wilson government's economic successes were remarkable. Devaluation apart, its record included keeping unemployment below 2.7 per cent, inflation (for most of the 1960s) below 4 per cent, and increased public spending on housing, social security, transport, research, education and health by an average of more than 6 per cent per annum for its duration. The real value of pensioners' benefits increased by some 20 per cent in the five years of Labour government between 1964 and 1969. Tapping into the Harold Macmillan playbook, Labour also ensured that in many ways people had it even better than before. For example, car ownership increased by some 3 million, so for the first time a majority of British households owned a car. At the same time – as Brian Lapping notes in his study of the Wilson governments – the percentage of house-holds with a television rose from 88 per cent to 90 per cent, those with a refrigerator from 39 per cent to 59 per cent and those with washing machines from 54 per cent to 64 per cent. When Labour left office in 1970, 1 in 4 people had central heating and 1 in 3 had telephones.[7]

Though the welfare state remained a contentious battleground, the notion of state intervention in the economy was, as the Minister of State for Economic Affairs from 1965 to 1967, Austen Albu, notes, a matter of relative consensus:

> Conservatives, under pressure in their last years in office, had introduced so many new ideas and created so many new institutions that I thought that the technical revolution had been almost achieved and that it only needed a final dash of government economic planning and industrial intervention to produce a *British Wirtschaftswunder*.[8]

There would not quite be the desired 'economic miracle' under Labour but the expansion of consumer goods to more homes and to more middle- and indeed working-class families was a big step forward, particularly given the 1945 government's (relative) failure in this area.[9] Indeed, Alice had pressed on these issues in the latter half of the 1945 Parliament as we have seen.

More broadly, according to the economic historian Nicholas Woodward:

> when judged against the standards of the 1970s and 1980s ... perfor-mance was fairly satisfactory ... When Labour left office it could argue that over the preceding six years there had been a reduction in economic inequality, a narrowing of regional disparities, a marked improvement in the balance of payments position and a slight improvement in Britain's productivity performance ... [and yet] a critic could point to the fact that

both unemployment and inflation were higher in 1970 than in 1964 ... and that it had only proved possible to rectify the balance of payments position by adopting a more deflationary stance than any previous post-war government.[10]

Debate on the successes and failures of Britain's economy in the 1960s continues to this day.

Amidst this changing economy it was for Alice Bacon to plough on in the social field – initially at Home Affairs and later at Education. In these areas this period marked, as the academic Peter Thompson notes, a victory for the party's revisionist wing, principally Roy Jenkins and Anthony Crosland. Here 'the politics of nationalisation and poverty (Labour's traditional agenda) could be replaced by other, and in the long run more important spheres – of personal freedom, happiness and cultural endeavour'.[11] With people freer from the grinding poverty seen in the interwar and immediate post-war period, it was up to a decent, reforming administration to deliver changes beyond the economic, and Alice Bacon was about to be a significant part of that.

According to Clive Ponting's study of the time, 'when it came into office the [1964] Labour government had no plans to transform the law in the moral and personal sphere but it did help pass backbench legislation which did so'.[12] To Ponting, what changed this nominal sympathy for reform to stronger tacit support were four major factors. The first was the personality of Roy Jenkins – 'without his help and advocacy the bills would have foundered amidst the doubts of his colleagues and the morass of parliamentary procedure'. The second was the election of 1966 bringing in a raft of new MPs determined to make an impact and feeling the social sphere was the most obvious area in which to do so. The third reflected 'the results of often long, drawn-out campaigns from pressure groups', and the fourth was due to 'public opinion which was going through one of its rare phases of support for reform'.[13]

On these we may stress that Jenkins was not the only minister minded towards reform – for, as we will see, his junior minister Alice Bacon had even previously attempted to bring forward a bill one of the subjects of reform. Equally, when it came to managing the new 1966 parliamentary intake, meeting with the various pressure groups, and monitoring public opinion, this was very much a task for a junior minister with her ear to the ground – again a job for Alice Bacon. What follows details the twists and turns in a key part of Labour history and that of wider British society.

Minister of State

Upon her appointment as Shadow Minister of State at the Home Office,
deputy to Shadow Home Secretary, Patrick Gordon Walker in 1959,
Charlie Pannell wrote a warm tribute to his friend Alice:

> Another Member who will be glad to put her feet up is Alice Bacon
> because after the election she was given the No 2 job to represent us on
> the Front Bench on Home Office affairs. As a holiday from her previous
> pre-occupation with education, she now has to look after prisons, proba-
> tioners, juvenile delinquents, and a whole host of other anti-social people.
> Alice believes, as becomes an ex-teacher, that you can't get your sums
> right, say your piece at the dispatch box, unless you do your homework.
> This she has done. She has visited all sorts of places where those of
> ill-repute are sent for correction, and she is already a walking encyclo-
> paedia on the subject.[14]

Few, Alice included, probably expected the 'holiday' from education
policy to go on for so long – eight years – but albeit unwittingly she had
stumbled into one of the most revolutionary eras of a great department
of state in twentieth-century British history. The achievements of the
period, the creation of a more 'civilised' society, came quickly – but the
process of managing this transformation was never an easy one. Wilson's
1964 pledge to offer a free vote on the death penalty was indicative of the
gift and the curse facing reformers – on the one hand, the government was
giving the green light to change, whilst still legitimising those, even on
the Labour benches, who were against it. Though this bill was eventually
passed fairly comfortably, its passage through Parliament was not without
its dramas – with Tony Benn compelled to call off a trip to Germany after
MP Sydney Silverman (sponsor of the bill) had warned him it was in
danger of foundering once more.[15] The margins on such issues were tight,
feelings were certainly strong, and in such an environment Alice had
much work to do.

Harold Wilson's first Home Secretary – and Alice's first boss in her role
as Minister of State – was Frank Soskice. Soskice had been one of the few
leading Labour lights in the 1940s willing to commit unreservedly to the
abolition of the death penalty, but he would require an able deputy.

Alice's appointment to the Home Office made her the first-ever woman
minister at the department, and local constituency party members in

Leeds, including Frank Pullan, remember Alice's pride in being appointed as a government minister. And it seems she was keen to protect her status. On 21 October 1964 – a week after the election victory – the Permanent Under Secretary to the Home Office, Sir Charles Cunningham, recorded that:

> Miss Bacon has ... spoken to me and said that she is very concerned that her special position as Minister of State should be recognised. While she is quite happy about the division of subjects which has been agreed, she is anxious that she should be in a position to act as the Home Secretary's deputy on any aspect of Home Office work and not be confined to exclusive consideration of the subjects allocated to her ... It would be helpful, I think, if it could be made clear in an Office Notice that Miss Bacon will help the Home Secretary generally over the whole field of Home Office subjects.[16]

The next day this bulletin was issued – Alice had won her first battle.[17]

In her role at the Home Office, Alice would oversee 'criminal, prison, probation and after care and charity departments', but informally her remit was much bigger. By the time Cunningham issued a new bulletin after the 1966 election, Alice was affixed to oversee 'general department' questions, as well as her specific brief.[18]

Soskice's successor at the Home Office, Roy Jenkins, later dismissed Soskice as a 'remarkably bad Home Secretary' and a man of chronic indecision.[19] This, to Andrew Holden, was 'both pompous and unfair'.[20] Whilst maintaining official neutrality he encouraged reformers to act on the Wolfenden Report of 1957 which had recommended the decriminalisation of homosexuality, for example. But, perhaps crucially for Alice, like Jenkins, Soskice was a Gaitskellite. Although all from the 'same side', upon succeeding to the office of Home Secretary in December 1965, Jenkins remarked how used Alice had got to Soskice's ways.[21] That Jenkins inherited a 'prickly' trio of junior ministers – Alice, Lord Stonham, and the future Commons Speaker George Thomas – did not necessarily impinge on policy making.[22] Nor it seems did Alice's suspicions regarding Jenkins' politics: 'she felt he liked duchesses too much', recalls Tam Dalyell. Alice had also apparently relished telling Nye Bevan (hardly a natural confidant) in the 1950s that someone had called Jenkins 'lazy', and was met by the comment from Nye that anyone who worked that hard on their accent could not be described in such terms.[23]

Alice's views about the moral and social issues that the Home Office had to grapple with in the 1960s are difficult to get a hold on at times. Councillor Bernard Atha's comment that she 'kept quiet' on abortion and homosexual reform whilst maintaining a broadly 'pro-liberal' stance seems accurate, but there were nuances here.[24] She trod an ambiguous path, but in doing so made reform ever more certain. Until the reshuffle of 1967 Harold Wilson never moved (or removed) her. The *Evening Standard* journalist, Robert Carvel, claimed no small credit here: 'many times I've saved Alice Bacon's job', he would say later.[25] Carvel would allegedly receive tip-offs that Alice was to be sacked, she would then read his report and weep on the phone to Wilson, who would duly relent. This remains unsubstantiated.

Crime and (Capital) Punishment

Alice had shown some interest in Home Office issues prior to her appointment, by Gaitskell, as shadow Home Office minister in 1959. In 1957, Alice attempted to introduce, through a Private Member's Bill, legislation to abolish hanging for murder. This was met by concerted Conservative filibustering – one MP, John Page, spoke for 67 minutes on minor provisions of the Advertisements (Hire Purchase) Bill to delay proceedings so Alice's bill on hanging would not be read. As Labour MPs cried 'agreed, agreed' to the majority of Tory amendments on the topic, Sydney Silverman (Labour MP for Nelson and Colne, in Lancashire) – a long-term proponent of the abolition of the death penalty – spoke for all those against the death penalty when he deplored the tactics of supporters who kept the debate going so that 'for four hours the Bill has been debated … (yet) there has not been a new argument advanced in the last two and a half hours. It is quite plain what the members opposite are doing.'[26] As the clock ran down on a debate that began at 11.06 a.m., Alice intervened shortly before the 4 p.m. adjournment to note that:

> no new argument has been put since 12 o'clock, and while I appreciate, as I am sure we all do, Mr. Speaker, your remarks about preserving the rights of private Members, I submit that what has been happening today has been a deliberate attempt to stop a private Member from introducing a Bill.[27]

Such tactics meant Alice's bill on capital punishment would have to wait for Silverman to return to it when Alice was a minister – but they do at least illustrate Alice's commitment to delivering on the issue when the opportunity arose.

That the Wilson governments should manage to chalk the death penalty off the statute book was a greater achievement than merely seeing off the filibusterers. As the historian Victor Bailey has shown, there were significant problems that needed to be overcome, and which had held back any legislation during the Attlee government. First, as with most issues of a moral nature, the Labour Party had been split over the issue. In the 1947–8 parliamentary session the Labour government attempted to introduce a new Criminal Justice Bill largely to deal with the question of *corporal* punishment. The question of *capital* punishment remained an issue Attlee's administration did not want to confront head-on due to internal splits within the PLP, and thus no clause dealing with the question was initially included. However, at the Report stage of the bill on 14 April 1948, the abolitionist MP Sydney Silverman proposed that a clause introducing a five-year temporary suspension of the death penalty be added to the bill.

When the Commons divided on the issue the vote came down in favour of Silverman's amendment, by 245 MPs to 222. Given there were then 640 MPs in the Commons, this implied a significant number of abstentions. Indeed, whilst 215 of the then 389 Labour Members voted in Parliament to abolish the death penalty in 1948, that left a significant percentage of the PLP either ambivalent to, or against, change.[28] Though the Cabinet decided that collective responsibility would be suspended to allow ministers to abstain rather than vote for the government position of keeping the death penalty, Bailey contends that most of the Cabinet were against repeal anyway.[29] The government was compelled to take Silverman's clause into the House of Lords where it was promptly rejected, to many in the Labour leadership's relief. After some internal wrangling, the issue was put into the long grass of a Royal Commission on the subject.

The key figures in the government – Attlee, Bevin, Morrison, and the Home Secretary James Chuter Ede – certainly all voted against repealing the death penalty. Important exceptions, it should be noted, were the future Prime Minister Harold Wilson (who abstained in the Commons vote), Alice's long-time friend Hugh Gaitskell (another abstention), and the first Home Secretary she directly served under, Frank Soskice, who argued that 'the case in favour of abolition of capital punishment seems ... overwhelming'.[30] Alice voted with Silverman's abolitioners (as well as the young Barbara Castle and Richard Crossman) and therefore against her friend Herbert Morrison – then Deputy Prime Minister – on this issue.[31] The death penalty was less an issue that divided left and right, and more one that split the different parliamentary generations.

But Labour was not just divided ideologically or in terms of age; there was also the pragmatic matter of public opinion. Whilst support for abolition was at an all-time high in 1939, this was not necessarily true in 1945. The executive committee of the National Council for the Abolition of the Death Penalty advised its members that the end of the war and the election of Labour 'should bring success to our efforts'. But the public mood was rather hard to gauge.[32] Whilst Bailey argues there is comparatively little evidence that abolition of the death penalty was a potential vote loser and had to be dropped, it is true to say that Herbert Morrison – who, though not Home Secretary, was leading on the matter – was determined not to get too far ahead of the voters. Polling indicated that by 1948 most people disapproved of even an experimental abolition (as eventually introduced in 1965). Mass Observation surveys in 1948 put the numbers against experimental abolition at 69 per cent to 13 per cent in favour. During the same year Gallup (66 per cent against abolition, 26 per cent for) and *Daily Express* polls (77 per cent against abolition compared to 14 per cent for) told a similar story. To have abolished the death penalty in the late 1940s would have required either a steadfast determination to go against public opinion, or a shift in it.

The other problem with reform was a lack of a clear mandate. There was a strong feeling that a Labour government trying to amend the law would need to do so with a fresh, unambiguous mandate. If the Conservative-dominated Lords (which was rabidly against abolition) scented any serious division in Labour, they would vote down any bill and challenge Labour to use the Parliament Act to force it through. This was particularly effective with bills of a moral nature – usually held under conditions of a free vote in the Commons, and thus making a party political intervention along the lines of using the Parliament Act rather hard.

That was all a world away by the 1950s, however. Three successive Conservative electoral victories provided a majority in the House of Commons unlikely to repeal the death penalty. In 1957 the House of Commons had passed the Homicide Act – which created the categories of 'capital' (punishable by the death penalty) and 'non-capital' murder (usually met with a life sentence) – but several Conservatives had been against this. One example was Henry Brooke, later Home Secretary, who noted in 1964 that:

> I should say that 10 years ago I firmly opposed the abolition of capital punishment. I did not like the Homicide Act. I was a junior Minister at the time. I did not take part in the debates, but I have recently come across copies of letters that I wrote to my constituents at that time, and I can see from them that I thought then that it was not a case for half measures. I started at the beginning of those discussions here with the firm belief that the death penalty should be retained for all murders.[33]

His views would eventually shift, but the Tory Party was not one predisposed for full repeal in the 1950s. Reforming MPs had to bide their time.

So part of Alice's early work shadowing the Home Office was in this defensive, rather than progressive role. Her conference speech in 1958 referenced this approach:

> I have been glancing through the Agenda of the Tory Party Conference. It made me think what a blood thirsty lot they are when they get collected together. There are no less than 32 resolutions on crime and punishment … We here this week are concerned with building schools, and we leave it to the Conference next week to discuss the cells, the cat and the gallows.[34]

There were several on the Tory right who fitted this description. Sir Thomas Moore, Conservative member for Ayr, saw the threat of physical punishment – both corporal and capital – as a far greater deterrent to crime than prison, and believed it was society's responsibility to lay down such conditions. Though a Commons Standing Committee rejected the introduction of corporal punishment by 26 votes to 6 in February 1961, Moore was determined to address the type of criminal where, he felt, 'the only thing they feared was getting flogged'.[35] One of the six votes in favour of corporal punishment was from Margaret Thatcher, in her first term as an MP. Alice, in rejecting the bill, flattered Moore by saying he himself would be too kind-hearted to administer the very punishment he proposed.

Two months later, however, Moore tried again with the passage of the Criminal Justice Bill. Moving a clause on 11 April 1961 that would bring in the cane (for those up to 17 years old) or the birch (17 to 20 years old) for young offenders, Moore again challenged Alice to respond. This she did in an astute manner, turning accusations of sentiment on their head:

> It has been said that those who are against corporal punishment are moved by sentiment and emotion. I believe that exactly the opposite is true. The emotion seems to come from those who advocate corporal punishment. There is the cry of 'flog 'em'. Those of us who are against corporal punishment are against it not because of emotion, but because of cold, hard facts … As my hon. Friend the Member for Chesterfield (Sir George Benson) said, there is no evidence to show that birching and flogging are any greater deterrent that any other method of punishment.[36]

In a measured, reasoned way Alice had destroyed the essence of the clause: 67 backed Moore, 259 rejected his measure.

That same day began, in Patrick Gordon Walker's words, the real debate over 'the big one' – capital punishment. Labour MP James MacColl's clause to raise the age at which the death penalty could be applied from 18 to 21 was arguably about as fertile a ground as Labour could play on with a Conservative-dominated Commons, and even then it was voted down by 144 votes to 229. Alice's speech during the debate might have been designed to play to Tory ears, but it did reveal something of her attitude which would come to light once in office. The age should be raised, she argued, because 'among a great many teenage people today there is an instability. They are impressionable, they lack judgment.'[37] Her future anti-drugs stance traced something of its lineage to this type of view. Nevertheless, her views on corporal – particularly for someone not afraid to use the cane in her teaching days – and capital punishment placed her firmly in the progressive camp.

The major charge levelled at those in favour of capital punishment was that if someone was not punished with their life for committing a murder, what incentive would they have for not killing again. To this Alice answered that:

> I know that they honestly believe that the death penalty is a deterrent, but will they honestly say that there is no other? Is not a further long period in prison for a man who has already done a long period in prison a great deterrent against committing a second murder?[38]

Other arguments made in the debate included the view that violent criminals could find ways to escape prison even were they given a life sentence, and that police recruitment numbers would suffer since wives would nag their husbands not to join the force now that murder would not be punished with death. These were largely suppositions, which Alice responded to with the available evidence from other European countries that had abolished the death penalty. As ever facts rather than emotion governed her politics.

In 1965, with Jenkins as Home Secretary and Alice as Minister of State, the Labour government passed the Murder (Abolition of Death Penalty) Act – removing the death penalty for an experimental period of five years. This was achieved through a Private Member's Bill from the Labour MP Sydney Silverman which, on its crucial second reading, was backed by 355 to 178 MPs. Alice Bacon, Tony Benn, Barbara Castle, Richard Crossman, Tony Greenwood, Harold Wilson and Shirley Williams were among the Labour MPs who voted 'aye'. Some liberal Tories (such as Norman St John-Stevas and Edward Boyle) joined them, but several Conservative leading (and future leading) lights including Margaret Thatcher, William Whitelaw and Quintin Hogg voted 'no'.

One Tory who voted for repeal was Henry Brooke, who had changed his mind since the 1950s. As Home Secretary Brooke had enquired as to the success of the 1957 Homicide Act – which, in creating two sentencing options of 'capital' and 'non-capital' murder, should have led to a significant shift in the types of crimes committed. Getting his civil servants to compare the types of murder committed pre- and post-differentiation between degrees of the crime, thereby comparing the likelihood that murder would equal the death penalty for the assailant, he found that:

Before the Homicide Act, the percentages were 14.4 per cent. capital and 85.6 per cent. non-capital. Since the Homicide Act, the percentages have been 13.5 capital and 86.5 non-capital. I do not see in those figures support, still less proof, of the argument that the death penalty is a uniquely powerful deterrent. To my mind, this is the best test which we can apply. The number of murders, both capital and non-capital, has increased since 1957, but it has increased in both categories rather less than the general increase in crimes of violence of all kinds. I make no claim that these figures afford final proof. They do not. But they throw doubt on the proposition that potential murderers are so much more afraid of hanging than of very long terms of imprisonment that, in making their plans, they carefully distinguish between the different statutory types of murder.[39]

Brooke voted for repeal – albeit under the initial time limited basis. Many Labour MPs were very forthright, with Frank Soskice calling the death penalty 'barbarous' during the December 1964 debate. Shirley Summerskill expressed the hope that:

> the Bill will pave the way to a new conception, a new system of punishing capital crimes. The argument has gone on for too long and public discussion about it should come to an end. After that, I hope that we can give more thought, time and the same enthusiasm to the fate of the victims and their dependants ... We are not tonight, fortunately, speaking for party or constituency in a doctrinaire manner and I find it an exhilarating feeling to be out of range of a Whip for one evening. We are voting as conscience dictates. I feel that in this House we adequately represent the conscience of this country and that our vote tonight will be welcomed by public opinion in general.[40]

It was 11.14 p.m. on the evening of 21 December 1964, after an eight-hour debate and getting on for two decades after Sydney Silverman had pushed the Attlee government to repeal the death penalty, that the House of Commons backed the bill at second reading. Subsequent attempts during committee stage to retain the penalty for instances where a convicted murderer killed again came to nothing and the Lords passed the legislation. Eight years after Alice Bacon had attempted to introduce a bill outlawing the death penalty as an instrument of state, she success-fully piloted the bill through Parliament as a Minister of the Crown.

Subsequently in 1969 the then Home Secretary Jim Callaghan brought forward an affirmative motion making the 1965 Act permanent – backed by all three main party leaders.[41]

Homosexuality

The reforming zeal at the Home Office continued. For 400 years male homosexuality was a crime in Britain, punishable by hanging (until 1861) or imprisonment. Prosecutions had increased since World War II, and by 1954 there were 1,069 men in prison in England and Wales for homosexual acts. In 1952 Alan Turing, one of the men to help break the

German Enigma code at Bletchley Park, was charged with gross indecency. As an alternative to prison Turing accepted 'treatment' with oestrogen injections (chemical castration) but was dead two years later, an inquest concluding that he had committed suicide. High-profile men were also caught up in the controversy, including Lord Montagu, his cousin Michael Pitt Rivers and Peter Wildeblood – all imprisoned for alleged homosexual acts with two RAF servicemen at Montagu's beach hut on the Solent.

The political atmosphere was poisonous. Conservative Home Secretaries, particularly Sir David Maxwell Fyfe (1951–4), promised 'a new drive against male vice' that would 'rid England against this plague'.[42] Yet these high-profile examples and the sheer growing volume of cases across the board led the Conservative government under Winston Churchill to commission Lord Wolfenden, vice chancellor at Reading University, to lead a review into the issue. The subsequent Report of the Departmental Committee on Homosexual Offences and Prostitution was published on 4 September 1957.

The general innovation of Wolfenden was to suggest that the law had no business in interfering in private matters. Should prostitutes be seen soliciting for business, or homosexual 'acts' be performed out in public then, it maintained, the state had a right to punish such activity. But what happened behind closed doors between consenting adults was not within the state's prerogative to pronounce upon. As such, the Wolfenden Report recommended the de facto decriminalisation of homosexuality, and after 400 years reform became a distinct possibility. Yet there was little political impetus at first – in part reflecting the position of the Conservative governments. Though groups such as the Howard League for Penal Reform and, perhaps surprisingly, the Church of England Moral Welfare Council supported reform, there was hardly a great groundswell of public opinion. A Gallup poll conducted just after the Wolfenden Report was published found 47 per cent against the legalisation of homosexuality, and 38 per cent in favour. Women, it appears, were a little more disapproving than men – though both sexes solidly rejected legalisation.[43]

Wolfenden was in many ways a gradualist product of a small 'c' conservative age. For the sake of the three ladies on his 15-person committee, Lord Wolfenden suggested at an early stage of proceedings that the terms Huntley and Palmers (after the biscuit manufacturers) be used for homosexuals and prostitutes respectively. Much was conducted under such pseudonyms, with evidence from two homosexuals being taken under the generic names of 'Mr White' and 'the Doctor'. But it did reach landmark conclusions – that the private life of individuals was of no concern of the state, and that there should be a new age of consent for homosexuals at the age of 21 (then the age of majority).

If Roy Jenkins has been hailed as the great liberal reformer on this matter, such perceptions have arisen in part due to the stark contrast between him, on the one hand, and on the other his Conservative predecessors and the conservative age in which they operated. Maxwell Fyfe (later Lord Kilmuir), the Conservative Home Secretary who first set the wheels in motion for Wolfenden's Report, was vehemently against lessening the penalties on homosexuality. To Andrew Holden, Kilmuir was using the enquiry to strengthen his hand on traditionally Conservative concerns – prostitution and general 'immorality'.[44] After Kilmuir's tenure at the Home Office came Gwilym Lloyd George, and, in 1957, Rab Butler.

Butler was personally rather sympathetic to reform, but unwilling to act on the issue. There were of course political and parliamentary obstacles beyond moral ones. In April 1964 Butler told a deputation from the HLRS that there was no point proceeding on Wolfenden until a new Parliament was elected.[45] He referred to the short amount of time prior to the forthcoming general election, but he could have been speaking of the need to fill the ranks of the Commons with more liberal-minded politicians, rather than the need for time to take the bill through.

As with the death penalty, it took a long time to change Labour minds on the issue too. Herbert Morrison had worried about the potential for moral decline should a bill be passed on decriminalisation of homosexuality, and had been concerned about the risk of getting too far ahead of public opinion. Alice's attitude is interesting. On 29 June 1960 the future Labour Minister of Health, Kenneth Robinson, had failed to get a motion passed calling upon the government to take early action on Wolfenden.[46] No surprise there: the Conservatives had won a 100-seat majority in 1959. Yet several high-profile Labour figures had joined the Tories in voting no, including James Chuter Ede, Ray Gunter and Margaret Herbison. Alice was one of the 99 who had voted for the motion, and was joined by Tony Benn, Tony Crosland and Roy Jenkins. Margaret Thatcher, surprisingly given some of her other views and the 1988 passage of Section 28 (which banned local authorities from promoting homosexuality), actually sided with Alice in urging the government to take action on implementing the recommendations of Lord Wolfenden.

The 1964 election was key to delivering reform: Labour's return to power also ushered in more university-educated, young, socially liberal Labour MPs replacing rather more senior, small and large 'c' Conservatives. Yet Alice's first two years at the Home Office were, according to Holden, 'a time of curious limbo'. Soskice, like Morrison on the death penalty, did not want to get ahead of public opinion – but interestingly, during a visit from Leo Abse and the HLRS to the Home Office on 4 May 1965, Alice agreed with Abse that the public simply did not care about the issue – potentially removing one of the barriers to action. Contemporary polling suggested she was probably correct: by November 1965 a NOP Poll indicated that only 21 per cent of people would even think about changing their vote because of any reform regarding homosexuality.[47] This suggested the government could act.

Three weeks after visiting Soskice and Bacon, Leo Abse introduced a Ten Minute Bill on implementing the spirit of Wolfenden. Labour split at the moment of the vote. Under pressure from Manny Shinwell, Labour MP and union leader, the trade unionists on the Labour benches appear to have voted against the reformism of 'middle-class liberals like Abse', with John Hynd joining Shinwell in voting no. Alice – this time of course voting with the weight of her office – voted with the man, Leo Abse, who thought her unqualified to be in her job. This left Shinwell and his followers allying themselves to Conservative reactionaries like Cyril Osborne, MP for Louth. Osborne's rants on matters of race we will encounter later, but he was equally forthright on homosexuality, and even made the logically questionable argument that homosexuality should not be legalised because previous 'homos' (Osborne's word) such as Guy Burgess and Donald Maclean had been ripe for blackmail because of their sexuality. By 19 votes the reformers failed to make progress. Even with a Labour majority, the bill failed to get a second reading (losing narrowly by 159 to 178 votes).[48]

The issue was kept alive in Parliament through predominantly upper-class pressure. In part this represented a certain liberal conservatism, and it is also true that the Wolfenden Report itself had been sparked by upper-class homosexuality.[49] The Conservative whip Lord Arran (Arthur Gore) managed to secure successful second and third readings in the House of Lords, whilst, in December 1965, the Tory MP (who later joined the Labour Party and the SDP) Humphrey Berkeley used his second place in the ballot for Private Members' Bills to introduce a further debate on Wolfenden. In February 1966, the bill passed its second reading (164–107) – with Hynd and Shinwell no longer voting against, and Alice, again, voting in favour.

The arguments in favour of decriminalisation were clear. Norman St John-Stevas – later Conservative co-sponsor of Leo Abse's bill on decriminalising homosexuality – simply noted that 'nobody would dream of enacting a law penalising homosexuality today. If we did not have it already, no one would support it.'[50] Roy Jenkins responded by first outlining the government's own neutrality and the free vote afforded to Labour members on the matter – before noting his personal support for reform:

> Homosexual inclinations are not often a matter of choice for the individual. Occasionally they may be, but this is the exception rather than the rule. In general it is, I am convinced, an involuntary deviation. But according to most medical opinion—I know that there are some differences about this—and certainly according to the Wolfenden Committee, it is not a disease in a sense of being, in the majority of cases, subject to medical treatment. It is more in the nature of a disability than a disease and, of course, it is a grave disability for the individual. It leads to a great deal of loneliness and unhappiness and to a heavy weight of guilt and shame. It greatly reduces the chance of the individual finding a stable and lasting emotional relationship.[51]

Given the still tricky political terrain, this was about as fervently pro-reform as one could get. But whilst the Commons voted in favour of reform, it was obvious dissent remained, and there remained hurdles to getting the bill through all its committee stages. From the Cabinet George Brown ranted against the changes in the law. As Barbara Castle records, the same day the bill was passed in second reading Brown declared that homosexuality was:

> how Rome came down. And I care deeply about it … Don't think teenagers are able to evaluate your library ideas. You will have a totally disorganised, indecent and unpleasant society. You must have rules! We've gone too far on sex already. I don't regard any sex as pleasant. It's pretty undignified and I've always thought so.[52]

Whilst the bill ran out of parliamentary time due to the March 1966 general election, by the summer of 1966 the passage of reform on the issue was becoming an increasing certainty. Abse reintroduced a Ten Minute Bill which passed easily this time by 244 to 100 votes. While Harold Wilson showed 'little interest in the subject', Jenkins as Home Secretary provided the final push needed.[53] Bizarrely, according to Clive Ponting's book on the Wilson government, 'the second reading of [Abse's decriminalisation of homosexuality] bill was agreed in December [1966] without a vote, mainly because the main opponent was too drunk to stand up and object at the right moment'.

Jenkins's professed attitude was that the government's position should be one of 'benevolent neutrality' towards the question of legalising homosexuality. In reality though, he, like Alice, was pushing for reform. Crossman records in his diary the worry that Labour members felt regarding the potential of working-class voters to move to the right on the issue, and, combined with the concerns over race we will touch upon, there was legitimate cause for concern. Crossman, like Jenkins and Bacon, nominally pledged to ministerial neutrality on an issue the government was keeping at arm's length. But despite such commitments they – along with John Silkin, who was Deputy Leader of the House and Chief Whip – lobbied Labour backbenchers mercilessly at the third reading of the bill in July 1967. Finally, on 28 July 1967 the Sexual Offences Act received Royal Assent, and homosexuality between consenting adults was decriminalised (from age 21 and up) in England and Wales (Scotland would have to wait until 1980, and Northern Ireland until 1982). Leo Abse was therefore successful in steering his Private Member's Bill on homosexuality through Parliament.

Abse was also a proponent of another, important social reform – legalising abortion. But it would be David Steel who took through the legalisation of abortion, despite the fact that Abse had started the ball rolling there too. Abse, despite his success with homosexuality, notes with some regret his inability to steer through reform on abortion too. As he recalls:

> I was politically blackmailed. It is the only time in my life that I have ever yielded to blackmail and it will be the last. My Homosexual Reform Bill was going through the House contemporaneously with the Abortion Bill and it was made clear to me by many Members, not a few of whom have since repented, that if I pursued my course on the Abortion Bill they would withdraw support for me on the Homosexual Bill.[54]

Even with the supportive Jenkins as Home Secretary reform had to be incremental. The essentially unanswerable trade-off always remained – do too little, and the changes would have no effect; do too much, and they might not get through both Houses of Parliament or cut it with the public. It was left to the Liberal MP David Steel to steer the next great reform.

Abortion

Reform over abortion was an easier sell for a Labour government than reforms governing homosexuality. But the tactics of reformers were similar – to underplay what were regarded as moral questions (in the case of abortion, the debate about the status of the foetus; with homosexuality, anything regarding the physical act itself), and to emphasise what was practical policy. To Labour – and particularly with a practical woman like Alice Bacon at the Home Office – there was much to be gained by such a strategy. The ALRA placed much importance, as did their parliamentary advocates, on the cost of illegal abortion (particularly to the NHS), the health issues raised by the recent thalidomide tragedies, and the inequality of treatment between the classes – whereby better-off women could travel abroad to get an abortion while working-class women were forced to use backstreet providers.

The ALRA, with which Alice Bacon would have many dealings, was formed in 1936. It was given some prominence in 1939 due to the case of Dr Aleck Bourne, who was acquitted of procuring an abortion for a 14-year-old girl who had been raped by four Guards Officers on the grounds that he had acted as a doctor in good faith. Bourne himself later failed to support legislative reform, and, crucially, had avoided prosecution largely because his defence team had established the girl in question had been of 'good character'. For many people, a concern that legitimising abortion would engender sexual promiscuity trumped the impact on individual families.[55]

In 1952 a Private Member's Bill on abortion reform was introduced by Joseph Reeves MP (Labour, Greenwich) but was talked out by a successful filibuster – as Alice saw with regards to her bill on abolishing the death penalty, the last refuge of Tory reaction. Then, for eight years Conservative governments made a concerted attempt to avoid the matter. But in 1960 Kenneth Robinson MP raised the issue again, with a bill, drafted by the Cambridge legal scholar and ALRA president Glanville Williams, that would decriminalise abortion by a medical practitioner until the thirteenth week of pregnancy. Upon the second reading of his bill, Robinson ruefully replied that:

> I am happy to have a little more time to discuss this subject than had my predecessor ... in 1952. He was slightly less successful than I in the [Private Members'] Ballot, and I think the House permitted him only one and a half minutes.[56]

But as with Reeves – albeit after two hours' debate this time – the bill foundered.

Though Robinson would never have been successful at this time under a Tory government, his efforts coincided with a wider cultural shift as it became increasingly clear that the status quo was neither fair nor safe. Alice Jenkins – the secretary of the ALRA – published a powerful text in 1960 entitled *Law for the Rich* which highlighted the class inequality in family planning. Middle-class women could easily obtain abortions in sanatoria abroad, whilst a working-class woman who had an unwanted pregnancy was forced to go to dangerous amateurs who were expensive and entirely unregulated. Indeed, in an answer to a parliamentary question tabled by Renée Short in February 1966, Alice Bacon revealed figures that showed 296 people had been convicted of providing illegal abortions in the five years between 1960 and 1964. The law, in other words, no longer worked. David Steel, who later moved the crucial bill that legalised abortion, noted that:

> I saw it as an issue of justice and hypocrisy really, because as Alice Jenkins' book showed, you could get round the law if you had enough money and contacts to persuade somebody in the private sector to carry out an abortion under some other title.[57]

In 1961, as the details of the thalidomide scandal became increasingly evident (with thousands of babies born with severe deformities after their mothers had been prescribed the drug Distaval to help alleviate morning sickness), public opinion began to soften towards legalising abortion, in part because pregnancy and childbirth became part of the wider discourse. Perhaps by now public opinion had got ahead of the politicians and the impetus for action was greater. By 1964, with Labour in office, Frank Soskice and Alice Bacon had both backbench pressure and a growing public demand pushing for reform.

But problems, and numerous ones at that, remained. First, a parliamentary majority of four in 1964 meant Wilson was not going out of his way to court controversy. Second, Soskice – as ALRA would find out – was rather on the fence on the issue. And third, a significant (enough that it mattered with a four-seat majority) number of Labour MPs were Roman Catholic (including future whip Bob Mellish and Shirley Williams, then a PPS), and were against abortion in any circumstances. As Roy Jenkins noted:

> I did not think it realistic to try to make these reforms Government-sponsored Bills, because although the majority of the Cabinet were in favour of them, they were in favour of them with differing degrees of enthusiasm. Out of a Cabinet of about 20 at that time, there were four or five people who were resolutely opposed to these reforms; there were eight or nine people who were strongly in favour and the rest probably wished they would go away. There would have been no chance of them becoming Government Bills. It would have been thought coercive by the four or five members who were strongly opposed if we made the Abortion Bill a Government Bill and whipped people into supporting it.[58]

Abortion was an issue which divided members across all parties. A final obstacle was a worry that a popular, pro-family, pro-Church Conservative message could undercut Labour's base and cost them office altogether. It is true that some Labour MPs were under significant pressure from their constituencies. Jeremy Bray MP received one letter signed by 456 constituents against abortion, with the total number of signatures he received in the thousands. Perhaps this explains why his stock reply to such inquiries was so carefully worded: 'I am in no doubt that our present laws, which cause so much unnecessary distress, need amending, but I also feel that we must be very careful about the way in which we amend them.'[59] An ALRA internal memorandum later recorded Bray as 'certainly not ... in favour of making it legal at the request of patient or her guardian'.[60]

Other Labour MPs were willing to be more outspoken. Dr David Kerr, Labour MP for Wandsworth Central was 'almost the only public supporter of "abortion on demand" in Parliament during the 1960s', along with Christopher Price (Labour MP for Birmingham Perry Barr), elected in 1966. Speaking in the Commons in February 1965, Kerr made the case that more children were being born to single mothers, still very uncommon in the 1950s and 1960s, and despite the difficulties that would present to the (often) young women, they had no choice but to continue with their pregnancies. Kerr pointed out that 'in England and Wales, between 1954 and 1963, the illegitimate birth rates rose from 4.7 per cent of live births to 6.6 per cent, an increase of nearly 50 per cent'. Knowing his audience, he also remarked that 'in the West Yorkshire conurbation the figures went from 5.5 to 7.9 percent, an increase of 45 per cent'. Though his general point was about sex education, he threw in a pointed reference to 'the inability of girls to have chosen what to do in the first place … and suffer, in the second place, from the inability to decide what to do in the context of their situation'. Alice remarked – paraphrasing an earlier comment by Kerr – that family planning advice was probably not sufficient to deal with the problem.

The gradual opening of this rhetorical space where the debate could be had was perhaps Alice's key role, as Frank Soskice was not going to force the issue. A deputation from the ALRA in February 1965 visited Bacon and Soskice. Alice was probably a welcoming voice here, for within a few months internal ALRA lists place her as an MP 'known or believed to be in support of abortion law reform'.[61] They were told the Home Secretary opposed abortion being available to all, though he did accept its use in instances of medical danger, rape, and cases of deformity (with the recent scandal concerning thalidomide very much in the public mind).[62] Full freedom of choice, however, was not yet on the cards.

Soskice's intransigence – and here one may agree with Jenkins' later, scathing comments – was at least in part down to his concern for public opinion. He asked that the ALRA should crystallise public opinion in favour of the legislation before he took any action.

But, unlike homosexuality, which left the public largely unmoved, and the death penalty – where attitudes were often more conservative than the government – a majority of the public was in favour of abortion reform. Renée Short reminded Alice Bacon in 1965 that 'a National Opinion Poll, as recently as last March, showed that over 72 per cent of the population was in favour of reform on the lines proposed by the [ALRA]'. Bacon responded that she was indeed aware, and that 'this might be a good subject for a Private Member's Bill in the new Session'. Dialogue between the ALRA and Alice was ongoing throughout this period, with Alice assuring the lobbyists she would be in the parliamentary chamber for a debate in January 1966.[63] But, as Wilson looked for a snap election to extend his majority, Simon Wingfield Digby's (Conservative, Dorset West) subsequent bill to reform the law had too little time to achieve anything prior to the general election in March 1966. Things would have to wait until the new Parliament.

Following the general election there was the usual ballot for Private Members' Bills. On this occasion David Steel, Liberal MP for Roxburgh, Selkirk and Peebles, came third in the ballot. Having come so high, various organisations began to lobby Steel. Among them was the ALRA to whom Steel had responded positively in 1964 when the ALRA were lobbying parliamentary candidates ahead of the general election to support abortion law reform. Steel took up the ALRA's cause and took forward the bill to legalise abortion. This bill had already successfully passed through the House of Lords, stewarded by Lord Lewis Silkin, a Labour peer. It also had much support among senior Labour figures in the Commons. Lord Silkin's son, John Silkin, for example, was the chief whip and helped Steel secure space for his bill in committee while opponents of reform were holding up the second Private Member's Bill to delay the abortion reform bill. Kenneth Robinson, who had previously tried to take through his own Private Member's Bill on the subject, was now Minister of Health and Dick Crossman, as Leader of the House was persuaded to give the bill an extra day on the floor of the House of Commons at its Report stage to see off the filibusterers. And Alice, a supporter of reform and in tune with party members, was the government minister from the Home Office on the Bill Committee. Harold Wilson, while not being a vocal supporter of reform, was allowing government time and effort to be put into allowing David Steel's abortion law reform bill to progress successfully through Parliament. Indeed, social reforms including on abortion and homosexuality are some of the most far-reaching, permanent legacies of Wilson's governments.

But the key to reform now was Jenkins, Home Secretary from December 1965 to November 1967. He – in the words of Holden – was the 'crucial' figure. Having replaced Soskice, he pressured the Home Affairs Select Committee of the House of Commons 'to take a more benevolent view of the progression of Private Members' Bills relating to abortion'. Importantly, Douglas Houghton, Chancellor of the Duchy of Lancaster and husband of ALRA lobbyist Vera Houghton, was appointed to chair the committee, to drive through reform. At the same time, lobbying was also taking place through doctors' organisations, with around 650 doctors writing to the Home Secretary expressing support for the reform. Addressing the committee on 12 January 1966, Jenkins even told them that the government should go further, since neutrality could be read as opposition. This was a far cry from the Soskice days, as Roy Jenkins himself later hinted at:

> Would the Abortion Bill have got through had not I, or somebody of like mind, been Home Secretary? It would not. I don't say I was unique, Kenneth Robinson for example would have had just as much conviction for those Bills. But I think you would certainly have needed a Home Secretary of similar disposition. I sat through all the nights and spoke on a lot of the amendments and on the Third Reading. We also provided, through the Home Office, a lot of drafting assistance to David Steel.[64]

Even with such assistance, the controversy of the bill meant a long parliamentary schedule, and overnight sessions for Alice. As Jenkins noted, part of this was about waiting out the filibusterers:

> What I was not able to do, I don't think I even attempted to do it, was to get convenient time for the Bills. In the key Committee Stages of these Bills we did not start until about 10.30 at night, and on the last night of the Abortion Bill sat through until nearly 1pm the next afternoon. And at times the progress was so slow it looked as though it would fall. But the way in which we defeated the filibuster was to make it clear that we were prepared to go on throughout the Friday night, the Saturday and the Sunday if our opponents insisted upon it. That of course made it clear that wasting a few hours was not going to be effective, so the ship came into harbour by lunchtime on the Friday.[65]

Seeing off the filibusterers was a huge challenge and a joint endeavour – from Silkin and Crossman giving the bill the time and space in Parliamentary Committee and on the floor of the House, to having a bill committee of dedicated and knowledgeable MPs. David Steel particularly acknowledges the support of the three medical doctors on the Committee (John Dunwoody – Labour, David Kerr – Labour and Michael Winstanley – Liberal) as well as the informal whips (as it was not a government bill, government whips could not officially steer the bill through the parliamentary process). Those informal whips were Peter Jackson, Labour MP for High Peak and Sir George Sinclair, Tory MP for Dorking, supported by Alistair Service, a lobbyist and supporter of the ALRA. Between them they had the largely thankless task of persuading MPs to stay in London for Friday sittings, when they would usually be in their constituencies, and to stay in Parliament for late night sittings, all to see off the filibusterers.

Lord Steel remembers their work, including Alistair Service ticking off the names of MPs as they arrived in the House of Commons. He also remembers the equal effort that went in to the work of those opposing the bill – chiefly the Tory MP Norman St John-Stevas and Labour MP Bernard Braine. 'At the Report Stage of the Bill they would pile in one after the other to talk the bill out', Steel remembers, 50 years on. Little wonder that Vera Houghton of the ALRA reported to Steel a conversation she had had with Dick Taverne who had reinforced 'how extremely important it is for you to go to the Whip's Office as soon as Parliament resumes (on the first day if possible) to make known your preferences about the members of the Committee for your bill'.[66] Other than Jackson and Sinclair, Steel succeeded in getting pro-reform voices such as Leo Abse, David Marquand and Lena Jeger onto the Standing Committee.

Despite such hard work, in some sense Steel, Jenkins and Bacon got lucky, as Lord Steel reflects on still. 'The timing of the March 1966 election gave an unusually long 1966–7 parliamentary session and we needed those eighteen months', remembers Steel. David Steel's Medical Termination of Pregnancy Bill was read for a second time on 22 July 1966, giving over a year to make its way through the parliamentary system.

In his speech introducing the bill, Steel noted 'that there has been a growing tide of public opinion in favour of such a change ... two National Opinion Polls carried out recently have indicated that three-quarters of the population are in favour of a reform of the law'. He certainly wanted to avoid the example of contemporary Sweden where women had to appear before a panel of:

> social workers, psychiatrists and medical practitioners to examine and pass each case. They are behind in their work, and many women are reluctant to appear before a panel of this kind. We have to avoid in the Bill wording which is so restrictive as not to have the effect which we are seeking— namely, the ending of the back-street abortions.

It was this desire – largely led by Steel, but supported by the three doctors on the Committee – to avoid the law being too restrictive that encouraged Steel to amend his own bill substantially compared with what he had taken on from the ALRA and from Lord Silkin's bill in the House of Lords. Lord Silkin's bill had given four categories in which abortion would be permissible. Steel did not want those restrictions and so after some disagreements with the ALRA Steel amended the bill to ensure that abortion would be more freely available with doctors less constrained.

Another area in which the bill was amended was on the right of medical practitioners to opt out of performing, or being involved with, abortions. This amendment, supported by Alice, was suggested to Steel by members of a Catholic seminary in Steel's Scottish constituency. Like many MPs, Steel was under some pressure by constituents, particularly Catholics, on abortion law reform, and this was one concession on conscience that Steel was willing, and indeed happy, to make.[67]

He ended with the pragmatic realities of the matter:

> those who wish to oppose the Bill have to consider the effect of their opposition. If they were opposing the Bill because they could devise some other means by which abortions would stop tomorrow and by which there would be no unwanted pregnancies and none of the tide of human misery which is developed by our uncertain state of the law, then they would have a strong case. But, as the Home Office statistics show, over the last few years an average of some 25 to 30 women have died as a result of complications following illegal abortions. Many more have been cluttering up hospital beds with the treatment required following these operations. Many lives have been lost through suicide following conditions in which it was impossible to obtain an abortion, or in which abortion was in some way involved.[68]

Such a view was not without contest. Speaking against Steel, William Wells, a long-time Labour member for Walsall, noted that in 'taking the stand which we take we are not only upholding the common tradition of Christianity, but are protecting principles which stand at the very root of an ordered society. We may be right, we may be wrong, but that is our position.'[69] The matter was not settled without something of a contretemps between Wells and Steel:

> William Wells (Labour): The hon. Member for Roxburgh, Selkirk and Peebles is, so far as I know, not yet a father. May I hope that he will become so. He may have a daughter.

> David Steel (Liberal): May I inform the hon. Gentleman that, although I am not yet a father, I hope to be one next month?

Wells: I congratulate the hon. Gentleman, as I am sure the whole House will. If he has a daughter, she may grow up to have a vocation for nursing. Let me ask the hon. Gentleman this question quite seriously. What does he think his feelings will be if his daughter becomes a nurse and if, when he sees her at the weekend and says, 'What have you been doing this week, darling?', she answers, 'I have been in the operating theatre terminating pregnancies':—

Roy Roebuck, MP for Harrow East (Labour) attempts an intervention: Will my hon. Friend allow me—

Wells: No, I am sorry.— 'and I have burned six embryos:'

(HON. MEMBERS: 'Oh'.)[70]

Anti-abortion MPs used arguments from Catholic doctrine and argued the need for an evidence-gathering commission to investigate the issue (as with Wolfenden and homosexuality). On the latter point, the argument that there was no need to rush reform fell down in two key ways. First, the abortion debate was hardly new and a major clamour for reform had existed since at least the aforementioned Bourne case of the late 1930s. But secondly it had taken ten years from Wolfenden's recommendations to eventually reform the law concerning homosexuality. With, as Steel pointed out, up to 30 women dying each year through botched 'backstreet' abortions, the lives of potentially hundreds of women were at risk should the issue be kicked even further down the road.

Eventually, in July 1967, after five hours of debate the House was ready to deliver its verdict at third reading. Aside from voting to back the bill (the count was 262–181), Alice played no part in the debate. Her real task came in piloting the bill through its committee. In contrast to her counterpart in the Lords, Lord Stonham, and his inconsistent, and strictly speaking improper, ministerial interventions (it was claimed rape should not be included as an acceptable reason for procuring an abortion within the legalisation as it would encourage slander), Alice trod a dispassionate and legalistic path during the Committee stage on the Steel bill. In essence, she argued that Clause (1,a) of the legislation – which took into account the 'mental health of the pregnant woman' – would, in practice, suffice as reason enough for termination under such circumstances. Once again, she avoided the emotive language of some of her peers in simply declaring that 'my advice is that subsection (1,a) covers the circumstances for which the Amendment seeks to provide'.[71] But this factual approach was welcome and helped clarify the scope and practical significance of the bill. The bill received Royal Assent on 22 October 1967, 15 months after the second reading. By now Jenkins was Chancellor and Jim Callaghan was Home Secretary, but it was Jenkins who held a party at the Treasury in November 1967 to celebrate the passage of the Abortion Act the previous month. Steel remembers the party – a small but significant gathering in Jenkins' private offices. Alice was one of the select members at the party that evening.

This was practical yet progressive politics in action. A controversial Act was passed – via the route of a Private Member's Bill, but tacitly supported by the government – through the allocation of parliamentary time, and a positive attitude with regard to the various votes and committees. The Wilson government did not publicly 'own' the legislation due to its controversial nature; this is perhaps why Labour in the 1960s sometimes flies a little under the public radar compared to the governments of 1945 or 1997. However, it did create the conditions whereby social reform was not only possible, but, with the help of an individual Member of Parliament willing to put their head above the parapet, virtually inevitable. This was a big moment indeed.

Race

Britain had changed substantially since the end of the war and the start of the 1960s, not least in terms of the large inflows of people from the Commonwealth. Though the arrival at Tilbury docks of 493 passengers on the *Empire Windrush* liner in June 1948 is referred to as the start of mass immigration to the UK, it was a piece of legislation introduced by the Attlee government that accelerated this trend. From 1 January 1949 the British Nationality Act gave, in effect, common citizenship of the United Kingdom to those from British colonies, dependencies and the burgeoning Commonwealth. Though its provisions were restricted in 1962, the number of British residents born in the West Indies increased from 15,000 in 1951 to 172,000 a decade later.

Immigration was not only from the Caribbean. Yorkshire saw the growth of significant eastern European populations (over 5,000 people in Bradford alone in 1951) as a result of the European Voluntary Workers scheme that helped plug gaps in the British labour market, and there were around 1,000 people of Asian origin in Bradford by the late 1950s, primarily working in the textiles industry.

On issues of race relations and community cohesion in Leeds, Alice proved (as in so many other areas) an invaluable source of information for Hugh Gaitskell. A note hastily scribbled – possibly for a speech, possibly in a Shadow Cabinet meeting – from Alice to Hugh survives in Gaitskell's papers at University College London. It is probably from 1961. Within these fragments we can glimpse not only Alice's knowledge of the local picture, but some of her views on the matter:

Leeds (South-East) – central:

Jewish, Irish, Hungarians, Poles, Lithuanians, West Indians and Pakistanis.

Problem – but no trouble.

Only (minor) tremble created by Fascist organisation – chiefly from outside Leeds. When a fascist chalks up 'Go home nigger' – only result 20 letters (chiefly from Jews) saying what are you going to do about these Fascist activities. The Chief Constable has detailed one police officer to whom immigrants can go with complaints + troubles. e.g. Recently some West Indians complained they had been refused a meal in a restaurant. They went to the police officer with their complaint. Officer went to the restaurant – which was a Chinese one – and found been a misunderstanding. They had been waving the West Indians out and asking them to go into another room as there was no service in that one. Chinese so concerned about the incident – they had a party in the restaurant for the West Indians.

Need for organisations – social + welfare. There is one in Leeds but I forget its name. Helps to settle etc – but ought to be checked from Leeds. Perhaps Mr Brookes [welfare officer] might know – or Bill Newitt. Voluntary organisations could help.

L[abour] P[arty] women ran a social event for women immigrants to meet others. In my opinion customs and social habits creates trouble as much as housing. Hence importance of organisations to help.

Some people don't object to coloured workers on buses – in hospitals – but object to them having houses. Ridiculous attitude.

G[rea]t contribution of immigrants to last 100 years – industry culture etc.[72]

Alice had always taken a liberal line on race. In 1961 the right-wing Tory Cyril Osborne asked the Tory Home Secretary Rab Butler 'if he will now give an estimate of the number of coloured immigrants which the United Kingdom can safely absorb; in view of the high birth rate amongst coloured immigrants'. After Butler had replied that the issue should be looked at 'without prejudice', Alice Bacon took aim:

> is the right hon. Gentleman aware that many of us deprecate the emphasis which is put by some Members opposite on coloured immigrants? Is he aware that the coloured immigrants are not the only immigrants among whom there is a high birth rate?

Later that year, the Conservative MP for Liverpool Kirkdale, Norman Pannell, a long-time ally of Osborne (they usually spoke on such matters in tandem) asked if the Home Secretary 'will, as a matter of urgency, appoint a small fact-finding committee to examine the question of immigration from the Commonwealth'. After a no from Butler, he pushed that 'with immigrants flooding into this country from every quarter of the Commonwealth in ever-increasing numbers, does not my right hon. Friend consider that there is urgent need for an impartial assessment of the position as a prelude to positive Government action?' To this Alice again leapt in: 'Is it not strange that hon. Members opposite always raise the question of immigration from the Commonwealth? Can it be that they are more concerned about the colour of the immigrants than the numbers of those coming in?' Before 1964 then, as with the death penalty, part of the battle Alice had to wage was in simply not making prejudice worse, rather than stamping it out altogether.

However, it was not just right-wing Conservatives who had concerns regarding immigration. John Hynd, the Labour MP for Sheffield Attercliffe, complained about the '11,000 or 12,000 immigrants pouring in every year' and excused local dance hall proprietors who imposed colour bars on their establishments. And on the far right, while Oswald Mosley concentrated his activities on London (with his Union Movement's involvement in sparking the Notting Hill riots of 1958), the National Front received average votes of around 10 per cent in the wards where they fielded candidates across the country by the late 1960s.[73]

That race discrimination issues were still being debated in the second half of the 1960s, after segregation had been successfully overturned in the

United States in 1964, indicated this was an issue the Wilson government would have to tackle head-on.

Unlike so many of the other social reforms of the 1960s, this was an area where the government, not backbenchers, led. In 1965 the Labour government introduced a bill – presented by Frank Soskice, Alice Bacon, Harold Wilson and others – which made it a civil offence to refuse to serve a person, unduly delay one's service towards them, or overcharge, on racial grounds. The 1965 Race Relations Act was a landmark piece of legislation and, though Enoch Powell's Rivers of Blood speech three years later showed racial prejudice was far from eliminated in British society, it was an important step forward. The 1968 Act which followed subsequently made housing and employment practices similarly colour-blind.

In office, Alice helped the race relations legislation make its way through the Commons. Her role was more procedural than rhetorical – Frank Soskice fielded all the questions in Parliament whilst Alice did little on the floor bar voting for the legislation.[74] What she did do, however, was toe a middle line between avoiding alienating the section of the working class affected by high levels of immigration, and helping the government to maintain a tolerant, liberal position. In 1965 she addressed the Labour Party Conference in Blackpool. A local activist had moved an emergency resolution describing government policy as 'a surrender, however disguised, to the currents of illiberal opinion'. Alice's response revealed the need to tread carefully:

> I say that this country of ours ought to be able to absorb one million immigrants, but I would ask the Conference to recognise that these immigrants are concentrated in those very areas where the supply of houses, schools, and teachers is already inadequate. Of course we know that the immigrants did not create the shortage. Of course we know that the immigrants are just making apparent a shortage which already existed, but until the Labour government can make good these shortages, to put more on the already over-burdened services could lead to a very serious situation.[75]

This was clearly difficult territory. Yet, more or less, Alice seems to have got it right. Working-class concern over the allocation of resources was real, understandable and needed to be addressed:

> The new immigrant children are coming into the schools at the rate of 24 a week, 100 a month, about a new school needed every three to four

months ... We must maintain our educational standards in this country for the immigrants and for everybody else, and it is not colour prejudice when a parent of somebody who has lived here all their lives comes along and questions whether or not their child is being held back because of these very necessary special steps (organising special classes to teach the children English) which are being taken for the immigrants.[76]

This was an environment in which Patrick Gordon Walker, Alice's former boss as Shadow Home Secretary, had lost his Smethwick seat on the day Labour won the general election against a candidate declaring 'if you want a nigger for a neighbour, vote Labour'. As with the other liberal measures Labour introduced, immigration needed to be carefully handled. Back at Party Conference, in Blackpool, Alice received backing for the NEC position (4,736,000 voted to 1,581,000). Finishing her address she then 'urg[ed] this Conference to ... go back to their trade unions and their constituencies resolved to do all possible to make at home those immigrants who are with us'.[77] *The Times* was almost effusive in its praise: 'loudly barracked through the first half of her speech, Miss Bacon ploughed on defiantly and subdued her audience by sheer weight of words ... Miss Bacon sat down to almost unadulterated applause.'[78] Even Richard Crossman, hardly a natural ally, was impressed:

> The most awkward moment came when Bob Mellish got up and made a rip-roaring speech which might have been tolerable from a Bermondsey docker but was really impossible for a Parliamentary Secretary of Housing and Local Government. Altogether it was a pretty unpleasant debate, until it was saved by Alice Bacon, who did magnificently. The row in the Conference Hall stimulated her. In that grating voice, she gave her clear, schoolmistressy, common-sense view of the White Paper, demonstrating what was in it to people who hadn't bothered to read it. It really was quite impressive.[79]

A battle won. Yet events in the coming years were going to stir matters up further. At half-past two in the afternoon on 20 April 1968, Enoch Powell gave a speech at the Midland Hotel in Birmingham. The following Tuesday, the 1968 Race Relations Bill was to have its second reading in the Commons, and Powell used his address – aside from famously referring to 'the River Tiber foaming with much blood' – to declare that:

we must be mad, literally mad, as a nation to be permitting the annual inflow of some 50,000 dependants, who are for the most part the material of the future growth of the immigrant descended population. It is like watching a nation busily engaged in heaping up its own funeral pyre.[80]

Powell was not the only parliamentarian making such points: Cyril Osborne had kept up his questions regarding 'coloured immigration', with Alice Bacon – as Minister of State – giving precise and factual, rather than emotive responses, trying to lower the temperature: 'in January 1967 there were about 144,000 immigrant pupils from the West Indies, Africa, India and Pakistan in schools with ten or more immigrant pupils on roll'.[81]

As odd a spectacle as the patrician, former classicist Enoch Powell leading a movement of the disgruntled working class was (particularly since Mosley had tried, and largely failed, in a similar bid during the 1930s), it certainly posed a problem for Labour. In May 1968 questions on race and immigration mushroomed in Parliament, and Alice, by then at the Department of Education and Science, often had to answer them. In 1968, the word 'immigrant' appears in her parliamentary speeches 29 times, compared to three in 1966 and two in 1967 – despite her move from the Home Office to the Department for Education.

Though the race relations legislation enacted by Labour could have gone further, the government did get much right. On 9 May 1968 *The Times* photographed a visit from Alice and the Education Secretary Edward Short to a comprehensive in North London. The caption recorded that 'the ministers are visiting schools with high numbers of immigrant children and discussing the problems of integration with members of the teaching staff'.[82] On 18 May Bacon and Short were again on the move, visiting schools in Wolverhampton (Powell's constituency) and West Bromwich. When Short asked how many immigrant pupils one teacher taught, he was told 'I don't know – I regard them as children'. In Wolverhampton, the pair met with little reaction regarding Powell's speech, bar the odd child repeating what they had heard.[83]

Despite this public relations drive, however, Alice and Short primarily got on with more constructive matters – such as encouraging a national conference on 'Immigration and the Education of Teachers', attempting to bolster the numbers (c.2,500 in 1966–7) of teachers and lecturers who attended courses dealing with the problems of immigrant children and racial issues, and increasing the one-third of Colleges of Education known to be teaching courses designed to increase the social integration of immigrant children.[84] Alice was hard-headed here; Britain owed her Commonwealth an innumerable debt for losses in the wars and Britain needed labour. But such immigration should be tightly controlled, showing particular concern for those communities most directly affected by large numbers of new arrivals. As demonstrated by her 1965 address in Blackpool, she tried to get this balance right.

War on Drugs

Although a liberal and reformer on the death penalty, homosexuality, abortion and immigration, Alice was certainly not soft on the issue of drugs, as Paul McCartney and others pushing for reform would learn. In this sense she was conservative with a small 'c', and, had it come to a vote, would have supported the Drugs (Prevention of Misuse) Bill that passed through the Commons in the late spring and early summer of 1964.[85] Bernard Atha recalls that many local members initially wondered why she was so exercised over what seemed a relatively minor concern, but later regarded her as a 'prophetess' for seeing that the problems experienced in the United States would soon travel over the Atlantic.[86]

It is fair to say that Alice Bacon was mistrustful of youth culture. Though she rejected the Thomas Moore approach regarding corporal punishment, she sympathised with views that the young were getting out of control. Speaking to the 1961 National Conference of Labour Women, she gave a speech that almost appeared to be drawn from a(n albeit Butler-ite) Conservative Home Secretary's notes.[87] The key, as she often repeated, was to get more policemen and women on the beat. That way – be it over it drugs or any other crime – the young would be scared straight.

Perhaps unsurprisingly, Leeds students were not so enthusiastic towards the views of one of their local MPs. In 1968, students at the University of Leeds, led by a young Jack Straw, occupied the campus's Parkinson Building in protest at what they saw as attempts by the institution's security service to spy on them. In this instance Alice, like her fellow Leeds MPs, was rather amused – but the danger remained of radicalising an essentially pacific youth. Jack Straw, after all, had canvassed for the party locally in 1964, and although he says he had never even been offered marijuana, from 1966 he felt 'ashamed to be Labour' at times due to what he saw as an authoritarian-leaning government.[88] These were fast-moving times for the political establishment to keep up with and, certainly, they did not always get things quite right.

Alice was later ridiculed for her opinion that the pop bands of the day – including the Beatles, but especially the Rolling Stones – were engendering some form of moral malaise, but she was hardly alone in such concerns. As historian Marcus Collins notes, 'general bewilderment testified to how the 1960s "counter revolution" exceeded the limits of the knowable and actionable in Westminster'. The Beatles or their members appeared in 57 parliamentary debates throughout the 1960s (this number was actually exceeded in the 2000s, presumably as youthful Beatles fans entered Parliament), with 15 mentions for the Rolling Stones. Labour MPs like Alice, actually, were more likely to be negative than positive. Tory members like Bill (later Lord) Deedes even occasionally declared themselves 'fans' of the band. Such members opposed the Labour government's so-called 'Beatle clause' in the 1969 budget, which sought to tax the foreign earnings of entertainers. In any event, MPs aged over 50 of whatever party tended to take a sterner line. The aptly named Conservative Tom Iremonger bemoaned in 1969 that 'for anything to be acceptable just now, it has to be said by Marx or Marcuse, or by Lenin or Lennon'. Whilst Harold Wilson was mostly positive – reopening the Cavern Club in 1966 and awarding the band MBEs (ostensibly for services to the export trade) – the political establishment was generally wary.[89]

A key part of this wariness was drugs. Renée Short, newly elected as an MP in Wolverhampton and latterly, like Alice, an NEC member, spoke of the publicly acknowledged statistics regarding drug addiction as 'only the tip of the iceberg'. 1960s youth, she argued, had peculiarly bad role models:

> There are thousands of young people, from the ages of 11 and 12 upwards, on drugs of all kinds—amphetamines, barbiturates and hard drugs, pills, purple hearts, black bombers, pot, heroin, cocaine, and LSD. It is regarded as the 'in' thing in many of the circles which young people frequent. Unfortunately many 'pop' stars are addicted to drugs, and some of the television programmes which we have seen recently, particularly the one on LSD, have not helped at all those who are trying to combat this dreadful menace.[90]

To Alice, as to Renée Short, television was a potentially morally corrupting influence. After an outbreak of violence at Dartmoor Prison in 1961 (in which two prison officers were attacked and one inmate died), Alice described the showing of the film *The Blue Lamp* – which depicted a policeman being killed – as 'provocative' and 'in bad taste'.[91]

Similarly, prior to ITV hitting the air, Alice told the Commons that 'the worst effects of allowing children's programmes to go into the hands of commercial interests would be that commercial television would become the greatest nuisance that parents of children under 16 had ever known'.[92] Though a reformer at the Home Office, she never completely shed her innate social conservatism.

There was a genuine debate about the scale of the problem and the appropriate policy response. In 1958 Conservative Home Secretary Rab Butler had commissioned the neurologist Sir Russell Brain to analyse the issues surrounding drug addiction then perceived to be growing. Brain's Committee considered whether drugs should be considered habit-forming, whether there was a medical *raison d'être* to implement new bespoke treatment facilities to deal with addiction, and how the government should approach the question. The first Brain Report, published in 1961, reached the same conclusions as the previous Rolleston Committee of 1926 – the incidence of addiction to dangerous drugs was minor in the UK. It noted that 'figures provided by the Home Office which might suggest an extension of addiction in Great Britain reflect, we think, an intensified activity for its detection and recognition over the post war period'. As such, 'because the overall problem is so small it is doubtful whether there is scope for establishing specialised institutions in Great Britain exclusively for the treatment of drug addiction'.

All seemed to be well. Yet three years later, in July 1964 (at the tail end of the Douglas-Home Conservative administration), Brain's Committee was reconvened. Given a significant rise in the number of addicts to 'dangerous drugs' – heroin and cocaine – and the shifting demographics of those using them (in 1959 only 11 per cent of heroin users were under 35, by 1964 the equivalent figure was 40 per cent), Brain and his committee set out to discover whether any reform was needed. Reiterating the view that 'the addict should be regarded as a sick person, he should be treated as such and not as a criminal, provided that he does not resort to criminal acts', the position on the creation of drug-treatment facilities had shifted dramatically: levels of usage had 'changed to such an extent that we consider that such centres should be set up as soon as possible, at least in the London area'.[93]

Whilst estimates in the mid-1960s that by 1972 there would be 11,000 heroin addicts in Britain were often 'treat[ed] with reserve' by even Conservative members (until the mid-1970s the figure of addicts known by the Home Office was under 2,000, but with a rapid increase occurring in the 1980s), that is not to say there was no issue.[94] 'The trend in heroin addiction is … serious', noted Alice in January 1967, 'the Home Office knew of 62 heroin addicts in 1958, of 132 in 1961; of 342 in 1964, and of 521 in 1965.'[95] By 1968 there were approaching 3,000 addicts.[96] This worrying pattern of increase was a source of concern to Alice as a minister and as an MP.

Part of the concern was that, while at the margins – or completely out – of society, this group was having a negative impact on others. In 1960 Alice had asked the then Home Secretary, Rab Butler, what steps he proposed 'to deal with the gang warfare and protection rackets which exist in London'. After Butler's response, Bacon commented that 'it is not now what might be called the underworld which is being affected by this gang warfare but ordinary people in London'.[97] As a minister she would later take action to curb the supplies of such destructive substances altogether.

In July 1967 Alice spoke in the Commons defending what would become the Dangerous Drugs Act. This legislation made good on the recommendations of the Second Brain Report which had noted that 'the major source of supply [of heroin] has been the activity of a very few doctors who have prescribed excessively for addicts'. The new Act tightened up prescription laws for the use of small quantities of heroin and cocaine to treat addiction, and required doctors to notify the Home Office of any addicted patients. Alice spoke in the Commons of the need for such action, but also for the need of the specific drug-treatment facilities the second Brain Report had backed:

> We need them because the Brain Committee laid stress in both its Reports on the view that institutional treatment offered the only satisfactory hope of cure and because the staffing and other facilities at treatment centres should offer a better assurance both of more accurate prescribing and more comprehensive treatment.[98]

Indeed, the only major facet of the Brain Report not taken on by the government was the recommendation to provide powers to detain addicts who broke off from voluntary treatment. Alice's view was that curbing the supply of dangerous drugs, rather than punishing those addicted to them, was generally the better course.

But she also firmly believed in taking action against the less dangerous, gateway drugs. Alice cited America as evidence of the horror to come:

'coffee bars, jazz clubs, bowling alleys' became the sites where 'young people can come into contact with those who have supplies to get rid of'.[99] On 24 July 1967 an advertisement was placed in *The Times* (signatories including the rainbow coalition of Paul McCartney, John Lennon, David Dimbleby, Brian Walden MP, the controversial psychiatrist R. D. Laing, and Francis Crick) calling for the legalisation of marijuana. The debate in the Commons that followed is worth repeating at some length – illustrating as it does the down-to-earth nature of Alice's rhetoric, the puritanical nature of Conservative Party discourse, and the broad, overarching fear concerning societal breakdown:

Alice Bacon: I believe that at present we are in danger in this country—I am not speaking only of cannabis but also of some other drugs which have been mentioned, particularly L.S.D.—of some people misleading young people by not only taking drugs themselves, but trying to influence the minds of young people and trying to encourage them to take drugs. I do not often read the magazine the Queen, but I was at the hairdresser's yesterday. [HON. MEMBERS: 'Hear, hear'.] This magazine was passed to me to while away the time when I was under the hair drier. There is a very long article in it called 'The Love Generation' with statements by various people who are pop singers and managers of pop groups. I was horrified at some of the things I read in it. For instance, Paul McCartney says among other things: God is in everything. God is in the space between us. God is in that table in front of you. God is everything and everywhere and everyone. It just happens that I realised all this through acid (L.S.D.), but it could have been through anything. It really does not matter how I made it ... The final result is all that counts.

Paul Channon (Conservative) Is the right hon. Lady quoting prominent people in favour of drug taking? It is terribly dangerous to quote people like that when we are against drug taking.

Tom Driberg (Labour): He is a very good man.

Alice Bacon: I am illustrating the argument. The hon. Member raised this question this morning and, running through his speech, I thought I detected a sort of feeling that we should relax on cannabis. Maybe I am wrong, but if he does not want any publicity to be given at all, this debate should not have taken place this morning.

The manager of the Beatles said in this article that there is a new mood in the country and this new mood has originated from hallucinatory drugs and I am wholeheartedly on its side. The only person with any sense at all quoted in the article seems to be a little pop singer called Lulu, who said: 'People talk about this love—love—love thing as if you had to be on drugs before you can be part of it. In fact, love is far older than pot and goes right back to Jesus. I'm a believer'. This may sound amusing to hon. Members, but young people take quite seriously what pop stars say. What sort of society will we create if everyone wants to escape from reality?[100]

This speech came only weeks before Alice's move to the Department for Education. The *Guardian* declared itself wryly amused:

Down among the nuts and bolts of the reshuffle there linger a few macabre delights. Alice Bacon's translation from Home Office to Education for instance. It's been an open Westminster secret (and joke) that Roy Jenkins and Alice didn't get on – a joke that reached its punchline a few weeks ago when Alice delivered a long homily on the evils of Beatle drug taking and the shining common sense example of 'little Lulu'. Roy ever conscious of his swinging image, wasn't amused. Alice has gone. But now she's responsible for universities, technical colleges, the whole shaggy-haired gamut. Hundreds more Bacon lectures to the young beckon.[101]

Whilst the Leeds University student newspaper found undergraduates almost unanimous in their support for McCartney, Jack Straw – on this occasion – sided with Bacon: 'it has not been conclusively proved that the taking of cannabis is not harmful … [Legalisation] would lead to a huge increase in consumption, and be a betrayal of the futures of many young people.'[102] Decades later, he recalls an article he wrote on the subject as 'pompous and obtuse', yet this was, broadly speaking, Alice's line too. Marijuana was the line in the sand: the gateway drug to heroin, and thereby to social decline. On this, albeit in a heavy-handed manner, Alice was determined to take a stand. After the Wootton Report of January 1969 recommended, in essence, the decriminalisation of possessing a small amount of cannabis, the passage of the Misuse of Drugs Act in 1971 would make that same substance a 'Class B' drug, in effect reducing the level of punishment for casual users with no intention to supply since most would be tried by a Magistrates Court (with a maximum of three months sentence open for possession, and six for possession with intent to supply). By this stage Alice was out of the Home Office.

Ideologically, the sixties had involved victories for both the Beatles and the Bacons of this world. What few perhaps realised was that the minister and her pop culture nemesis had actually met. Alice was helping organise a communications and media training session on party election broadcasts. She waited outside a radio studio with Roy Hattersley (then Under Secretary of State for Employment) when John Lennon, Paul McCartney, Ringo Starr and George Harrison came out. Alice accosted Lennon by saying he 'ought to be more like that little Lulu rather than promoting the drug culture'. Lennon, probably not expecting such a rebuke, asked Alice who she was. Once told, he remarked that 'I don't know you from Adam'.[103] By the late 1960s few engaged in the politics of drugs could have said that.

Concluding Thoughts

Alice was responsible for the Home Affairs brief for almost eight years – a long break from her passion, education. Yet she accomplished much during this break. For all the veiled criticism that she was an administrator and not an innovator, this was precisely what was required after 1964. A wafer-thin majority in the Commons required careful management by not only party whips, but by those framing policy. Even with a more substantial majority in 1966 bills still needed to be piloted through at the right time and pace, as Leo Abse found when trying to change the laws on homosexuality and abortion at the same time.

When Alice left the Home Office Britain's social landscape had been transformed in three years. The death penalty off the statute book. Abortion legalised. Homosexuality no longer a crime. The race relations bill about to come in to law. Alice had helped Soskice, Jenkins and Callaghan steer them all through Parliament – working with backbenchers to achieve lasting change where government could not, or would not, lead.

As historian Andrew Holden notes, even as the shine came off the 1964–70 Wilson governments – with increasing criticism from the left on support for the Americans in Vietnam and criticism from the right on economic policy and the devaluation of the pound in 1967 – there was an acceptance, certainly in retrospect, that Labour's social reforms had been significant and transformational.[104] With Jenkins as the determined and enthusiastic minister, backbenchers like Abse, Steel and Silverman, along with parliamentary practitioners, often behind the scenes, such as Alice Bacon, reform came. In social policy it was probably the biggest set of reforms ever legislated for in the Houses of Parliament.[105]

Change in her ministerial portfolio was, however, by 1967, afoot. As Quintin Hogg, the many-time Tory minister noted in early 1968, there was something of a continuity for Alice, however:

> As it is St. Valentine's Day, I pause in the explosion of raspberries which I propose to blow across the Floor of the House to say how pleasant it is to be sitting once more opposite the right hon. Member for Leeds, South-East (Miss Bacon). She and I have a tolerable working relationship in home affairs. It is a pleasant surprise to find that we are now moving ahead to the next logical phase, which is to discuss the education of children.[106]

The education of the nation's children was about to undergo a revolution that even Mrs Thatcher could not overturn – and Alice was to realise one of her long-cherished goals: the rolling out of comprehensive education.

∞ 5 ∞

EDUCATION REFORMER
(1967–70)

The Impact of Crosland

Alice's views on comprehensive education were well known even before
she was an MP. And it was an area where Alice's ideological, rather than
practical, politics showed itself. Alice said in Parliament in 1954 that
'my belief in the comprehensive school is based on educational grounds,
and I believe that the minister's opposition is nothing but party political
prejudice against giving all children a fair chance'.[1] Yet when Alice made
this statement, and at the time future Education Secretary Tony Crosland
was beginning his famous book on *The Future of Socialism*, there were
'only some 14 comprehensive schools as yet in being' and thus 'there is
naturally no conclusive evidence [as to their efficacy]'.[2] Though Crosland
argued that 'there is no sign of any levelling-down of standards', the key
argument against comprehensive education were that bright children
would see their horizons lowered by the comprehensive structure. The
battle to achieve comprehensive education was what Alice – and
Crosland – fervently believed in, a belief in equality essentially. It was
not just an 'evidence-based' approach driving the march to abolish the
secondary modern/grammar model and put the comprehensive in their
place. This was an argument of the heart as well as the head.

Tony Crosland is remembered for many reasons. His book, *The Future
of Socialism*, plotted a course for the Labour right that has by and large
held: that the market should be centre stage in any Labour administration,
but it should be regulated to curb its excesses. Thus did Gordon Brown
remark that 'no post-war Labour writer has had such an impact on Labour

thinking as Anthony Crosland'.[3] *The Future of Socialism*, completed after Crosland had lost his parliamentary seat in 1955, with an increased Conservative majority in Parliament, made its author 'an instant hero on the [Labour] Right and a hate figure on the left', according to Richard Crossman, Labour MP and diarist.[4] Its principal message was encapsulated in its concluding sentence: 'we do not want to enter an age of abundance, only to find that we have lost the values which must teach us how to enjoy it'.[5] Unlike the Bevanites, who believed Gaitskell and his acolytes were plotting 'to abolish socialism and lead the people to a hell of TV sets and home ownership', Crosland saw such trends as, barring the necessary correctives a Labour government would provide, a good thing.[6] Alice, as illustrated by her earlier questioning of the rationing and austerity of the 1940s, similarly embraced 1950s consumerism and the benefits it brought in her usual practical manner:

> One of the good things in the post-war years has been the fact that ordinary working women have been able to take advantage of electrical appliances which were once considered to be luxuries. Only those who live among working people know the difference which it makes on washing days when the woman of the house can use an electric washing machine instead of having to do a big weekly wash in the old-fashioned way.[7]

If Bevan believed a Labour government should be doctrinaire socialist or it would be nothing, Bacon and Crosland placed greater stock in engaging with the changing realities of 1950s and 1960s Britain. The creation and manufacture of the washing machine might have helped big businesses to grow wealthier, but it also allowed working-class women a greater degree of comfort in their lives. There were merits to both sides in this debate, but the process of arguing the point led, as Andrew Marr put it, 'after due thought and consideration, [Labour] to tear itself into small pieces'.[8]

Despite such a broad influence over Labour thought in the 1950s and 1960s it is an off-the-cuff remark by Crosland to his wife Susan that arguably has constituted his political epitaph – 'If it's the last thing I do, I am going to destroy every fucking grammar school in England. And Wales. And Northern Ireland.'[9] If Alice ever made similarly coarse remarks, they are not on the record. Yet she was of the Croslandite mindset on this issue – in fact her views pre-date Crosland's. Whilst the two would never serve together in the Department of Education and Science (Crosland became President of the Board of Trade in the same reshuffle that brought Alice into the Department of Education and Science on 29 August 1967), Crosland was a clear intellectual fellow traveller.

For all their similarity, however, the Croslandite theorists at the top of the party have taken some of the credit that should go to junior ministers such as Alice Bacon. Alice had taught in an interwar secondary modern, had fought to get comprehensive education to the top of Labour's offer to the electorate in the 1950s, and would be the minister – after some sidelining of Shirley Williams, which we will get to – who would ultimately manage much of the battle that would determine the success or failure of the comprehensive drive. We begin the comprehensive story with its origins in the 1940s.

The Drive towards Comprehensive Education

The march towards comprehensive education was long and full of pitfalls. In the 1940s there was no accepted definition of what a 'comprehensive' school would mean except for teaching children of all abilities. A 1947 circular from the Ministry of Education stressed that such schools needed to be large enough (over 1,500 pupils) to teach the full range of subjects and maintain viable sixth forms. Given that the final say over the education system lay with the local authority, there was inevitably a lack of uniformity across the country. The West Riding of Yorkshire, for example, pursued what became known as the 'Thorne scheme' – whereby, to address the harsh reality of a life-altering exam at 11, grammar school places were allocated to the ablest pupils based on the recommendations of primary school teachers. In Yorkshire there was something of a cross-party consensus – in the West Riding some Conservatives favoured a fully comprehensive system as early as the 1940s, and two new comprehensive schools opened in the local authority area in the early 1950s. But divisions across the country remained – including in the Labour Party.

In 1942 Labour's NEC, which included Alice who had been elected the previous year, passed a resolution compelling the wartime coalition government to introduce comprehensive schools for *all* children – thus, in essence, calling for the abolition of private schools, as well as grammar schools and secondary moderns. In 1943 the NALT – still including Alice Bacon in its ranks, if not then its leadership – sent a letter to all Labour MPs criticising Education Secretary Rab Butler's White Paper commitment to a tripartite system of post-war education to 15

– secondary modern, grammar, and technical school. In April 1945, the Yorkshire Regional Council of the Labour Party expressed its concerns with the newly passed Education Act. Although broadly acknowledging it was a step forward, Alice's local Regional Council noted that the legislation still heavily depended on a progressive council making good on the powers it had been conferred, and also that nominal equality of status was no guarantee of equality of opportunity:

> A reactionary Local Authority could nullify many of the concessions obtained [in the Act] ... The Act provides for three types of school, Grammar, Technical and Modern Schools, and it is intended that these shall be on the same social scale. There is a danger that the grammar schools will be regarded as having a higher social status than the other two and this must be guarded against.[10]

But party policy would not be mandated from the bottom up. Caroline Benn writes of a shift in the sources informing Labour's educational policy after 1945 – from grass-roots activists such as the NALT, to Fabian 'elitist and meritocratic thought'. This was important because it prevented a clear party line being taken on the comprehensive until the early 1950s – and, given Labour would be out of office by then, no government action was taken on the issue until 1964.

By the late 1950s, there was relative cross-party consensus that Butler's tripartite system needed reform. The post-war baby boom had created a pressure on the grammar system that was beginning to worry contemporary Tories. Edward Boyle, a Conservative junior minister at the Ministry of Education, commented that 'the proportion of Tory voters in the electorate is more than double the proportion of grammar school places, and over ten times the proportion of those who can afford to educate their children privately in a good fee-paying school'. Such tactical concern in part led mainstream Conservative opinion against the 11-plus by the late 1950s and early 1960s. Indeed about 90 of 162 LEAs had completed or were beginning a reorganisation of their local education system to either move the age at which pupils were selected for the grammar or secondary modern to a later point in the child's development, or build in greater possibility of transfer should the 11-plus to be retained. There was an economic argument here too: by the 1960s Britain was a more high-skill and service-based economy than 20 years earlier, and it was felt that the secondary modern was not delivering the tools to enable businesses to hire people with the skills needed to create the growth of the future or to compete internationally. A 1964 Fabian pamphlet, *New Patterns for Primary Schools*, recommended the West Riding model of transfer at 13 to be standardised across the country.[11]

Despite such political to-ing and fro-ing for over a decade, when things began to move towards comprehensivisation, they moved quickly. According to the academic Nirmala Rao this was for three reasons. First, the election of a Labour government meant that a desire for reform could be seized upon by those, such as Alice, who fervently believed in the comprehensive system. That studies in the 1950s were increasingly showing that the 11-plus exam was skewed towards benefiting middle-class children lent great weight to the reformers' arguments. Second, techno-logical and industrial changes opened up a policy space that was also consistent with the 'White Heat' Wilsonian agenda. There was, in other words, a positive goal to complement the slightly negative goal of ridding Britain of the worst of the secondary moderns. Lastly, an upsurge in educa-tional ambition had occurred amongst lower-middle and working-class parents. In an era of increasing equality, parents were demanding a better education than the secondary moderns could provide for their children. Reform, in short, was in the offing and the new Education Secretary, Anthony Crosland, set to work relatively swiftly in January 1965.[12]

A few months after Crosland's appointment as Education Secretary he started encouraging local authorities to establish comprehensives in their areas by offering financial assistance to build new schools and classrooms – if, and only if, they moved towards ending the 11-plus. The deal was set out in Circular 10/65, released by the DES in July 1965. It was a piece of tactical mastery, broadly reflecting the twin issues Alice Bacon had been campaigning on for the previous 20 years: overcrowded lessons taking place in dilapidated buildings, and the drive for comprehensive education to end the spectre of a life-defining exam at the age of 11. Yet it also attempted to overcome an at least nominal roadblock – the fact that local authorities, not the Department, would have the final say on changes. To accomplish all of this, Crosland 'request[ed] that local authorities ... prepare and submit to him plans for reorganising secondary education in their areas on comprehensive lines'.[13] Alice, as one would suspect, voted with the government on this measure.[14] The key point, however, was that, in an increasingly overcrowded school system, Crosland promised only those local authorities moving towards comprehensive education access to funds for new buildings. Councils either toed the line, or would face the financial – and electoral – consequences. This did not initially affect the grammar schools directly, as much as secondary moderns (their ability to pick and choose pupils keeping numbers, and therefore the need for new buildings, down); but nonetheless the number of grammar schools did fall from 1,285 to 1,155 in the three years after Crosland took office.[15]

Two years after Circular 10/65 was issued, in late August 1967, Alice was appointed Minister of State at the Department of Education and Science (DES). The October 1967 Party Conference in Scarborough plunged Alice straight into the battlefield. Rejecting a resolution to compel local authorities to introduce comprehensive education (by 500,000 votes), a measure was later passed calling upon the government to use all their power, including legislation, to introduce comprehensive education. This went beyond Crosland's nudge for authorities to establish comprehensives by withholding building subsidies to nonconformists and instead called for a legislative commitment to make the comprehensive mandatory. Alice told conference that it was 'absolutely unthinkable' that there should be permanent division under which children were selected at the age of 11. 'The Government could not tolerate such a situation', she thundered. 'If local authorities refuse to comply with requests to change to a non-selective system or delay unreasonably, I give you my pledge that the Government will not hesitate to legislate.'[16]

Comprehensive education was clearly Alice's passion and now at the DES she had a chance to do something about it. And unlike other Labour ministers, Alice had been educated at a state school and was from a working-class background. The three Labour Education Secretaries under Wilson's leadership up until Alice's appointment to the Department for Education had all been privately educated: Michael Stewart (Christ's Hospital School), Tony Crosland (Highgate School) and Patrick Gordon Walker (Wellington College). Alice's passion for educational reform came from her experience growing up in Normanton and then as a school teacher there.

Alice's drive for comprehensive education and her determination to reform the system is illustrated by some internal battles at the DES. Shirley Williams remembers the 1967 reshuffle when Patrick Gordon Walker, Alice's former boss whilst shadowing Rab Butler at the Home Office, became Education Secretary and Alice a Minister of State at the Department. Alice soon discovered that Shirley was to be appointed to oversee schools. Whilst Shirley was on holiday, Alice asked for her files to be moved so that she would be attached to comprehensive education policy, and Shirley be put in charge of Higher Education and Science on the grounds that Shirley had been a lecturer. Shirley was horrified when she found out, but Alice had succeeded in getting her way.[17]

Alice was not the only former teacher at the Department – indeed Harold Wilson's only mention of her in his *Personal Record* of the 1964–70 governments was to make this very point:

> Joan Lestor's appointment (Autumn 1969) meant that all the minis-
> terial appointments at Education were filled by former teachers: former
> headmaster Ted Short as Secretary of State, Oxford don and Lancaster
> lecturer Gerry Fowler as Minister of State for Higher Education, Alice
> Bacon and Jennie Lee, former secondary school teachers, and Joan Lestor,
> a nursery school teacher who continued to run her own class until shortly
> before becoming a minister.[18]

While Crosland's reforms had a big and lasting impact on state education, private or public schools were left largely untouched during his tenure. The Croslandite approach was that the public school would wither away (or gradually reform), rather than be eradicated in one fell swoop.[19] When asked whether a private system could exist in tandem with the comprehensives, Alice remarked that 'personally I would answer no' because for a school to be properly comprehensive you need the range of children from across the income and ability scale.[20] However, as with her earlier battles with Gaitskell on the issue in the early 1950s, she knew that making the state sector deliver for the majority of children within it had to be the priority. Concentrating on a comprehensive system was far more likely to have more 'comprehensive' outcomes. Certainly there were limits to what could be achieved in moving towards a totally comprehensive system in the short term, but, where she could, Alice was determined to get around them. It was best to implement workable reform that would have impact across the board rather than spend political capital on issues at the fringes. Despite her dislike for private schools, government for Alice was about delivery for working-class families.

Towards a Comprehensive Consensus

For Alice, becoming a minister at the DES meant fulfilling some of her dreams. In many ways reform was already underway by the time Circular 10/65 was issued, but the circular gave local authorities clear and important incentives to act. A 1947 survey of LEAs showed that over half were thinking of introducing at least one non-selective secondary school.[21] In rural areas, including in Yorkshire, even Conservatives generally favoured a fully comprehensive system. By 1962, 90 of the 146 LEAs had made tentative moves towards the comprehensive model.[22] What Crosland, and subsequently Short and Bacon, did, however, was to speed up the process and encourage some of the wavering LEAs to act. For example, some progressive LEAs, such as Leicestershire and the West Riding, which wanted to move faster, were constrained by demography and the suitability of buildings. But after Circular 10/65, central government was simply able to increase the school building programme for those LEAs which fell into line.[23] Alice was also able to provide direct support and encouragement. With prior experience of teaching and her ear still pressed to the grass roots, the new Education minister was an excellent conduit for a change in policy emphasis which, as the historian David Crook notes, was likely to rely on '"bottom up" rather than "top down" initiative'.[24] By 1969 only 20 of the 146 LEAs in England and Wales had failed to respond positively to the circular (most were Tory-led) – and over 1,200 comprehensive schools were now in existence.[25] As Alice noted in 1976, at local government level there was relative bi-partisan acceptance that the push towards comprehensive education was a good thing. As Alice reflected upon in the House of Lords in 1976:

> At local level—with a few exceptions—many Conservative and independent local authorities were as keen on getting their schemes of comprehensive education through as were Labour local authorities. From 1967 to 1970 I was in charge of the comprehensive scheme part of the Department of Education and I know that pressure was coming from local authorities for us to approve the schemes of comprehensive education and that that pressure was coming not only from Labour authorities but also from Conservative and independent authorities. Indeed, some of the best and most successful comprehensive schools in the country are down in the West Country in Devon and Cornwall.[26]

Yet despite such bi-partisanship, these school reforms were not without controversy. The historian Nirmala Rao argues that the comprehensive system simply replaced an imperfect educational structure where a test determined fates at age 11, with one where, due to the catchment area model of the new comprehensive, geography determined your fate instead. Geographically concentrated comprehensives, to Rao, saw a reduction in social mixing (clever children from 'rougher' areas being lumped in with less academically minded pupils) and encouraged parents to move to better catchment areas, or – if affordable – to send their children to private schools. Crosland saw the possibility of this – scribbling in one note that authorities 'must try to draw catchment areas' to minimise the risk of a postcode lottery. Some promising children, no doubt, were victims of this – with the neighbourhood comprehensive replacing any chance of attending a nearby grammar in a different part of town.

On the right, the Conservative press and some Conservative MPs hammered the Labour Party over the issue of choice. Local Conservatives in Wilson's third Education Secretary, Patrick Gordon Walker's, Leyton constituency declared that 'in this the citadel of freedom, we are facing the little dictators with their wanton disregard for the individual. Socialism does not only mean nationalisation but dictatorship and loss of freedom.'[27] Given their local MP was simply moving with trends to some degree encouraged even by the previous Conservative Education Secretary Edward Boyle, this was pretty strong stuff. A big part of the uproar was caused across the North Circular from Leyton in nearby Enfield, where Iain Macleod, prominent Tory (and then Shadow Chancellor) was the Member of Parliament. In Enfield the local grammar school wished to go comprehensive – but the local authority was taken to court by local ratepayers and parents who believed that the consultation process had not been sufficiently long. The parents' QC was a highly politicised choice – the recently deposed Conservative MP and future Deputy Prime Minister, Geoffrey Howe. Whilst the *Daily Express* foamed about choice, and Howe was a skilled barrister, the anti-comprehensive case was fundamentally undermined by the fact that of the 177 pupils affected by the proposed change, only eight had expressed a preference as to their desired school.[28] Iain Macleod complained that 'Mr Gordon Walker has a closed mind on this issue … He regards the articles of government in the same way as he regards the courts of this country – merely as obstructions to his socialist will.'[29] In the event, Gordon Walker conceded to the introduction of a statutory consultation period, but nothing else. The drive for comprehensives rolled on.

Dealing with cases such as these was a large part of Alice's job, and she was lobbied from both sides of the comprehensive debate. Lord Bertram Bowden was one Labour parliamentarian and former minister who lobbied

Alice. Bowden, a scientist, had been ennobled by Harold Wilson in 1964 to become a Minister for Science and Education and drive forward the 'White Heat' of the technological revolution. Less than a year later, with progress not being made as quickly as planned, Bowden was out of office, leaving him free to write to Alice on comprehensives. Having heard her speak at a conference in Leeds in the autumn of 1967, he wrote to highlight a conversation he had had with a grammar schoolmaster from Sidcup (near Chislehurst) who was anxious about the coming of the comprehensive. In response, Alice laid out the plans for the new system and how it would 'still produce sufficient academic sixth formers to help Chislehurst' turn out well-educated boys and girls. Bowden was still not satisfied and locally there were problems.[30] Chislehurst and Sidcup School was a high-performing grammar whose headmaster resigned in protest at the proposals for comprehensive schools (the headmaster noted that it would be 'over my dead body that the best grammar schools would be abolished'). In the end, sweeping Conservative gains in the local elections of 1968 saw Labour lose control of the London Borough of Bexley anyway and plans for comprehensive schools in the borough were shelved.

All this showed the great challenge facing reformers like Alice – even on the left there was disagreement as to the utility of the comprehensive, and, should such debates be won, the comprehensive system still needed to be got through sometimes obstructive local authorities. The Tory rhetorical argument was about 'choice', but the practical issue was that the way Crosland was trying to drive the comprehensive system through – the withdrawal of subsidy for new school buildings – mattered less in more affluent (and largely Conservative) councils where local taxes were not required for social service budgets to a degree seen in many Labour authorities. There were funds left over, in other words, to ride out the Labour government and await the coming of a Heath administration.

But there was also criticism at the time from the left who did not think that Edward Short and Alice Bacon were going far enough in forcing through change. At the Labour Party Conference in 1968 Alice had promised legislation if comprehensive reform was being blocked by local authorities. But Caroline Benn, writing in *Tribune* ahead of the 1969 Labour Party Conference, accused local authorities (predominantly Conservative, but not all so) of 'subtly' blocking reform by, for example, not setting out a date for changes, not reorganising schooling in the whole of the authority area or through introducing different selection criteria. Benn urged the party to act, and introduce 'strong and effective' legislation, for she argued 'it is one thing to nominally end the 11-plus, quite another to establish a comprehensive system'. Benn recommended an 'end-date' for reform along comprehensive lines of 1980, and a withdrawal of funding for councils who would not cooperate.

On 3 October 1969 the comprehensive issue once again made the floor of conference. Composite Resolution 37, moved by the Post Office Engineering Union and seconded by Cambridgeshire CLP, called upon the Labour Party to deliver 'an education system ... less autocratic in structure and more comprehensive by nature'. Within this the motion compelled 'the Labour Government [to] enact immediate legislation to implement the principle of comprehensive education'. The mover of the motion, Brian Stanley of the Post Office Engineering Union, noted that 'the move towards comprehensive education has begun, but it is being delayed by reactionary authorities in various parts of the country'. This was met with applause from the hall, as was his comment that 'we cannot allow these inequalities to go on developing and the new Act must prohibit selection for secondary education in all areas'.[31]

It was Alice's job to respond on behalf of the NEC, and also, essentially, the government. She maintained that a broad-based Education Bill which would have settled the comprehensive issue had been delayed by wider local government reorganisations. However, she told the delegates in 1969 that this could no longer block progress. Quite apart from a wider Education Bill, she was pleased to promise that 'in the next session of parliament, we shall introduce a short Bill dealing with this one specific subject [of the comprehensive]'. The intention of this bill would 'make selection illegal' and continue the expansion of comprehensive schools seen under the Wilson government – from 262 such schools in 1965 to 900 by 1969. Composite Resolution 37 was passed unanimously.[32]

While Alice herself would have liked to go further and faster, and move education up the political calculus, as a minister she had to recognise differences and the limitations as well as the benefits of forcing change. That she had helped shift public opinion and, just as crucially, convince sceptical people within the Labour Party can be gleaned from the manifesto the party would put before the electorate in 1970. The progress of the comprehensive, that document argued, 'must not be checked; it must go forward'. If elected, 'we shall legislate to require the minority of Tory education authorities who have so far resisted change to abandon eleven plus selection in England and Wales'. Alice had helped move the debate virtually full circle.

Alice could be proud of her record as an Education minister. The net effect of the Wilson governments was a marked rise in educational standards. In 1962 15 per cent of students were in full-time education aged 16, and 7 per cent aged 19. By 1970 these two figures had risen to 20 per cent and 14 per cent respectively. Part of this was down to the increasing aspirations of working-class families, in part engendered by moves towards comprehensive education, though the rise in those undergoing teacher training, another priority of the Wilson government (from 55,000 in 1962/3 to 124,000 by 1970/1), also helped.[33] From 1970, acting under pressure from Alice's former associates in the NUT, teachers in maintained schools were required to undergo some form of professional training – something which aimed to level out the discrepancy whereby three-quarters of grammar school teachers had a degree, compared to only one in five teaching in a secondary modern.[34] The proportion of pupils educated under the comprehensive system increased from 10 per cent to 32 per cent during the Labour administrations. The tools for making this change happen had existed essentially since 1944 (and, as we have seen, some Conservatives such as Edward Boyle – later vice chancellor of the University of Leeds – had been advocates). But the process set in motion in 1965 made change happen.

Even Margaret Thatcher, as Education Secretary, who was determined to preserve the grammar, did not roll back the process set in train by Crosland. Though she issued Circular 10/70 which essentially reversed Crosland's edict, she turned down less than 10 per cent of the proposals for schools to go comprehensive during her tenure at the DES (326 out of 3612). The proportion of pupils attending such comprehensives thus rose again from the 32 per cent Alice Bacon had left behind in 1970 to 62 per cent by 1974.[35] Through the 1970s around 90 grammar schools closed each year as authority after authority moved to the comprehensive model. By 1982 nine in ten children across England and Wales were being educated at comprehensive schools. As with the welfare state and National Health Service established by the 1945–51 Labour governments, the Tory Party might have questioned the idea of comprehensive education before it came to pass, but could do little to stop the process once in motion. Consistently arguing for the end of the 11-plus and helping achieve the roll-out of comprehensives in the late 1960s was arguably Alice Bacon's greatest personal and political legacy and certainly the reform she was most proud to have been part of.

Dealing with the Cuts

The introduction and expansion of comprehensive education was the upside to Alice's tenure at the Department of Education and Science, but the late 1960s also bore witness to an economic contraction which placed severe strain on departmental ambitions. Such strain, at times, exposed divisions within the department. Facing cuts after the devaluation crisis, on 14 February 1968 the former Tory Education minister Edward Boyle begged to move that 'this House regrets that the education service should have been subjected to cuts which are educationally damaging, based on a wrong choice of priorities, and disproportionate in relation to the economy measures as a whole'. Boyle and Bacon actually got on rather well. Boyle wrote to Alice in July 1968 asking if she could confidentially look into schools in Eastbourne for the daughter of an acquaintance he had met at the American Embassy, the author Cyril Connolly, and she did so readily – offering advice on schools that were 'small but well accommodated', 'well directed by a good headmaster', and 'good modern premises with a comparatively new head'.[36] She was a diligent minister and not party political to the point of personal antipathy.

But in the debate of February that year Boyle had opened up a fissure in the Labour education team.

The debate progressed fairly predictably, and the vote divided on party lines, with Labour winning by 323 to 244. All Labour's big names in education policy – Bacon, Fowler, Lee, Lestor, Short and Williams – voted with the government, as one would suspect. Yet the latter name's appearance in Hansard is interesting. Shirley Williams had been due to travel up to Birmingham to open an education institute when she received a phone call from the Leader of the House, Richard Crossman, who recorded in his diary that:

[Shirley Williams] came in looking very disturbed but before she could begin a speech I said, 'you ought to be here for the big censure debate'. 'This debate has nothing to do with me', she said. 'I deal with universities'. Of course there is an impossible relationship between Shirley on the one hand and Gordon Walker and Alice Bacon on the other. I don't blame her for finding Patrick pretty miserable and Alice Bacon's voice unbearable but I do blame her for the kind of disloyalty which makes her absent herself during a vote of censure. She's trying to avoid responsibility for the education cut of which she doesn't approve.[37]

This was quite possibly in response to Alice's poaching of her comprehensive school remit the previous year. Yet it was also symptomatic of
Alice's steadfast loyalty to the Labour Party, typified by Alice's complete
disinterest, despite being on the right of the party, in joining Williams'
fledgling SDP in the early 1980s.

In the shorter term, cuts were coming thick and fast. In what became
known as the '20 July measures' Wilson opted in 1966 for a strategy of
a balance of payments surplus (which was indeed achieved by 1969).
Devaluation, despite, famously, not affecting the 'pound in your pocket'
was also long mooted, and finally arrived in 1967.[38] A letter from John
Silkin, government whip, to Labour MPs prior to a vote on spending
measures in January 1968 illustrated that this course was far from univer-
sally popular:

> Dear Colleague, I have always believed that the strength of the
> Parliamentary Labour Party depends upon the free expression of sincerely
> held opinions. In a very real way this gives to the Party a sense of purpose
> and of unity which no other system can guarantee. Such a system,
> however, demands the self-discipline implicit in the understanding that
> on a vote of confidence the Government must be able to depend on the
> support on each one of us. It is because the Government intends to put
> before the House what it regards as the fairest possible set of measures in
> the prevailing economic climate that the main division on Thursday will
> be on a vote of confidence.[39]

Labour MPs whispered against Wilson. Silkin wrote to the Prime Minister,
referencing one of Alice's close colleagues, urging a careful eye be kept on
the PLP:

> Charlie Pannell has put forward the intriguing idea that each member
> should be allowed 3 consciences a year. I do not advocate that. All I say
> is, watch it. Every dog is allowed one bite. But a different view is taken of
> a dog that bites all the time ... He may not get his license renewed when
> it falls due.[40]

On 22 January 1968 15 junior ministers met to discuss the situation
including Shirley Williams, Roy Hattersley, Eirene White and Tam
Dalyell. Tam Dalyell's papers at Churchill College contain scribbled notes
from the occasion, which while not fully highlighting who said what, give

a flavour of the passions at the gathering. Scribblings include 'if Barbara [Castle] resigned there would be a leadership battle', 'it was the PLP – vote to destroy credibility of the Govt', 'misunderstood in the country'.[41] In the end the government survived this confidence vote to fight an election in 1970 that it expected, incorrectly, to win.

At a meeting at Chequers prior to the initial round of cuts, Crosland had spoken of wanting a raft of new school buildings, and a wider programme to tackle poverty.[42] George Brown's National Plan of 1964 had been predicated on steady spending levels (and was negotiated with the CBI and unions on such an understanding). The trick for Alice was to try and push through some measure of this early spirit of reform and investment in the new circumstances – of cuts. These cuts were felt keenly in the Department for Education. In January 1968 the raising of the school leaving age to 16 was to be postponed once more (eventually occurring in September 1972 after Labour had left office). Given this had been a pressing issue since the Butler Act of 1944, this was a blow to the ambitions of education policy and progress. Similarly, spending cuts hit local authority budgets, and thus had a direct effect on education spending. On 16 October 1969, for example, the Cabinet discussed the spending estimates for 1971/2: £355 million was to be cut – with £60 million from Defence, and £34 million from the local authorities. Alice had been invited along to this meeting, and her Secretary of State, Edward Short, protested that this would mean fewer teachers. 'More than a quarter of Local Authority current expenditure', he protested, was on 'teachers' salaries'.[13] Previously in February 1968 Alice had declared that 'the last thing Local Authorities should do is cut the employment of teachers'.[44]

These cuts hit Alice particularly hard. To begin with, her former associates at the NALT (by the 1960s, the – SEA) and at the NUT were not shy about trying to exploit prior connections. In 1965, even when she was at the Home Office, the SEA had written to her asking to renew her vice presidency of the organisation.[45] This she accepted with the proviso that she would hardly have much time to concentrate on it. By 1969, according to the SEA records, Alice had ceased to pay her subscription to the body – but was still viewed as a friendly voice for teachers, with Labour trying to placate SEA concerns over school meals by invoking Alice Bacon's reputation as a parliamentary ally to the teaching profession.[46] Her commitment to the principle of good nutrition was, after all, long-standing, as she told the 1967 Party Conference:

> I remember when I first started teaching it was at a time when school meals were first being inaugurated and at that time school meals were being introduced because of the very severe malnutrition in our schools. I remember that my first job was at a mining town in Featherstone in the Yorkshire coal-fields, where the boys I taught were deemed by the school medical officer to be suffering, 73 per cent of them, from malnutrition.[47]

She was committed, she told conference, to backing the £80 million cost to subsidise school meals.

But, tough choices clearly needed to be made and, whether deliberate or not, it certainly did not harm Wilson to have a cadre of former teachers to sell them at the DES. Alice set out to achieve what she could subject to such constraints by prioritising children in poorer areas and of greater need. As she told the Labour Party Conference that year:

> You will have seen that the Government has decided to have an urban programme to provide assistance for areas facing acute social problems. We were asked at the Department of Education and Science what we thought were the priorities as far as our department was concerned, and we had no hesitation whatsoever in saying that our number one priority in this would be the establishment of some nursery schools and nursery classes.[48]

The money saved by postponing the school leaving age rise was largely invested elsewhere in the education budget. 'In recent years we have given high priority to building allocations for schools for handicapped children. Up to 1970/71 we have sanctioned buildings which will mean a further 21,000 places.' One hundred and fifty old schools – Alice's long-standing bug-bear from her speeches in the 1940s and 1950s – were also to be pulled down and replaced, to avoid the 'double deprivation of attending old schools and coming from deprived homes'.[49]

Labour also made significant strides in many areas of improving primary school education – including implementing many of the recommendations of the Plowden Report set up under the Tory Edward Boyle in 1963 and carried out by the educational reformer Bridget Plowden. These included headline targets such as reducing class sizes, raising standards in the most deprived areas, improving the provision of English language teaching for immigrant children and getting more male teachers into primary schools.

In the 1970 manifesto Labour was able to point to 'Britain ... now spending more on education than ever before. This has brought improvements in the quality of education – more teachers and better schools.' This document lauded the programme of expanding the comprehensives:

> our first priority has been to end the system under which 80 per cent of our nation's children were, at the age of eleven, largely denied the opportunity of a broad secondary education with the chance of higher education beyond ... In the past six years 129 of the 163 English and Welsh local education authorities have agreed plans for reorganising their secondary schools.

With 13 new schools a week being completed in the first five years of the Labour government – up from fewer than nine in the last five years of Tory rule – there was much to be proud of. New priorities, had Wilson retained office in 1970, included expanding nursery provision, reducing class sizes to 30 in all schools, introducing a new Education Bill to update the Butler Act of 1944 and 'bring parents and teachers into a closer partnership in the running of our schools', and legislation to impose the comprehensive model of schools on reluctant local authorities.[50]

For someone who never served in Cabinet, the achievements for which Alice could claim at least partial credit for were considerable. By the time Labour left office, comprehensive education had clearly been established as the political direction of travel. Alice had nursed this issue as a teacher in the 1930s, within the Labour Party from the early 1940s when it had few backers, in opposition in the 1950s, through to ministerial office in the 1960s. This was a long battle, and one which in many ways had driven her political career. Alice would continue to press the Heath government on its education policy from the Lords after her frontline political career ended. But given the fact that even Margaret Thatcher, who clearly didn't shy away from taking radical new courses, could not reverse the direction of travel Alice had helped establish seems to attest to the scale of her achievement. Alice retired from the House of Commons in 1970 bearing the scars of battles both within the Labour Party and against the Conservatives across the aisle, but she left frontline politics both undefeated in a general election and with the issue she had so long campaigned for moving decisively in her favour. It was testament to a career that had delivered much practical and real change ultimately for the people she went into politics to serve.

$\backsim$ 6 $\backsim$

FINAL YEARS (1970–93)

Baroness Bacon

Alice chose not to stand for re-election in 1970. Aged 60, with an aunt who needed a carer, and after a quarter of a century as an MP, Alice left frontline politics. Her retirement as an MP coincided with her standing down from Labour's National Executive Committee. Reflecting her contribution as an MP, minister and to the Labour Party, Alice was ennobled in Harold Wilson's dissolution honours list, alongside George Brown, Tony Greenwood, Jennie Lee and Eirene White.

The job of introducing Baroness Bacon of the City of Leeds and of Normanton in the West Riding of the County of York to the House of Lords fell to an old friend, Dora Gaitskell, wife of the former leader and the chair of the Leeds Women's section back in the 1950s. Denis Healey remembers her being greeted by the then Lord Chancellor, Lord Hailsham (previously Quintin Hogg, Alice's shadow at the Home Office and Department for Education) with the words 'Bacon meet Hogg'. With Stan Cohen replacing her as MP in Leeds South East, Cohen knew he had a hard act to follow, remarking to Tam Dalyell that he had 'broken the Leeds tradition of sending national figures to Westminster'.[1] He did, however, vote for Denis Healey in the 1976 leadership election that saw Callaghan victorious, which Alice would have approved of.

Alice was not entirely at home with the pomp and ceremony of the upper chamber. It was, according to Baroness Gould (another Labour activist from Leeds) a 'total culture shock to her'. There was no sense of politics, let alone Labour politics, especially with all the 'hereditaries' in there. To Frank Pullan's request that she sign a card with her full title, she replied that 'I am just Alice Bacon as I have always been'.[2]

Alice kept a close eye on education policy under the new Secretary of State for Education, Margaret Thatcher. Alice was particularly concerned about Thatcher's withdrawal of Crosland's 1965 circular and its replacement with guidance which *requested*, but did not compel, authorities to take action in establishing comprehensive schools. Alice told an approving Labour Party Conference in 1970 that this 'shows that Butler in 1944 was more progressive than Thatcher in 1970. She is yesterday's woman with yesterday's ideas.'[3] Alice also told conference that had they been re-elected, the party would have ensured that direct-grant schools should cease to exist from 1973–4. Independent schools, she also noted, would have been subject to special licence and allowed only where they fulfilled some need the state could not.

Alice's *Times* obituary in 1993 gave a generous account of her service in the Lords: 'she proved to be as industrious and diligent … as she was in the Commons and spoke on the subjects which dominated her life – education, domestic affairs, and her native Yorkshire.'[4] The *Independent* was a little more prosaic, highlighting the fact that she became 'more and more remote from politics. The Yorkshire lass did not seem to fit into the House of Lords. Her old chum Charlie Pannell … did not like it either. He died and she liked it even less.'[5] Alice's first address in the Lords, as she noted, occurred in the same building as her first House of Commons speech a quarter of a century earlier (the Commons having been bombed during the war with MPs temporarily relocating to the Lords).

From the red benches, in 1971, Alice gave a trenchant attack on Thatcher's policies at the Department of Education and Science. 'The clock has been set back several years' by 'sixteen months of reactionary policy', she said. Having played a part in extending new primary school places 'from just over 100,000 in 1963–4 to 230,000 by 1968–9', she deplored Thatcher saying that the 'money which she has saved on [withdrawing free school] milk has gone to the primary school building programme':

This is complete nonsense. It is completely misleading to give the impression that the money being spent on the improvement of primary schools is an extra expenditure on school building, because it quite clearly is not. The amount spent on major school building programmes, excluding the special allocations for the raising of the school-leaving age [is as follows]. It was £132 million in 1969–70; in 1971–72 including the primary improvements, it will be only £125 million; and in 1973–74 it will have gone up to only £140 million.[6]

This was not merely opposition for opposition's sake. When two former Conservative Education Secretaries, Edward Boyle and David Eccles, were in the Lords, Alice was prepared to offer some words of praise. 'They accepted some forms of comprehensive education, even if they were not prepared to go as fast as the Labour Party would go ... the difference seemed one of degree and timing.' Thatcher was simply a different case, however: 'there seemed to be a change in Conservative policy at national level ... now it seems not so much to be one of timing and degree, but opposition to the comprehensive system.'[7] She carried this attack into the pages of *The Labour Woman* when Thatcher repealed Crosland's Circular 10/65:

> Many local authorities, including Conservative ones complied with the circular, but we all know that in some areas this has been done against the objections of a few of the most reactionary Tories. By withdrawing this circular Mrs Thatcher has given encouragement to these reactionary elements who are already demanding the scrapping of plans already adopted. She has ranged herself with the reactionaries and backwoodsmen in her own party who have always been opposed to Comprehensive Schools. Had Edward Boyle been Secretary of State he would not have compelled local authorities to adopt comprehensive education but I do not believe he would have withdrawn a circular which gave encouragement to the system. Mrs Thatcher's action has certainly shown her anti-progressive attitude to education and the fight in localities will be all the harder in the coming months.[8]

Beyond education, Alice paid attention to her other previous ministerial brief. Recalling that between 1959 and 1964 'I had a lot to learn [on home affairs] as it was a sphere in which hitherto I had not taken a great deal of interest', Alice acknowledged that many of the problems she had discovered then were still realities – and indeed getting worse – in the early 1980s. 'There were too many people in prison who ought to have been treated outside. There was a rising crime rate among youth. What are the problems today? They are exactly the same, but much worse and much more serious.' Denouncing the borstal system for not knowing whether it should punish or rehabilitate, she urged more emphasis on the latter. Visiting an institution in the 1960s, she remembered meeting a 'cherub-like face[d]' youth smiling at her. To Alice's question as to why he was there, the boy replied 'breaking and entering'. 'I should', she continued, 'not be surprised if today he is doing his third or fourth term in prison.'[9]

Alice was concerned to break the cycle of deprivation and delinquency. In education this meant the comprehensive school where more working-class children would have the chance of a decent education. In terms of law and order, it meant dealing with offenders, but not in a manner which would likely lead to reoffending. Thus detention centres should 'relate in some way to the environment in which the young person will live on leaving the establishment or on completing his treatment'. And, ultimately, the best solutions would come before any crime had been committed. 'We must look at the child in his community and, at the first signs of any criminality, bring together parents, teachers, social workers, community police, and so on, and try to deal with the problem first of all in the locality.' Tory minister William Whitelaw's 'short, sharp shock' – trialled in West Yorkshire, a few miles from Alice's home – was but a series of slogans for Alice. The solution would only come, as ever, in policies that were practicable, moderate and affordable.

The Poulson Affair

One of the last episodes of Alice's Commons career was the gradual uncovering of what would become known as the Poulson Affair, a murky set of political and financial dealings that Alice pursued after she had left the House of Commons, and that bears some resemblance to the 'cash for questions' scandal of the 1990s.

In 1966 the former Colonial, and future Home, Secretary, Conservative MP Reginald Maudling had accepted (for a fee of £5,000) the chairmanship of Construction Promotion, an export company run by the businessman and architect John Poulson. Crucially, Poulson conducted his business through the extensive use of bribes and was, in the words of the QC at his later trial, 'hypocritical, self-righteous, and perhaps something of a megalomaniac'.[10] Leeds Crown Court would be told in 1974 that Poulson had given away more than half a million pounds (equivalent to over five and a half million today) in various holidays, suits, flowers and other items as sweeteners to ease the planning process for his various projects. Over 300 individuals (and 23 local authorities) were implicated in the scandal. Unfortunately one of these, Reginald Maudling MP, was in one of the highest positions in the land.

As Colonial Secretary in the early 1960s 'Reggie' Maudling had paved the way for Maltese independence, and the provision of £50 million worth of economic aid to help the fledgling country through the transition period after leaving British control. There was initially more or less consensus between Labour and the Tories on this, for both strategic and social justice reasons. However, this inflow of money to Malta meant, for Poulson, an opportunity. He therefore lobbied the Maltese government to allow his construction company to build a hospital on the island of Gozo. Although Poulson was not even on the list of potential architects for the Gozo project at first, a call from Maudling to the Maltese Minister of Public Works soon saw him awarded the contract.

Such direct intervention to secure what was British taxpayer money for a personal acquaintance was a problem for three reasons. First, the ties between Maudling and Poulson were fairly deep: Poulson secured Maudling's son a place on the board of one of his other companies despite his having no prior management experience (by April 1967 the son had been paid £1,000 in director fees). Second, Maudling had previously, more or less, sold his parliamentary time. On 2 February 1967 the normally mild-mannered Conservative had lambasted the government for even contemplating including Malta in its list of economies for overseas military expenditure. Over time, he helped move the Conservative Party away from a position where it backed Labour's proposals for a 50/50 split between grant and loan from the British government for the new Maltese State, to one where the Tories backed a 75/25 split in favour of a grant. Poulson's money had therefore helped shift Tory policy. And third, Poulson's ties piqued the interest of Alice Bacon.

In her last few months at the Home Office, Alice became suspicious about Poulson's activities in West Yorkshire. This is revealed in a set of notes from the journalist Alistair Hetherington, held at the London School of Economics' Archive. In July 1972, as Maudling resigned from office when the scandal began to break, Hetherington met Harold Wilson to discuss the matter. Despite the impropriety of his dealings, Wilson recognised that Maudling would be a loss to the Tories: 'he said that Maudling's sleepy manner was deceptive ... Reggie had a very quick mind.'[11]

Although a scandal engulfing of a Conservative Home Secretary was seemingly good news for the Labour Party, it was not altogether straight-forward. Poulson had ties to Labour-supporting regions too and had used T. Dan Smith (former Labour leader of Newcastle council) as his pivot into local government circles. Indeed Maudling's biographer Lewis Baston suggests that this is part of the reason that Labour did not pursue the issue of his dealings with Maudling with much vigour. Suspected of financial impropriety with regard to housing contracts in Wandsworth, it was eventually his dealings in Bradford – where there was a series of corrupt transactions, expenses fiddles and freeloading at the expense of municipal contractors at the City's Architects department – that brought the net closer around him. Maudling's involvement was almost exclusively limited to the Maltese episode but – according to Wilson – by 'late 1969 or early 1970' Alice was beginning to piece together the puzzle. This was largely because Alice was so diligent a local MP, and the fact that the impact of Poulson could be seen in the Yorkshire she knew so well.

Alice raised Maudling's involvement with Poulson in a meeting with the Prime Minister just before the 1970 general election. Hetherington recorded Wilson telling him that:

> her suspicion had been aroused among other things because buildings appeared on land previously zoned as country and close to where she had her own cottage (I think in the Leeds area). She thought that there had been some peculiar handling of changes in planning decisions.

Wilson asked for a memorandum on the subject, but did little on the issue partly, as Baston notes, for fear of exposing T. Dan Smith's involvement and also because, according to Wilson's then adviser Gerald Kaufman, giving such an issue to the press was not the 'done thing' at the time. Alice, 'a little reluctant to get involved' herself, had moved to the House of Lords by the time the case came out. She had been reticent to overly involve herself, according to Hetherington, 'partly because she herself was a Home Office minister'.[12]

But the prospect of a criminal investigation meant there was no lid that could be kept on the story. Maudling's involvement with a man under police investigation for corruption forced him to resign as Home Secretary in 1972 and Poulson was jailed in 1974. The main political legacy was to create a Register of Members' Interests.

Leeds and Other Interests

As the years went on Alice's speeches became fewer and far between, as the health of her aunt and herself deteriorated. Her last speech in the Lords was in 1986 and dealt with an issue of concern to those in West Yorkshire. An outbreak of salmonella in Stanley Royd Hospital – the new name for Menston, the institution Alice had highlighted in the House of Commons in the 1950s – had contributed to the death of 19 patients. Alice told the Lords:

> As I have lived the whole of my life within two or three miles of Stanley Royd Hospital, I realise only too well the appalling tragedy which happened in our area and the suffering not only of the patients but of the relatives of patients who were in the hospital at the time ... I am personally acquainted with the doctors, nurses, patients and others at the hospital, and, in spite of this tragedy, I feel that the patients are receiving all the medical care and attention from doctors and nurses which they would receive in other hospitals.

She went on to question whether the claim by the government that 'finance did not enter into this' could be true because Stanley Royd was 'one of the old Victorian hospitals—like so many others in the country—that need either demolishing and rebuilding or a great deal of money being spent on them'.[13]

Her parliamentary career had come neatly full circle. Beginning with problems of concern to the locals of West Yorkshire, and moving through issues of inadequate public services and institutions and the problems they brought, she had returned to local concerns by the end of her public life.

Back in Yorkshire in 1972, Alice had been awarded an honorary degree by the University of Leeds, and two years later was appointed a deputy lieutenant for West Yorkshire. Alice liked to keep busy, and her remark that 'I have never been a part-time MP, or come to that, a full-time MP. I have always been an overtime MP' seems to ring true.[14] Yet there was an inevitable slowdown as the years passed. Merlyn Rees, whom she had helped to secure Hugh Gaitskell's former parliamentary seat in Leeds South, tried with some success to interest her in women's charities in Northern Ireland. She took part in, and helped co-ordinate, other charity events such as carol concerts – 'none of which', her *Independent* obituary notes, 'was ever quite her scene'.[15] After the election of Michael Foot to the Labour leadership in 1980, she took less and less interest in the party. That said, she retained her loyalty, and denounced those who joined the SDP – even if she may have held a sympathy with their more centrist (than Foot) aims:

> I remember sitting in the House of Commons dining room, sitting with David Owen, having lunch, discussing the Labour Party. It is quite true he was being critical, but then a few days later there was the announcement that the SDP had been formed and I thought that quite apart from politics and the issues involved, it was a terrible way to set up a new party like that. They owed everything to the Labour Party. They had become Labour Party candidates, Labour Party members of parliament. They had been ministers. They had everything from the Labour Party and to throw everything to one side like that was absolutely despicable.[16]

Alice's loyalty was first and foremost to the Labour Party, not to any faction within it, and certainly not outside it. Shirley Williams 'never heard anything that would lead me to believe she would join the SDP – Europe, for instance, was a key policy for us, but was not an issue Alice greatly cared about'.[17] As an interesting brief coda to this, her successor as member for Leeds South East, Stan Cohen, was approached by the SDP after expressing pro-European and anti-unilateral disarmament views at odds with Foot. He was promptly deselected by the local party, a circumstance he took with good grace. Having had such a loyal MP in Alice Bacon, Cohen's discussions with Shirley Williams and David Owen were no doubt rendered all the more unpalatable to the local Labour Party members and activists.[18]

Private Life

Two figures dominated the last years of Alice's life – her aunt Sarah Handley, and Edward Painter 'Staccy' Stacpoole, a journalist. After leaving the Commons Alice lived in Yorkshire and accepted what was still, to her, the unquestioned duty of an unmarried daughter or niece: the care of an elderly relative. Whilst it was still possible, she would occasionally take Sarah to the Lords, as she had taken her to the House of Commons, and according to all sources she 'was very attached to Sarah and used to look after her well'. When Frank Pullan visited Alice's bungalow in Normanton with Bill Merrit, Alice's former local agent, he noted Sarah's love of Rugby League as he left Alice, her aunt and Merrit to watch a game on television in the next room. Alice and Sarah, it seems, lived a happy few years together.

Alice was almost zealously protective of her own private life – perhaps the reason, more than factual accuracy, that rumours of affairs with Gaitskell and Morrison floated around the Commons. But she did seem to let her guard down over time, and developed a close relationship with Staccy Stacpoole. Stacpoole was a highly regarded journalist – as his *Times* obituary put it: 'his generosity made him pick up a junior colleague's dinner bill as readily as he would share his knowledge with him ... Never once [when receiving] private confidences did he betray a trust.' His work on the Suez Crisis in 1956 met with particular praise, and 'played a vital part in giving the Press Association its reputation for total reliability'.[19] As head of the Press Association's parliamentary office Stacpoole and Alice, in her role as head of Labour publicity in the early 1960s, had encountered each other on numerous occasions.

There is an oblique reference to Alice's friendship with him in the diaries of Richard Crossman. During February 1966 Wilson held a meeting at Chequers planning the impending election campaign. The NEC and Cabinet were both invited and, once it was over, Wilson held a gathering of trusted associates to discuss what had happened. Sara Barker milled around, much to the discomfort of Wilson's inner circle, before finally leaving:

> Finally, Sara [Barker] withdrew and after that Harold came and said, 'There are still two journalists, old Stacpoole of Exchange Telegraph and someone else, filing their stories. After we and they have both eaten let's have them in for a cup of coffee'. Marcia said, 'if you don't take care they will record who's here tonight and who is not'. And Harold said, 'Oh yes, I must be careful about that', and the idea fell through. Though he is the most powerful man in the country he is still anxious lest Alice Bacon should be upset to read that Dick Crossman and Peter Shore stayed behind at Chequers to discuss things privately with the Prime Minister at a meeting from which she was excluded.[20]

Whether that entry says more about Bacon and Crossman's rivalry, or Alice's friendship with Stacpoole, is open to debate, but certainly many found Alice and Stacpoole 'cosily gossiping, or just silently together in the corridors of the Commons, a touching sight'.[21] *The Times* described

Alice as 'for many years the inseparable companion' of Stacpoole, with a 'deep, public' friendship between the two. Some 'assumed they would get married', and Betty Boothroyd reflects that Alice was 'sweet on him' while others believed 'there never seemed any question of that'. Certainly the Westminster corridors might have approved of any relationship between Alice and Staccy, yet it does not seem to have come to pass. In 1979 Stacpoole married Enid Hanson, giving 'his last 18 months an exceptional dimension of happiness'. In 1981 he died.[22]

Bernard Atha recalls Alice's final years being plagued by ill-health, loneliness and occasional bouts of depression.[23] As rheumatoid arthritis reduced her mobility, this isolation only increased.[24] She left the bungalow she had bought in Normanton, and with it lost one of her other pleasures – tending (or sometimes having others tend) to her garden. Her final days were spent in a nursing home with only sporadic visitors.[25] It was certainly a sad way to end a full and varied life.

Conclusion

Alice died of bronchopneumonia on 24 March 1993 and was buried in Normanton Parish Church with her parents.[26] She bequeathed £80,000 and £40,000 respectively for the benefit of the people of Leeds and Normanton, with her remaining relatives, and political friends such as Bernard Atha, also mentioned in her will. Normanton Town Council used the money to hold a series of meetings with senior citizens which led to the creation of a committee to allocate Alice's bequest on a long-term basis. The Alice Bacon Foundation organises an Easter Friday meal of pie and peas or fish and chips (with a concert and bingo), and has organised trips to take over 150 old age pensioners to Bradford to see pantomimes over the years. Today, Normanton councillors hold their surgeries at the Alice Bacon Community Centre on Market Street.

Throughout her life Alice campaigned for a fairer, more equal country and for a better deal for her constituents. Her politics were the product of her experiences. Her teaching career told her that poorly funded schools brought poor life opportunities and the perpetuation of inequality. The comprehensive system aroused debate at the time it was being rolled out, but it served to elevate the life-chances of many children whom both the interwar and tripartite systems had locked out of opportunity and prosperity. Few could doubt her commitment to the cause, and even political opponents conceded she knew what she was talking about. In many ways the roll-out of comprehensive education constitutes one of the most enduring legacies of the 1964–70 Labour governments, and Alice played a significant role in its implementation – laying the arguments in the 1950s for a policy she could then implement in office a decade a later.

Education may have been her primary motivation, but she also sat in the committee rooms, in the parliamentary debates and put in the hard yards to change British society. Alice Bacon may have been relegated to the historical margins until now, but her impact continues to be felt to this day. For the gay man fearful of arrest and public shame, or the woman unable to get access to an abortion under anything like safe conditions, the ramifications of Alice's dependable, determined work in the Home Office were clearly life-changing

In this light the view of Alice as a 'predictable right-wing loyalist' perhaps does not do her justice. If Labour's Deputy Leader George Brown could regard homosexuality as 'how Rome came down' and the Catholic bloc of MPs including ministerial colleague Shirley Williams rejected abortion reform, it is clear that Alice was not as 'predictable' as all that. In many ways small 'c' conservative on drugs, she could take distinctly liberal positions elsewhere.

Alice had been as willing to get stuck in in Labour's wilderness of 1950s opposition as she would prove in government. Her role in modernising the Labour Party under Gaitskell and later Wilson was not without controversy, and perhaps explains both the mixed opinions towards her in later years, and the tendency (her neighbour Denis Healey is an important exception) to write her out of the post-1945 Labour story. Alice was ferociously loyal to Labour – from her expelling communist members in the Yorkshire Labour Party in 1950s to her decision to remain within a Michael Foot-led party in the early 1980s – and this produced a degree of ruthlessness in her too. She was a forceful and continual advocate of moderation (or as others would say, a tribal right-winger) on an NEC that, due to the nature of its annual elections, could often rapidly change composition. And she had a strong bond and valued her friendship with Hugh Gaitskell. Whilst a loyal member of Wilson's government (and certainly, unlike her sometime boss Patrick Gordon Walker, not one of those plotting for his overthrow in 1968), she regarded Labour's leader from 1963 to 1976 as clearly inferior to his predecessor, Gaitskell. Better Wilson, perhaps, than George Brown (whose drinking Alice found distasteful), and the Yorkshire connection between Alice and Wilson helped build a relationship between them which helped her serve for six years as a minister in his government.

Alice's relationship with Gaitskell was not just important in a personal sense. Alice Bacon filled a role for the leadership in linking high politics to the grass roots. It was disparagingly claimed that Alice's sole purpose was to keep Leeds safe for Gaitskell, but this, even if so, underplays her role in the wider party structure. Alice provided a political haven away from the national squabbles of the late 1950s, kept her leader focused and in good spirits, and supported him through thick and thin. When she suffered a minor heart attack in 1961 Gaitskell dropped everything to visit her.[27]

Because of his early death at the age of 56, a Gaitskell administration would never come to pass, but one could imagine that had it lasted as long as Wilson's, Alice might well have pushed for a Cabinet post. Alice was no theoretician, and played little part in the Campaign for Democratic Socialism, even though she sympathised with its aims. Yet her practical, down-to-earth politics gained her much sympathy in the (non-Bevanite) Labour grass roots, and her teaching background provided gravitas for her speeches and campaigns on a number of issues, not just education. If people did not always like her, they usually respected her. The divide between her and Wilson can be summarised by the way they recounted their youth. Both had grown up in the poverty of interwar Yorkshire, yet both attended grammar schools which opened up paths closed to most of their contemporaries. While Wilson was mocked (rather unfairly) for delivering a Dickensian speech in 1948 that suggested 'more than half the children in my class never had any boots or shoes to their feet', Alice provided a more measured, yet also compelling, narrative of her own reasons for why she was Labour and why she entered politics. The left may not have liked her rampant loyalty to Gaitskell, but they knew where she stood and knew she was sincerely, authentically and unequivocally Labour.

Apart from her ministerial achievements, Alice's major historical contribution was her long service as a woman in Parliament and within the Labour Party. In the interwar period only 3 per cent of parliamentary candidates and, at most, 2 per cent of MPs were female. If the proportion of women MPs remains low (29 per cent at the 2015 general election – a record high, but still a long way from equality), it was figures such as Alice who helped achieve this increase. She also operated from a Yorkshire constituency, in itself a rarity for a woman. From the general election

of 1945 – when Alice and Muriel Nichol of Bradford became the first
women members of the PLP to represent a Yorkshire seat – to 1987, there
were only six female MPs in the region. Alice's 25 years in the Commons
as a Yorkshire-woman was easily longer than her nearest rivals, Shirley
Summerskill (Halifax, 1964–83), and Yvette Cooper, who has served
since 1997.[28]

Alice helped change Labour politics too. Three decades (1941–70)
on Labour's NEC, including through Gaitskell's struggles to keep hold
of the party in the late 1950s and early 1960s, showed that the numbers
mattered – particularly given the ability, often utilised by Alice, for the
NEC to deselect those parliamentary candidates deemed 'unsuitable'.

There is a tendency to write up the Fabian reformers of this era:
Crosland's *Future of Socialism*, for example. But the revisionism of the
Labour movement did not occur in the Oxbridge seminar room or the
pubs and buildings of the Fabians' Dartmouth Street headquarters alone.
It took practical politicians like Alice to orient Labour away from a
blanket commitment to nationalisation and suspicion of the consumer
society of the 1950s to a more nuanced position where socialism could be
asserted whilst not repudiating the socially useful elements of the market.
It was in many ways people like Alice who sold reform to the Labour
movement at conference and in party meetings.

Her accomplishments came without any partner at home. Whilst
Barbara Castle could rely on Ted, as Denis Healey pointed out, Alice 'had
more than a touch of Jane Eyre about her, [but] no Rochester ever entered
her life'.[29] As Walter Harrison (former deputy chief whip) remarked,
Alice was 'as good as married to the Labour Party'. To help break the
glass ceiling without a partner to come home to suggested a woman of
real resolve. If figures such as Richard Crossman felt Alice could defend
her corner too vigorously, it must be said that politics, for her, was an
all-consuming business. The Labour Party was the love of her life. Few
others made such sacrifices.

Her achievements resonated wider than Labour. As Margaret Thatcher
acknowledged in a 1966 interview, Alice's contributions to areas not seen
as 'women's issues' helped open doors. The future Prime Minister told her
local paper, the *Finchley Times*, that women such as Alice had produced a
shift in attitudes as to what women were capable of:

> In days gone by [women] were used almost exclusively on the welfare
> side. It was common for Prime Ministers to select women politicians to

go to the Ministry of Pensions, the Ministry of Health ... Or Ministries with a quasi-social responsibility. Now while we are still expected to have a special knowledge of those subjects modern Prime Ministers have also sent women to the Home Office ([the first ever female Minister of State] Miss Alice Bacon), Commonwealth Relations (Mrs Judith Hart); and the Foreign Office (Mrs Eirene White).[30]

There was still more to do. The *Finchley Times* might have underestimated its local MP in describing Thatcher as someone 'who personified beauty and intelligence on the British political scene [and] may well go down in history as our first woman Chancellor of the Exchequer'. But Thatcher, as with later women MPs and ministers, owed something to the path trodden with determination and ability by women like Alice Bacon for so many years.

It has been the aim of this work to place on record Alice's historic contribution to the politics of the Labour movement, Leeds, and Britain in the post-war period. Alice was a woman who, to quote her obituary in the *Wakefield Express*, 'never forgot her roots and would not allow anyone else to forget them either ... She was able to deal with world leaders and Leeds pensioners in the same honest, forthright manner.'[31] Alice made significant contributions to the rolling out of comprehensive education and social reform as Minister of State at both the Home Office and DES. She was a down-to-earth woman, but one who helped shape some extraordinary times. She put politics in front of her personal life – both romantic and family – but she was happy to do so: the Labour Party, all our interviewees acknowledge, was her life. Merlyn Rees reflects that 'to serve the body politic was her ideal. It was an aim that guided her like a beacon all her political life.' The political journalist Robert Carvel described Alice as having an 'instinctive feel for the Labour movement' and that while 'she looks a homely, simple, plump Yorkshire lass, she was extremely shrewd, at times even hard'. The last word we may leave to Bernard Atha:

Alice was like a rock for the Labour Party. She was very strong. Without being an exhibitionist, she got things sorted. She was sound, solid, and with common sense. She was not dour though, and had a good sense of humour. There was no messing with Alice![32]

APPENDICES

Appendix 1

Use of the phrase 'Comprehensive schools' in the House of Commons, 1950–69* – The Labour Party top 4

	Politician			
Year	Alice Bacon	Anthony Crosland	Michael Stewart	Stephen Swingler
1950	2	0	0	0
1951	1	0	0	0
1952	2	0	0	3
1953	1	0	0	1
1954	3	0	1	4
1955	3	0	4	0
1956	2	N/A	4	2
1957	2	N/A	6	4
1958	1	N/A	3	7
1959	0	0	6	2
1960	0	0	0	4
1961	0	1	0	4
1962	1	0	1	1
1963	0	0	0	2

Year	Politician			
	Alice Bacon	Anthony Crosland	Michael Stewart	Stephen Swingler
1964	0	0	9	0
1965	0	27	13	0
1966	5	29	0	0
1967	5	7	1	0
1968	22	0	1	0
1969	29	0	1	0
TOTAL	79	64	50	50

* The phrase was not used by any of these four MPs prior to 1950 though was discussed in the Commons during and immediately after the war.

Appendix 2

Alice Bacon's parliamentary election results, 1945–66

Leeds North East

Election	Electors	Turnout	Candidate	Party	Votes	%	Maj.	Lab Swing	AB Swing
1945	75,886	71.7	A. Bacon	Lab	28,870	53.1	8,464	+11.7%	+17.9%
			J. J. C. Henderson	Cons	20,406	37.5			
			F. C. Wilson	Lib	5,097	9.4			
1950	48,131	82.3	A. Bacon	Lab	21,599	54.6	6,819	−1.6%	+1.5%
			J. C. Bidgood	Cons	14,780	37.3			
			W. G. V. Jones	Lib	2,612	6.6			
			B. Ramelson	Com	612	1.5			
1951	47,461	80.9	A. Bacon	Lab	22,402	58.3	6,411	+2.7%	+3.7%
			J. C. Bidgood	Cons	15,991	41.7			

Leeds North East

Election	Electors	Turnout	Candidate	Party	Votes	%	Maj.	Lab Swing	AB Swing
1955	57,211	67.9	A. Baccn	Lab	25,714	66.2	12,572	-2.4%	+5.7%
			W.W.J. Dunn	Cons	13,142	33.8			
1959	48,457	70	A. Baccn	Lab	21,795	64.2	9,649	-2.6%	-2%
			J.B. Womersley	Cons	12,146	35.8			
1964	38,326	64.3	A. Baccn	Lab	16,672	67.7	8,708	+0.2%	+3.5%
			J.E. MacDonald	Cons	7,964	32.3			
1966	33,199	61.4	A. Baccn	Lab	14,633	71.8	8,890	+3.9%	+4.1%
			Mrs J.G. Todd	Cons	5,743	28.2			

Appendix 3

Unemployment in the Normanton area during the 1930s

Employment Exchange	26 May 1930	14 May 1934	20 May 1935
Pontefract	1,180	1,757	1,864
Castleford	2,034	4,000	3,784
Normanton	392	876	852
Barnsley	4,523	6,624	7,842
Wakefield	2,589	3,635	3,659
Goole	739	1,316	1,390
Total	11,457	18,208	19,391

Appendix 4

Female Labour MPs first elected in 1945

Name	Constituency	Length in the Commons	Married	Children	Highest Rank
Clarice Shaw	Ayrshire & Bute	1945–6	Y	N	backbench
Grace Colman	Tyneside	1945–50	N	N	backbench
Barbara Gould	Hendon North	1945–50	Y	Y – 1	backbench
Muriel Nichol	Bradford North	1945–50	Y	Y – 1	backbench
Florence Paton	Rushcliffe	1945–50	Y	N	backbench*
Mabel Ridealgh	Ilford North	1945–50	Y	Y – 2	backbench
Edith Wills	Birmingham Duddeston	1945–50	Y	Y – 1	backbench
Caroline Ganley	Battersea South	1945–51	Y	N	backbench
Lucy Middleton	Plymouth Sutton	1945–51	Y	N	backbench
Jean Mann	Coatbridge, Coatbridge & Airdrie (1950–9)	1945–59	Y	Y – 5	NEC committee
Alice Bacon	Leeds North East, Leeds South East (1955–70)	1945–70	N	N	minister, NEC committee
Bessie Braddock	Liverpool Exchange	1945–70	Y	N	NEC committee
Margaret Herbison	Lanarkshire North	1945–70	N	N	minister

Name	Constituency	Length in the Commons	Married	Children	Highest Rank
Freda Corbet	Camberwell North West, Peckham (1950–74)	1945–74	Y	N	backbench
Barbara Castle	Blackburn, Blackburn East (1950–5)	1945–79	Y	N	minister (Cabinet)

* Served as the first female chair of a parliamentary standing committee.

Appendix 5

Power blocks amongst Labour parliamentary candidates and the Parliamentary Labour Party, 1935–55

General Election	Classification of Candidates						
	Trade Union	% of Total	Co-op	% of Total	CLP	% of Total	Total
1935	132	23.9	21	3.8	399	72.3	552
1945	125	21	33	5.5	438	73.5	596
1950	140	22.9	33	5.4	439	71.7	612
1951	139	22.7	38	6.2	436	71.1	613
1955	128	20.7	38	6.2	451	73.1	617

General Election	Candidates Returned						
	Trade Union	% of Total	Co-op	% of Total	CLP	% of Total	Total
1935	79	51.3	9	5.8	66	42.9	154
1945	120	30.5	24	6.1	249	63.4	393
1950	110	35	18	5.7	186	59.2	314
1951	106	35.9	16	5.4	173	58.6	295
1955	96	34.6	19	6.9	162	58.5	277

NOTES

Chapter 1: From the West Riding of Yorkshire (1909–45)

1   HC Debs, vol. 414, c.292–3, 10 October 1945.
2   Ben Pimlott, *Harold Wilson* (London, 1992), 35–6.
3   Via the ONS: http://www.ons.gov.uk/ons/dcp171778_270487.pdf (accessed 20 July 2012).
4   See 1911 Census, www.1911census.co.uk. George and Alice had five children in total, one of whom had died by 1911.
5   Atha interview.
6   Ibid.
7   'Labour of Love', BBC Radio Interview, 1986.
8   Various interviews.
9   For such details, see C. M. P. Taylor, 'Alice Martha Bacon' in the *Oxford Dictionary of National Biography*, www.odnb.com (accessed 3 September 2014).
10   *Yorkshire Evening Post*, 20 December 1950.
11   See the history section on www.wakefield.gov.uk (accessed 12 February 2013).
12   Goodchild interview.
13   Pickard quotes in HC Debs vol. 104, c.1131–36, 12 March 1902.
14   Adrian Gregory, *The Last Great War* (Cambridge, 2008), 72, 88, 101 and 268.
15   All via the *Manchester Evening News*, http://www.manchestereveningnews.co.uk/news/nostalgia/world-war-one-search-soldiers-7519123 (accessed 5 November 2014).
16   *Yorkshire Evening Post*, 8 November 1915.
17   *Yorkshire Evening Post*, 12 July 1915.
18   *Yorkshire Post*, 23 August 1918.
19   See e.g. *The Times*, 22 January 1929.
20   Lisa Martineau, *Politics & Power: Barbara Castle, a Biography* (London, 2011), 5.
21   Ibid., 17.
22   Kathleen E. Gales and P. H. Marks, 'Twentieth Century Trends in the Work of Women in England and Wales', *Journal of the Royal Statistical Society*, 137 (1974): 60–74.

23 Martineau, *Politics & Power*, 11.
24 See HL Debs, vol. 373, c.1471 onwards, 29 July 1976.
25 A speech published online at http://labourlist.org/2014/04/keir-hardies-sunshine-of-socialism-speech-full-text/ (accessed 11 April 2014).
26 See http://labourlist.org/2014/04/keir-hardies-sunshine-of-socialism-speech-full-text/ (accessed 11 April 2014).
27 For all this see Harold Macmillan, *The Middle Way* (London, 1938), Chapter 4.
28 See *Leeds Weekly Citizen* clipping of 3 June 1960 in Charles Pannell's diary, Parliamentary Archives [PARL], Westminster, PAN/2/D2; John Grayson, *Solid Labour* (Wakefield, 1991), 34.
29 'Labour of Love'.
30 See Andrew Meiklejohn, 'History of Industrial Diseases of Coal Miners in Great Britain, 1920–1952', *British Journal of Industrial Medicine*, 9 (1952): 208–20.
31 G. I. Twigg, 'The Distribution of the Underground Rat Population of a South Yorkshire Drift mine', *Journal of Hygiene*, 60 (1962): 283–8.
32 Anne Perkins, *A Very British Strike, 3 May–12 May 1926* (Basingstoke, 2006), 129.
33 Jack Reynolds and Keith Laybourn, *Labour Heartland: A History of the Labour Party in West Yorkshire during the Inter War Years 1918–1939* (Bradford, 1987), 77.
34 'Labour of Love'.
35 See *British Gazette*, 6 and 8 May 1926 and *Daily Mail*, 10 May 1926.
36 *The Times*, 20 May 1929.
37 Martineau, *Politics & Power*, 50.
38 'Labour of Love'.
39 Williams interview.
40 AV Hoskins reference, 1 September 1936, Alice Bacon collection [ABC], privately held.
41 See HL Debs, 29 July 1976, above.
42 *The Times*, 23 April 1935.
43 *History Today*, 58 (2008).
44 HC Debs, vol. 531, c.54–5, 26 July 1954.
45 Ibid.
46 See HC Debs, vol. 513, c.821–2, 26 March 1953.
47 HC Debs, vol. 540, c.770, 26 April 1955.
48 See NUT Annual Report (1943), 249 and 1007.
49 See the 8 April 1942 and 27 April 1943 entries in the 1942–1946 Executive Committee Minutes of the NALT, London Metropolitan Archives [LMA], A/NLT/I/2.
50 See ibid., 6 October 1945 and A/NLT/I/3 12 July 1947 minutes and November 1947 letterhead.
51 *Independent*, 29 March 1993.
52 Leopard Abse, *Private Member* (Wiltshire, 1973), 228.
53 See Michelle Webb, 'The rise and fall of the Labour league of youth' (University of Huddersfield PhD thesis, 2007), 67.
54 Webb, 'The rise and fall', 66.
55 Webb, 'The rise and fall', 65.
56 Jack Prichard to Alice Bacon, 21 June 1939, ABC.

57 Webb, 'The rise and fall', 68, 78 and 100.
58 *The Times*, 29 August 1967.
59 *Leeds Weekly Citizen*, 25 January 1963.
60 Anonymised clipping, ABC.
61 See 19 February 1936 Report of International Sub-Committee, People's History Museum [PHM], Manchester, WG/ISY/4.
62 See minutes of the Brussels meeting, WG/ISY/8vi, and 8xxv–8xxvi.
63 For the statistics, see R.S. Hudson's statement in the Commons, HC Debs, vol. 302, c.1516, 3 June 1935.
64 For all this see Richard Carr, *Veteran MPs and Conservative Politics in the Aftermath of the Great War: The Memory of All That* (Farnham, 2013), Chapter 4.
65 George Lansbury, *My England* (London, 1935), 59.
66 Macmillan, *Middle Way*, 32.
67 *Yorkshire Post*, 3 April 1933.
68 *Yorkshire Post*, 17 March 1933.
69 Anonymised clipping, ABC.
70 *Yorkshire Post*, 5 December 1936.
71 The Missing Women script for NOVA, London School of Economics [LSE], JEGER/6/36, November 1972.
72 Kaufman interview.
73 Undated clipping, Bodleian Library, University of Oxford [BOD] – BCP MS. Martineau, *Politics & Power*, 62.
74 Grayson, *Solid Labour*, 17.
75 *The Times*, 25 May 1945.

Chapter 2: Picking Your Battles (1945–64)

1   House of Commons Research Paper 12/43, 7 August 2012.
2   Nova essay, JEGER/6/36, LSE.
3   Martin Pugh, *Speak for Britain: A New History of the Labour Party* (London, 2010), 311–12.
4   Amy Black and Stephen Brooke, 'The Labour Party, Women, and the Problem of Gender, 1951–1966', *Journal of British Studies*, 36 (1997): 419–52.
5   Ibid., 420.
6   Martineau, *Politics & Power*, 87.
7   Ibid., 81.
8   1960–1974 Leeds Women's Luncheon Club Minutes, 29 June 1961 press clipping, WYL1642/1, West Yorkshire Archives Centre, Leeds [WYA].
9   For all these statistics, see the excellent article by Brian Harrison, 'Women in a Men's House: The Women MPs, 1919–1945', *Historical Journal*, 29 (1986): 623–54.
10 Nova essay, JEGER/6/36, LSE.
11 Ibid., 430.
12 Morris interview.
13 Nova essay, JEGER/6/36, LSE.
14 Morris interview; Lord Morris interview.

15 *Observer*, 17 February 2002.
16 Millie Toole, *Mrs Bessie Braddock MP* (London, 1957), 188.
17 Williams interview.
18 Nova essay, JEGER/6/36, LSE.
19 HC Debs, vol. 500, c.1785, 16 May 1952.
20 For this issue, see Katie Haessly, 'British Conservative women MPs and 'women's issues' 1950–1979' (University of Nottingham Phd thesis, 2010), Chapter 3.
21 Williams interview.
22 30 September 1963, Ruth Winstone (ed.), *Tony Benn: Out of the Wilderness. Diaries, 1963–67* (London, 1987), 66.
23 Ibid.
24 There is no letter in BCP, BOD – MS Castle 267.
25 Abse, *Private Member*, 101.
26 Martineau, *Politics & Power*, 99, 55, 66–7.
27 Williams, *Gaitskell*, vii, 14 October 1954, 25 March 1955, 338 and 391.
28 Gaitskell–Murray letters, 1–4 December 1955, WYA, WYL1257/13.
29 Skelly Murray letter, 6 December 1956 and Murray to Gaitskell, 5 February 1961, ibid.
30 See Alice Bacon to Beryl Skelly, 17 January 1961, University College London [UCL], GAITSKELL E/27.
31 See Alice Bacon to Beryl Skelly, 16 November 1960, GAITSKELL E/26, UCL.
32 See 20 February 1953 letter from 'Brenda' to Murray, WYL1257/13, WYA.
33 10 October 1958 and 26 May 1960 correspondence, ibid.
34 Gaitskell to Murray, 15 May 1956, ibid.
35 *Leeds Weekly Citizen*, 25 January 1963.
36 Gaitskell to Murray, 10 January 1962 and 11 July 1956, WYL1257/13, WYA.
37 *Leeds Weekly Citizen*, 25 January 1963.
38 See Pannell Diaries per se, but in this instance 3 June 1960 clipping of the *Leeds Weekly Citizen*, PAN/2/D2, PARL.
39 Melanie Phillips, *The Divided House: Women at Westminster* (London, 1980), 167.
40 Ibid.
41 Draft notes for speakers, Nuffield College, University of Oxford [NUO], Williams [PWP] 11/7.
42 See PWP Williams 11/6, NUO.
43 See Crosland's note for Gaitskell, November 1960, CROSLAND 6/1/10 and /16, LSE.
44 See *Pathé News*, 'LABOUR CRISIS', 1960.
45 Philip M. Williams, *Hugh Gaitskell: A Political Biography* (London, 1979), 757, 760.
46 Williams interview.
47 Atha and Williams interviews.
48 Merlyn Rees to Kate Taylor, 29 January 1998.
49 Healey interview.
50 Ralph Miliband, *Parliamentary Socialism* (London, 1979), 327.
51 *The Times*, 30 March 1993.
52 *Queen Magazine*, 15 January 1964.

53 Kaufman interview.
54 *Spectator*, 25 February 1966.
55 See 23 April 1956, Philip M. Williams (ed.), *The Diary of Hugh Gaitskell 1945–1956* (London, 1983), 506–15.
56 *The Times*, 23 December 1961.
57 *The Labour Woman*, February 1963.
58 *Leeds Weekly Citizen*, 25 January 1963.
59 Ibid.
60 HC Debs, vol. 670, c.50, 22 January 1963; *Leeds Weekly Citizen*, 25 January 1963.
61 Atha interview.
62 Rodgers interview.
63 Atha interview.
64 Morrison talk to sixth form students, 1962, Morrison [HMP] D2/11, NUO.
65 *Derby Daily Telegraph*, 4 February 1950. Many thanks to George Jones for his thoughts.
66 *Yorkshire Post*, 14 March 1951.
67 Undated via ABC.
68 *Tribune*, 18 March 1955.
69 *The Times*, 15 April 1954.
70 *The Times*, 3 May 1954.
71 *The Times*, 4 May 1954.
72 Gaitskell to Pearce, 20 July 1954, UCL, GAITSKELL/C118, UCL.
73 Ben Pimlott (ed.), *The Political Diary of Hugh Dalton 1918–1940, 1945–60* (London, 1986), 16 March 1955, 558.
74 See 'Backbench Technocrat', Chapter 4.12, Churchill Archives Centre, Cambridge [CAC], ALBU file 15.
75 HC Debs, vol. 540 c.773, 26 April 1955.
76 Kaufman interview.
77 Bacon to Gaitskell, 2 August 1954, ibid.
78 Gaitskell to Bacon, 3 August 1954, ibid.
79 See Ian Mikardo, *Back-bencher* (London, 1988), *passim* for this.
80 Pullan interview.
81 Pimlott, *Harold Wilson*, 177; Dalyell interview.
82 *The Times*, 23 April 1951.
83 Healey, *Time of My Life*, 153.
84 Ibid., 158.
85 EC/GC, Leeds City Council Minutes, 20 January 1960 meeting, WYL 853/4/33, WYA.
86 Ibid.
87 Grayson, *Solid Labour*, 58–9.
88 Ibid., 60–1.
89 Ibid., 59.
90 See *The Times*, 3 December 1954 and *Tribune*, 8 October 1954 and 24 December 1954.
91 See undated 'Manifesto to the Labour Movement' signed by Rodgers et al. in GNWR 1/14, CAC.
92 For all this see GS/LEAK/5, 18 and 19, PHM.

93   Lewis Minkin, *The Labour Party Conference: A Study in the Politics of Intra-Party Democracy* (London, 1978), 256.

94   See the 2011 BBC Documentary, *Heath v Wilson, the 10 Year Duel*.

95   Williams interview.

96   See *The Acland Travelling Scholarship Booklet*, 1939, GS/ACL/102, PHM.

97   Howson to Phillips. 23 August 1945.

98   GS/ACL/81, undated letter, PHM.

99   Paraphrasing the comment regarding John Jennings (MP for Burton), HC Debs, vol. 1758, c.1466, 14 February 1968.

100   Lord Rodgers comments thus: 'In the 1950s, I was running the Fabian Society and we had a strong local Fabian group in Leeds. I cannot remember Alice playing any part in the Fabians.' The correspondence of Shirley Williams (FABIAN SOCIETY/A/16/3, LSE) as head of the Fabians in 1963 likewise reveals nothing relevant to Alice.

101   See Agreement between the Labour Party and the Co-operative Union Limited, GS/CO-OP/542, PHM.

102   Greg Rosen, *Serving the People: Co-Operative Party History from Fred Perry to Gordon Brown* (Norfolk, 2007), 19.

103   See Andrew Thorpe, 'Reconstructing Conservative Party Membership in World War II Britain', *Parliamentary Affairs*, 62 (2009): 227–41, 230.

104   David Butler and Gareth Butler, *Twentieth Century British Political Facts 1900–2000* (New York, 2000), 158–9.

105   See Transport House Meeting Note, 29 March 1957, GS/CO-OP/469ii, PHM.

106   Calculated from the data in NEC meeting 27 February 1957, GS/CO-OP/446i, PHM. As the figures are rounded up to a single decimal place, the percentage totals do not all equal 100 per cent. It is, however, broadly indicative.

107   Co-operative and Labour Relations Paper, GS/CO-OP/445v, PHM.

108   See Report of Activities for Submission to National Council of Labour note, 19 March 1945, GS/CO-OP/20i, PHM.

109   Rosen, *Serving the People*, 25.

110   *Pathé News*, 1946, 'LABOUR AND TORY CHIEFS ON BATTLES AHEAD.'

111   See Anthony Eden note, 4 July 1944, National Archives, Kew, London [TNA], CAB/66/56/22.

112   See *Yorkshire Evening Post*, 19–22 August 1946.

113   See *Yorkshire Evening Post*, 19–20 August 1946.

114   Martineau, *Politics & Power*, 58–61.

115   Via Gapminder, http://www.gapminder.org/data/documentation/gd004/#.U-s5PPldW yo (accessed 2 January 2012).

116   For all this, see *Yorkshire Evening Post*, 22 August 1946.

117   *The Times*, 31 May 1948.

118   *The Times*, 29 December 1949 and 26 July 1949.

119   Churchill to Bacon, November 1950, ABC.

Chapter 3: Leeds and Westminster (1945–64)

1   Pullan interview.

2   October 1964 General Election leaflet, COLL MISC 0401/2/2G, LSE.

3   *Yorkshire Post*, 14 September 2007.
4   See Appendix 2.
5   Pullan and Atha interviews.
6   *Yorkshire Post*, 12 August 1953.
7   Ferdinand Mount, *The New Few or a Very British Oligarchy: Power and Inequality in Britain Now* (London, 2012), 133.
8   Boothroyd interview.
9   Atha interview.
10   Martineau, *Politics & Power*, 84.
11   1945 Labour Manifesto, http://www.labour-party.org.uk/manifestos/1945/1945-labour-manifesto.shtml (accessed 11 April 2014).
12   Kaufman interview.
13   Grayson, *Solid Labour*, 34.
14   Ibid., 20.
15   Kaufman interview.
16   See Bevin to Wilkinson, 14 March 1945 and TGWU to Bevin 19 March 1945, BEVN 5/24, CAC.
17   'Labour of Love'.
18   *The Labour Woman*, September 1945.
19   'Labour of Love'.
20   HC Debs, vol. 414, c.293–6, 10 October 1945.
21   HC Debs, vol. 422, c.110, 30 April 1946.
22   Ibid., c.111.
23   Ibid., c.115.
24   *Yorkshire Post*, 11 April 1946.
25   Ira Zweiniger-Bargielowska, 'Rationing, Austerity and the Conservative Party Recovery After 1945', *Historical Journal*, 37 (1994): 173–98, particularly 177–97.
26   *Yorkshire Evening Post*, 21 August 1946.
27   HC Debs, vol. 502, c.1094–1095, 17 June 1952.
28   *The Labour Woman*, September 1952.
29   HC Debs, vol. 415, c.10–11, 29 October 1945, vol. 419, c.1550–1, 25 February 1946, vol. 445, c.1856, 18 December 1947, and vol. 444, c.820–1, 17 November 1947.
30   HC Debs, vol. 425, c.1658–9, 22 July 1946.
31   Pullan interview.
32   See Zweiniger-Bargielowska, 173–98.
33   See 'Backbench Technocrat', Chapter 4.12, ALBU file 15, CAC.
34   Herbert Morrison, *Lord Morrison – An Autobiography* (London, 1960), 286.
35   Kaufman interview.
36   Michael Sanderson, *The Missing Stratum: Technical School Education in England, 1900–1990s* (London, 1994), 119.
37   Kenneth O. Morgan, *Labour in Power, 1945–51* (Oxford, 1984), 176–7.
38   *Scotland on Sunday*, 3 March 1996.
39   Martin Francis, *Ideas and Policies under Labour: 1945–1951; Building a New Britain* (London, 1997) 142–54.
40   *The Labour Woman*, September 1951.

41   Labour Party Conference proceedings, 1953.

42   HC Debs, vol. 531, c.48, 26 July 1954.

43   http://www.labour-party.org.uk/manifestos/1950/1950-labour-manifesto.shtml (accessed 2 January 2012).

44   http://www.conservative-party.net/manifestos/1950/1950-conservative-manifesto.shtml (accessed 11 April 2014).

45   HC Debs, vol. 531, c.86, 26 July 1954.

46   HC Debs, vol. 531, c.50–3, 26 July 1954.

47   All via Greg Rosen, *Old Labour to New: The Dreams that Inspired, the Battles that Divided* (London, 2005), 177–9.

48   Ibid.

49   See Home Affairs (5/1/6) document, 2 March 1954, PHM.

50   Labour Party Conference proceedings, 1953.

51   http://news.bbc.co.uk/onthisday/hi/dates/stories/july/20/newsid_3728000/3728225.stm (accessed 23 February 2012).

52   HC Debs, vol. 540, c.769, 26 April 1955.

53   Richard Crossman, *Labour in the Affluent Society* (1960).

54   Grayson, *Solid Labour*, 47.

55   *Leeds Toryism Exposed* in WYL853/176, WYA.

56   Butler and Butler, *British Political Facts*, 357.

57   *Leeds Toryism Exposed.*

58   *The Times*, 22 September 1933.

59   See *The Times*, 8 December 1937.

60   See the 1945 campaign leaflet in HYND 2/3, CAC.

61   David E. Butler and Anthony King, *The British General Election of 1964* (London, 1965), 281.

62   Kaufman interview.

63   HC Debs, vol. 494, c.2298, 4 December 1951.

64   Grayson, *Solid Labour*, 93. Per 1,000 people, Leeds built only six houses compared to the 13 in Halifax, 14 in Wakefield, 23 in Pudsey and 34 in Morley.

65   See the Writers' Panel on Conservative Policy, April 1955, WOOD 15, CAC.

66   Anthony to Castle, 16 April 1955, BCP MS. Castle 62, BOD.

67   See HC Debs, vol. 607, c.689–94, 18 June 1959.

68   See HC Debs, vol. 494, c.2297, 4 December 1951 and vol. 607, c.691, 18 June 1959.

69   HC Debs, vol. 494, c.2300, 4 December 1951.

70   HC Debs, vol. 544, c.1082, 26 July 1955.

71   See Richard Carr, *One Nation Britain: History, the Progressive Tradition and Practical Ideas for Today's Politicians*, passim.

72   HC Debs, vol. 607, c.692, c.694, 18 June 1959.

73   Ibid., c.693.

74   HC Debs, vol. 544, c.1082, 26 July 1955.

75   HC Debs, vol. 550, c.2191, 28 March 1956.

76   HC Debs, vol. 550, c.2191, 28 March 1956.

77   See Labour Party Conference proceedings, 1957.

78   Lansbury, *My England*, 104–5.

79   HC Debs, vol. 505, c.1248–9.

80 HC Debs, vol. 535, c.1377, 13 December 1954 and vol. 547, c.129–30, 12 December 1955.
81 Atha interview.
82 Straw interview.
83 For all this, see HC Debs, vol. 618, c.1571–1632, 4 March 1960.
84 *The Times*, 23 April 1956.
85 Miliband, *Parliamentary Socialism*, 354.
86 Ibid.
87 Castle transcript, SUMMERSKILL/1/46, LSE.
88 Ruth Winstone (ed.), *Tony Benn: Years of Hope. Diaries, Papers and Letters, 1940–1962* (London, 1994), 2 March 1960, 325.
89 See NEC minutes of 21 May 1958, 25 February 1959 and 24 June 1959 in BCP, BOD – Castle 174.
90 28 November 1959, ibid., 320.
91 See *The Times*, 7 October 1964 and Report of the National Executive Committee to the 63rd Labour Party Conference, Brighton 12–13 December 1964, accessed through TADA Box 106, CAC.
92 *The Times*, 20 May 1963.
93 See NEC minutes, 28 March 1962, BCP, BOD – MS. Castle 174.
94 The paragraph here is all ibid.
95 Mark Abrams, 'Opinion Polls and Party Propaganda', *Public Opinion Quarterly*, 28/1 (1964), 13–19.
96 See Political Education Sub-Committee minutes, 9 July 1959, in BCP, BOD – MS. Castle 174.
97 Talk to London and Home Committee marginal candidates, ABMS 86, CAC, 15 December 1963.
98 *The Times*, 22 April 1963.
99 See election material in ABMS 68, CAC.
100 'Labour of Love'.

Chapter 4: Home Affairs (1959–67)

1 See the 2011 BBC Documentary, *Heath v Wilson, the 10 Year Duel*, for information in this paragraph.
2 New themes for Labour undated typescript, HWP, BOD – MS Wilson, c.1516.
3 See Thomas Balogh, *Planning for Progress: A Strategy for Labour* (1963), 3.
4 For the 1964 manifesto see www.labour-party.org.uk/manifestoes/1964/1964-labour-manifesto.shtml (accessed 17 March 2013).
5 T. Hennessey, 'Harold Wilson', in C. Clarke and T. S. James, *British Labour Leaders* (London, 2015), 216.
6 Hennessey, 206.
7 For these, see Brian Lapping's *The Labour Government 1964–70* (London, 1970), *passim*.
8 See 'Backbench Technocrat', ALBU, CAC file 15.
9 Richard Crossman, *Paying for the Social Services* (1969), *passim*.

10   N. Woodward, 'Labour's economic performance', in R. Coopey, S. Fielding and
     N. Tiratsoo, *The Wilson Governments 1964–1970* (London, 1993), 72, 72–101.
11   P. Thompson, 'Labour's Gannex conscience? Politics and popular attitudes in
     the '"permissive society"', in R. Coopey, S. Fielding and N. Tiratsoo, *The Wilson
     Governments 1964–1970* (London, 1993), 137, 136–50.
12   C. Ponting, *Breach of Promise, Labour in Power 1964–1970* (London, 1989), 264.
13   Ibid., 264, 269.
14   3 June 1960 clipping of the *Leeds Weekly Citizen*, PAN/2/D2, PARL.
15   22 June 1965, Winstone (ed.), *Tony Benn*, 279.
16   HO 223/7, 21 October 1964 note, TNA.
17   HO 223/7, 22 October 1964 note, TNA.
18   HO 223/7, 21 April 1966, TNA.
19   Roy Jenkins, *A Life at the Centre* (London, 1991), 184.
20   Andrew James Holden, 'Public morality, politics and "permissive" reform under the
     Wilson Governments, 1964–70' (Queen Mary, University of London PhD Thesis,
     2000), 97.
21   Jenkins, *Life at the Centre*, 184.
22   Ibid.
23   Dalyell interview.
24   Atha interview.
25   *Guardian*, 7 July 1994.
26   See *The Times*, 2 February 1957 and HC Debs, vol. 561, c.1391, 1 February 1957.
27   HC Debs, vol. 561, 1 February 1957, c.1391.
28   Victor Bailey, 'The Shadow of the Gallows: The Death Penalty and the British
     Labour Government, 1945–51', *Law and History Review*, 18 (2000): 305–49, 334.
29   Ibid., 331.
30   Ibid., 322.
31   HC Debs, vol. 499, c.1097, 14 April 1948.
32   Bailey, 'Shadow of the Gallows', 308.
33   HC Debs, vol. 704, c.910, 21 December 1964.
34   Labour Party Conference proceedings, 1958.
35   *The Times*, 15 February 1961.
36   HC Debs, vol. 638, c.98, 11 April 1961.
37   HC Debs, vol. 638, c.281, 12 April 1961.
38   HC Debs, vol. 709, c.528, 24 March 1965.
39   HC Debs, v. 705, c.910–12, 21 December 1964.
40   HC Debs, v. 704, c.950, 21 December 1964.
41   Holden, 'Reform under the Wilson governments', 11.
42   Michael McManus, *Tory Pride and Tory Prejudice: The Conservative Party and
     Homosexual Law Reform* (London, 2011), Chapter 1.
43   Holden, 'Reform under the Wilson governments', 87.
44   Ibid., 76.
45   Ibid., 91.
46   Ibid., 87.
47   Ibid., 113.
48   Ibid., 96.

49 For the father, see Bradley W. Hart, 'Watching the 'Eugenic Experiment Unfold: The Mixed Views of British Eugenicists Toward Nazi Germany in the Early 1930s', *Journal of the History of Biology* (2011).
50 HC Debs, vol. 724, c.845, 11 February 1966.
51 HC Debs, vol. 724, c.850, 11 February 1966.
52 11 February 1966, Barbara Castle, *The Castle Diaries, 1964–1970* (London, 1974), 103.
53 Holden, 'Reform under the Wilson governments', 102.
54 Abse, *Private Member*, 228.
55 See Holden, 'Reform under the Wilson governments', Chapter 4.
56 HC Debs, vol. 634, c.857–92, 10 February 1961. There was no intervention (or vote) from Alice on this day, but she may still have attended the debate.
57 See interviews in BPAS, 'Pioneers of Change', at http://www.abortionreview.org/images/uploads/Abortion_Pioneers_(1).pdf (accessed 12 February 2015).
58 'Pioneers of Change'.
59 See Bray's papers at Churchill College.
60 List 'C' of MPs, 25 October 1965, Wellcome Library, London [WELL] ALRA, SA/ALR/A.15/19.
61 'Labour MPs who are known or believe to be in support of abortion law reform', 5 May 1965, ALRA, SA/ALR/A.15/19, WELL.
62 Holden, 'Reform under the Wilson governments', 144.
63 Replies from MPs to ALRA, January 1966, WELL.
64 'Pioneers of Change'.
65 'Pioneers of Change'.
66 Houghton to Steel, 17 October 1966, SA/ALR/A.15/10/1, STEEL, WELL.
67 As an amusing aside: There was a Liberal activist in Steel's Peebles constituency called Ronald Ogilvie who was also a Catholic. He dropped out of the party after the abortion law reform led by Steel. He returned to the campaign trail in 1974. Steel noted the reappearance of Ogilvie to his wife and she told him that Ogilvie had told the local priest that he had always been a Liberal but Steel's views on abortion made it hard for him to vote for him. The priest replied to Ogilvie that he had never let it stop him.
68 HC Debs, vol. 732, c.1079, 22 July 1966.
69 HC Debs, vol. 732, c.1080, 22 July 1966.
70 HC Debs, vol. 732, c.1087–8, 22 July 1966.
71 HC Debs, vol. 750, c.1177, 13 July 1967.
72 See scribbled note, GAITSKELL/C238, UCL.
73 For this see Grayson, *Solid Labour*, 108–13.
74 HC Debs, vol. 711, c.926–1059, 3 May 1965 and vol. 716, c.969–1088, 16 July 1965 for the clauses.
75 See 1965 Conference Report in TADA Box 106, CAC.
76 Ibid.
77 Ibid.
78 *The Times*, 30 September 1965.
79 Richard Crossman, *The Diaries of a Cabinet Minister, Volume 1: Minister of Housing, 1964–66* (London, 1975), 29 September 1965, 339.

80   Simon Heffer, *Like the Roman: The Life of Enoch Powell* (London, 1999), 449.

81   HC Debs, vol. 758, c.200–1, 8 February 1968.

82   *The Times*, 9 May 1968.

83   *The Times*, 18 May 1968.

84   HC Debs, vol. 769, c.233–34, 26 July 1968.

85   HC Debs, vol. 694, c.600–78, 30 April 1964.

86   Atha interview.

87   See *The Times*, 16 March 1961.

88   Straw interview.

89   See Marcus Collins, 'The Age of the Beatles: Parliament and Popular Music in the 1960s', *Contemporary British History*, 27/1 (2013): 85–107.

90   HC Debs, vol. 733, c.644, 3 August 1966.

91   *The Times*, 13 June 1961.

92   *The Times*, 21 May 1954.

93   All via the Second Brain Report, available at http://www.dldocs.stir.ac.uk/documents/2nd-brain-report.pdf (accessed 12 February 2015).

94   HC Debs, vol. 740, c.121–2, 30 January 1967; Alex Nicola Mold, 'Dynamic dualities: The "British system" of heroin addiction treatment, 1965–1987' (University of Birmingham PhD thesis, 2004), 100.

95   HC Debs, vol. 740, c.168, 30 January 1967.

96   Mold, 100. This was a temporary spike.

97   HC Debs, vol. 623, c.1469–70, 19 May 1960.

98   HC Debs, vol. 744, c.472, 6 April 1967.

99   HC Debs, vol. 733, c.890, 5 August 1966 and vol. 740, c.147, 30 January 1967.

100   HC Debs, vol. 751, c.1163–4, 28 July 1967.

101   *Guardian*, 29 August 1967.

102   *Guardian*, 1 October 1997.

103   Hattersley interview.

104   Holden, 'Reform under the Wilson governments', 9–10.

105   Ibid., 10.

106   HC Debs, vol. 758, c.1457, 14 February 1968.

Chapter 5: Education Reformer (1967–70)

1   HC Debs, vol. 531, c.56, 26 July 1954.

2   Anthony Crosland, *The Future of Socialism* (London, 2006 edn), 229.

3   See the foreword to Crosland, *Future of Socialism*, vii.

4   Dick Leonard's Introduction to Crosland, *Future of Socialism*, xvi.

5   Ibid., 409.

6   Andrew Marr, *A History of Modern Britain* (Basingstoke, 2007), 185.

7   HC Debs, vol. 544, c.1084, 26 July 1955.

8   Marr, *Modern Britain*, 183.

9   Susan Crosland, *Tony Crosland* (London, 1982), 148.

10   *Leeds Weekly Citizen*, 13 April 1945.

11   Fabian Group, *New Patterns for Primary Schools* (1964), 11.

12 For all this see Nirmala Rao, 'Labour and Education: Secondary Reorganisation and the Neighbourhood School', *Contemporary British History*, 16/2 (2002): 99–120.
13 DES Circular 10/65.
14 HC Debs, vol. 705, c.535–41, 21 January 1965. The vote was not on the circular per se, but it was used as the justification for it.
15 *The Times*, 25 April 1969.
16 *The Times*, 3 October 1967.
17 Williams interview.
18 Harold Wilson, *The Labour Government 1964–70: A Personal Record* (London, 1971), 714.
19 See Crosland, *Future of Socialism*, 231–4.
20 See 1967 Conference Report in TADA Box 106, CAC.
21 David Crook, 'Local Authorities and Comprehensivisation in England and Wales, 1944–1974', *Oxford Review of Education*, 28 (2002): 247–60, 248.
22 Marr, *Modern Britain*, 248.
23 Crook, 'Comprehensivisation', 254.
24 Ibid., 257.
25 *Tribune*, 26 September 1969.
26 HL Debs, vol. 373, c.1500–1, 29 July 1976.
27 *Leyton Guardian*, 22 September 1967.
28 *Guardian*, 12 September 1967.
29 *Daily Express*, 22 October 1967.
30 For the Bowden–Bacon correspondence (September–November 1967) see University of Manchester [UMN], BVB/1/65.
31 All paragraph quotes via 1969 Conference Report. Many thanks to Darren Treadwell at the People's History Museum for locating.
32 All via the 1969 Conference Report, 335–43.
33 For all these stats, see Butler and Butler, *British Political Facts*, 366.
34 For the pressuring on this point, see 8 March 1969 resolution at Modern Records Centre, Warwick University [MRC] MSS.179/EXEC/1/1/3/3. For the decision see *The Times*, 16 October 1969.
35 Marr, *Modern Britain*, 248–9.
36 See Bacon–Boyle correspondence July 1968, University of Leeds [ULD], EBP/27907 and 27919.
37 Richard Crossman, *The Diaries of a Cabinet Minister, Volume 2: Lord President of the Council and Leader of the House of Commons, 1966–68* (London, 1976), 14 February 1968.
38 Including in Michael Shanks, *Is Britain Viable?* (1966), *passim*.
39 In TADA Box 32/TADA 2/67, CAC.
40 Silkin to Wilson, 2 March 1967, SLKN/11/2/1, CAC.
41 Junior Ministers Meeting notes, 22 January 1968, TADA 2/68. CAC.
42 6 February 1966 entry, Winstone (ed.), *Out of the Wilderness*, 384–5.
43 16 October 1969 Cabinet Meeting, CAB/128/44, TNA.
44 *The Times*, 15 February 1968.
45 Bacon to Ron Wallace, 29 July 1965, A/NLT/III/2/3/29, LMA.

46 See Betty Lockwood to Ron Wallace letter, 2 July 1968, A/NALT/VII/1/C, LMA.
47 2 October Speech, 1967 Conference Report, within TADA Box 106, CAC.
48 1968 Conference Report, ibid.
49 Ibid.
50 1970 Labour Manifesto via http://labourmanifesto.com/1970/1970-labour-manifesto.shtml (accessed 12 February 2015).

Chapter 6: Final Years (1970–93)

1 *Independent*, 25 February 2004.
2 Pullan interview.
3 *The Times*, 29 September 1970.
4 *The Times*, 30 March 1993.
5 *Independent*, 29 March 1993.
6 HL Debs, vol. 325, c.498, 11 November 1971.
7 See HL Debs, vol. 373, c.1501–3, 29 July 1976.
8 *The Labour Woman*, July–August 1970.
9 For all this see HL Debs, vol. 431, c.4–72, 7 June 1982.
10 BBC News Online, 'On This Day, 1974: Architect Jailed Over Corruption,' http://news.bbc.co.uk/onthisday/hi/dates/stories/march/15/newsid_4223000/4223045.stm (accessed 14 December 2014).
11 See HETHERINGTON/19/2, LSE.
12 For Hetherington's account, see 19 July 1972 meeting, HETHERINGTON/19/2, LSE.
13 HL Debs, vol. 470, c.141, 21 January 1986.
14 *Yorkshire Post*, 10 July 1985.
15 *Independent*, 29 March 1993.
16 'Labour of Love'.
17 Shirley Williams letter.
18 Michael Meadowcroft describes on www.bramley.demon.co.uk/obits/cohen (accessed 12 February 2015).
19 *The Times*, 16 September 1980.
20 6 February 1966, Crossman, Vol. 1, 448.
21 *Independent*, 29 March 1993.
22 See *Independent* and *The Times* obituaries, above and *The House Magazine*, 10 June 2002, 25.
23 Atha interview.
24 Taylor, 'Alice Martha Bacon'.
25 Atha interview.
26 Moran interview.
27 See *Leeds Weekly Citizen* clipping, undated, within WYL1642/1, WYA.
28 Grayson, *Solid Labour*, 37.
29 Healey, *Time of My Life*, 153.
30 Accessed via margaretthatcher.org (accessed 12 February 2015).
31 *Wakefield Express*, 2 April 1993.
32 Atha interview.

SELECT BIBLIOGRAPHY

Archival Material

Though much material has unfortunately been lost, Mrs Elaine Bacon (the wife of Alice's cousin Harold) holds several documents of interest, and has very kindly allowed the authors to see this material. It is cited here as Alice Bacon collection (ABC). Otherwise we have used:

Bodleian Library, University of Oxford (BOD): Barbara Castle (BCP), Harold Wilson (HWP).

Churchill Archives Centre, Cambridge (CAC): Mark Abrams (ABMS), Austen Albu (ALBU), Ernest Bevin (BEVN), Jeremy Bray (BRAY), Tam Dalyell (TADA), Patrick Gordon Walker (GNWR), John Hynd (HYND), Michael Stewart (STWT), George Strauss (STRS), John Wood (WOOD).

London Metropolitan Archives (LMA): National Association of Labour Teachers (NALT).

London School of Economics (LSE): Anthony Crosland (CROSLAND), Hugh Dalton (DALTON), General Election Ephemera (COLL MISC), Fabian Society (FABIAN SOCIETY), Anthony Grey (HCA), Peter Hetherington (HETHERINGTON), Lena Jeger (JEGER), Herbert Morrison Material (MORRISON), Edith Summerskill (SUMMERSKILL).

Modern Records Centre, Warwick University, Coventry (MRC): Maurice Edelman (EDEL), National Union of Teachers (NUT).

National Archives, Kew, London (TNA): Cabinet Papers (CAB), Home Office Papers (HO).

Nuffield College, University of Oxford (NUO): Herbert Morrison (HMP), Phillip Williams (PWP).

Parliamentary Archives, Westminster (PARL): Charles Pannell (PAN).

People's History Museum, Manchester (PHM): Acland Scholarship Correspondence (GS/ACL), Labour/Co-Operative Party Correspondence (GS/CO-OP), Leaked Material

(GS/LEAK), Labour Party National Executive Committee (GS/NEC), Pensions Material (GS/PENS), Socialist International Documents (WG/ISY), Home Policy (within GS/NEC).

University College London (UCL): Hugh Gaitskell (GAITSKELL) – currently housed at TNA.

University of Leeds (ULD): Edward Boyle (EB).

University of Manchester (UMN): Lord Bowden (BOW).

Wellcome Library, Euston, London (WELL): Abortion Law Reform Association Papers (ALRA), David Steel (STEEL).

West Yorkshire Archives Centre, Leeds (WYA): LLD1/2/834562, WYL1642/1, WYL853/176, WYL 853/4/33, WYL1257/13.

Interviews and Correspondence

Cllr Bernard Atha, Tony Benn, David Clark, Tam Dalyell, John Goodchild, Baronness Joyce Gould, Lord Roy Hattersley, Lord Denis Healey, Fred Jarvis, Sir Gerald Kaufman MP, Lord Anthony Lester, Charles Morris, Lord John Morris, Mr Roland Frank Pullan, Lord William Rodgers, Lord Tom Sawyer, Lord David Steel, Rt Hon. Jack Straw, Lord Dick Taverne, Baroness Shirley Williams.

Published Diaries

Castle, Barbara, *The Castle Diaries 1964–70* (London, 1984).

Crossman, Richard, *The Diaries of a Cabinet Minister, Volume 1: Minister of Housing, 1964–66* (London, 1975).

———, *The Diaries of a Cabinet Minister, Volume 2: Lord President of the Council and Leader of the House of Commons, 1966–68* (London, 1976).

———, *The Diaries of a Cabinet Minister, Volume 3: Secretary of State for Social Services, 1968–70* (London, 1977).

Pimlott, Ben (ed.), *The Political Diary of Hugh Dalton 1918–1940, 1945–60* (London, 1986).

Williams, Philip M. (ed.), *The Diary of Hugh Gaitskell 1945–1956* (London, 1983).

Winstone, Ruth (ed.), *Tony Benn: Years of Hope. Diaries, Papers and Letters, 1940–1962* (London, 1994).

———, *Tony Benn: Out of the Wilderness. Diaries, 1963–67* (London, 1987).

———, *Tony Benn: Office without Power. Diaries, 1968–72* (London, 1988).

Contemporary Publications

Crosland, Anthony, *The Future of Socialism* (London, 2006 edn).

Macmillan, Harold, *The Middle Way* (London, 1938).

Hansard (HC Debs – Commons, HL Debs – Lords).

The Times.

Tribune.

Contemporary Fabian Society Pamphlets

Balogh, Thomas, *Planning for Progress: A Strategy for Labour* (1963).
Crossman, Richard, *Labour in the Affluent Society* (1960).
———, *Paying for the Social Services* (1969).
Fabian Group, *New Patterns for Primary Schools* (1964).
Shanks, Michael, *Is Britain Viable?* (1966).

Memoirs

Abse, Leo, *Private Member* (Wiltshire, 1973).
Brockway, Fenner, *Towards Tomorrow* (London, 1977).
Healey, Denis, *The Time of My Life* (Middlesex, 1989).
Heffer, Eric, *Never a Yes Man: The Life and Politics of an Adopted Liverpudlian* (London, 1991).
Jenkins, Roy, *A Life at the Centre* (London, 1991).
Mikardo, Ian, *Back-bencher* (London, 1988).
Morrison, Herbert, *Lord Morrison – An Autobiography* (London, 1960).
Wilson, Harold, *The Labour Government 1964–70: A Personal Record* (London, 1971).

Secondary Books

Baston, Lewis, *Reggie: The Life of Reginald Maudling* (Stroud, 2004).
Butler, David and Butler, Gareth, *Twentieth Century British Political Facts 1900–2000* (New York, 2000).
Butler, David E. and King, Anthony, *The British General Election of 1964* (London, 1965).
Carr, Richard, *Veteran MPs and Conservative Politics in the Aftermath of the Great War: The Memory of All That* (Farnham, 2013).
Coopey, R., Fielding, S. and Tiratsoo, N., *The Wilson Governments 1964–1970* (London, 1993).
Crosland, Susan, *Tony Crosland* (London, 1982).
Donoughue, Bernard and Jones, G. W., *Herbert Morrison: Portrait of a Politician* (London, 1973).
Francis, Martin, *Ideas and Policies under Labour: 1945–1951; Building a New Britain* (London, 1997).
Graves, Pamela M., *Labour Women: Women in British Working-Class Politics 1918–1939* (Cambridge, 1994).
Grayson, John, *Solid Labour: A Short History of the Yorkshire Regional Council of the Labour Party 1941–1991* (Wakefield, 1991).
Heffer, Simon, *Like the Roman: The Life of Enoch Powell* (London, 1999).
Lawrence, Jon, *Electing Our Masters: The Hustings in British Politics from Hogarth to Blair* (Oxford, 2009).
Marr, Andrew, *A History of Modern Britain* (Basingstoke, 2007).
Martineau, Lisa, *Politics & Power: Barbara Castle, a Biography* (London, 2011).
Marwick, Arthur, *British Society since 1945* (London, 1990).

Miliband, Ralph, *Parliamentary Socialism* (London, 1979).

Minkin, Lewis, *The Labour Party Conference: A Study in the Politics of Intra-Party Democracy* (London, 1978).

Morgan, Kenneth O., *Labour in Power, 1945–51* (Oxford, 1984).

Mount, Ferdinand, *The New Few or a Very British Oligarchy: Power and Inequality in Britain Now* (London, 2012).

Perkins, Anne, *A Very British Strike, 3 May–12 May 1926* (Basingstoke, 2006).

Phillips, Melanie, *The Divided House: Women at Westminster* (London, 1980).

Pimlott, Ben, *Harold Wilson* (London, 1992).

Ponting, Clive, *Breach of Promise: Labour in Power 1964–1970* (London, 1989).

Pugh, Martin, *Speak for Britain: A New History of the Labour Party* (London, 2010).

Reynolds, Jack and Laybourn, Keith, *Labour Heartland: A History of the Labour Party in West Yorkshire during the Inter War Years 1918–1939* (Bradford, 1987).

Rosen, Greg, *Old Labour to New: The Dreams that Inspired, the Battles that Divided* (London, 2005).

Rosen, Greg, *Serving the People: Co-Operative Party History from Fred Perry to Gordon Brown* (Norfolk, 2007).

Sanderson, Michael, *The Missing Stratum: Technical School Education in England, 1900–1990s* (London, 1994).

Toole, Millie, *Mrs Bessie Braddock MP* (London, 1957).

Williams, Philip M., *Hugh Gaitskell: A Political Biography* (London, 1979).

Secondary Journal Articles

Abrams, Mark, 'Opinion Polls and Party Propaganda', *Public Opinion Quarterly*, 28/1 (1964): 13–19.

Bailey, Victor, 'The Shadow of the Gallows: The Death Penalty and the British Labour Government, 1945–51', *Law and History Review*, 18 (2000): 305–49.

Black, Amy and Brooke, Stephen, 'The Labour Party, Women, and the Problem of Gender, 1951–1966', *Journal of British Studies*, 36 (1997): 419–52.

Collins, Marcus, 'The Age of the Beatles: Parliament and Popular Music in the 1960s', *Contemporary British History*, 27/1 (2013): 85–107.

Crook, David, 'Local Authorities and Comprehensivisation in England and Wales, 1944–1974', *Oxford Review of Education*, 28 (2002): 247–60.

Gales, Kathleen E. and Marks, P. H., 'Twentieth Century Trends in the Work of Women in England and Wales', *Journal of the Royal Statistical Society*, 137 (1974): 60–74.

Harrison, Brian, 'Women in a Men's House: The Women MPs, 1919–1945', *Historical Journal*, 29 (1986): 623–54.

Rao, Nirmala, 'Labour and Education: Secondary Reorganisation and the Neighbourhood School', *Contemporary British History*, 16/2 (2002): 99–120.

Thorpe, Andrew, 'Reconstructing Conservative Party Membership in World War II Britain', *Parliamentary Affairs*, 62 (2009): 227–41.

Zweiniger–Bargielowska, Ira, 'Rationing, Austerity and the Conservative Party Recovery after 1945', *Historical Journal*, 37 (1994): 173–98.

Academic Theses

Freedman, Des, 'The television policies of the British Labour Party 1951–2000' (University of Westminster PhD thesis, 2000).

Haessly, Katie, 'British Conservative women MPs and "women's issues" 1950–1979' (University of Nottingham PhD thesis, 2010).

Holden, Andrew James, 'Public morality, politics and "permissive" reform under the Wilson Governments, 1964–70' (Queen Mary, University of London PhD thesis, 2000).

Mold, Alex Nicola, 'Dynamic dualities: The "British System" of heroin addiction treatment, 1965–1987' (University of Birmingham PhD thesis, 2004).

Webb, Michelle, 'The rise and fall of the Labour League of Youth' (University of Huddersfield PhD thesis, 2007).

INDEX